Seeing Double

Revisioning Edwardian
and Modernist Literature

Edited by Carola M. Kaplan
and Anne B. Simpson

ST. MARTIN'S PRESS
NEW YORK

ISBN 0-312-15896-3

Library of Congress Cataloging-in-Publication Data

Seeing double : revisioning Edwardian and modernist literature /
   edited by Carola M. Kaplan and Anne B. Simpson.
      p. cm.
   Includes bibliographical references and index.
   ISBN 0-312-15896-3
   1. English fiction—20th century—History and criticism.
   2. Modernism (Literature)—Great Britian.   I. Kaplan, Carola M.,
   1942- . II. Simpson, Anne B., 1956- .
   PR888.M63S46 1996
   823'.91091—dc20

                                             96-34457
                                                 CIP

Book design by Milton Heiberg Studios

First edition: October 1996
10 9 8 7 6 5 4 3 2 1

Permissions

From *The Collected Poems of Edward Thomas* edited by R. Gregory Thomas. Copyright © 1981, by Oxford University Press, Inc. Reprinted by permission.

Photographs of Munstead Wood and Wilsford Manor have been reproduced with the permission of Country Life Picture Library.

Extracts from Rudyard Kipling's "Hobden the Hedger," from *Puck of Pook's Hill;* "A Charm," from *Rewards and Fairies;* and "The Glory of the Garden," from *The Definitive Edition of Rudyard Kipling's Verse* are reprinted with the permission of A.P. Watt Ltd. on behalf of The National Trust for Places of Historical Interest or Natural Beauty.

Contents

For Bruce and Ben

Introduction

Edwardians and Modernists: Literary Evaluation and the Problem of History

Carola M. Kaplan and Anne B. Simpson

In the creation of literary history, as in the writing of history itself, those who make claims of "fact-finding," "truth-telling," "objectivity," and "accuracy" often mask underlying—if unconscious—special interests. "A literary work," writes Hans Robert Jauss, "is not an object that stands by itself and that offers the same view to each reader in each period. It is not a monument that monologically reveals its timeless essence. It is much more like an orchestration that strikes ever new resonances among its readers" (165-66). In the ongoing process through which authorial purpose is forever mediated and text forever modified, each new audience shapes and reshapes literary works in its own image. The aim of this volume is to interrogate the critical tendency to designate literary periods under constricting aesthetic rubrics and to define them by discrete thematic preoccupations, as if these pursuits lead to "truths" about literary history. We see, rather, that acts of appropriation are performed by successive generations of readers, with far-ranging and often unforeseen results.

In the twentieth century, the crucial relationship between critical interpretation and cultural trends is typified by the shifting evaluations of writers labeled, sometimes disparagingly, sometimes approvingly, "Edwardian."

After World War I, in the wake of the destruction and bloodshed that had ravaged Europe, it became a truism to assert that the culture immediately preceding the chaos had offered an idyllic interval for a mindless British populace. Writers who had been highly respected and widely read as artists, critics, and reviewers in the epoch spanning King Edward VII's ascension to the throne in 1901 and extending to the outbreak of the war in 1914 were now grouped together, their differences and disagreements forgotten, as fervent agitators who had tried to rouse the complacent English from their cultural slumber. Rather than crediting Edwardian artists for their efforts, the postwar generation of writers viewed these elders, whom they arbitrarily limited to a composite Bennett-Galsworthy-Wells caricature, as rather pedestrian craftsmen who had spoken with a single, too-strident voice in an earnest-minded literature protesting the smugness of the Edwardian age. The younger writers self-consciously set themselves apart with the label "Georgians" (eventually the positive and innovative-sounding title "Modernists" was accorded them), launching and winning a battle against the Edwardian writers whom they identified as their most immediate rivals. It was not sufficient, the Modernists proclaimed, to use literature as a tool for prodding the middle class out of its inertia. Art could, and should, do more. Characterizing the Edwardians as simple-minded liberals obsessed with thematic issues at the expense of artistic considerations, the Modernists forged a powerful and persuasive assessment of those whom they saw as the enemy. Their denigrating view of the Edwardians as well-meaning, socially conscious hacks became deeply lodged in the critical unconscious.

Certainly the Edwardians were preoccupied with culture, and in recent years this preoccupation has gotten its due consideration. Since the mid-1960s, with the publication of Samuel Hynes's literary study *The Edwardian Turn of Mind* and Barbara Tuchman's historical account *The Proud Tower,* one popular version of Edwardianism has lauded the very tendencies that were rejected by the younger Modernist writers. The Edwardian generation was suddenly quite appealing to those caught in the crossfire of sixties disruption and unrest; they loomed larger than life, these refashioned Edwardians, as significant, early heralds of social instability. Change and insecurity were seen as hallmarks of the Edwardian age, and Edwardian writers were cited for their keen awareness. Historians of the 1960s noted that the country-house weekend that delighted the upper strata and has served as stereotype of the Edwardian age actually signaled a need for escape from general social distress (Nowell-Smith 46-47). They observed, too, that the period opened in the midst of the Boer War, a war that divided the Liberal party into factions and that proved a national embarrassment because of staggering British losses (Minney 15). Tuchman points out that although the war ended in 1902, as the Edwardian era progressed, an increasing paranoia about international affairs and specifically about the German threat, expressed itself in a virtual "invasion psychosis" among the general public (380). Similarly, Tuchman cites contemporary disruptions of the established order: the rise of English Socialism and, most significantly, of the Labour Party, a growth that suggested the beginnings of a shift in power from one class to another. This shift was to cause "upheaval in the components of society," an upheaval that could already be felt (Tuchman 367). It was a period, historians observed, of vigorous trade unionism; of dock and railway strikes in 1911; of coal strikes and the Port of London strike in 1912; and of fervent discussion everywhere of "a civil war between labour and capital" (Nowell-Smith 97-98). The militant tactics of the Edwardian suffragettes were repeatedly cited as evidence of the violent, agitated Edwardian frame of mind (Hynes 353). As cultural markers of social change, chroniclers listed Edwardian advances in technology (the ever-increasing popularity of the typewriter, telephone, airplane, and automobile) and significant contributions in physics and psychology, with Einstein's relativity theory appearing during the Edwardian years and Freud's *Interpretation of Dreams* translated into English in 1913.

Commentators of the 1960s recurrently pointed to the work of the M. P. Charles Masterman, who in his 1909 study of the state of England had remarked on the disruptive effects of technology and of a speeded-up, mechanized culture lacking direction and vision; and on the staggering disparities and social inequities between rich and poor (28, 150). From the vantage point of fifty years later, Masterman seemed remarkably prescient in his assessments of his own generation, its instabilities and its terrors. His text *The Condition of England* therefore became a touchstone for serious analyses of the Edwardian age.

This conception of the opening of the twentieth century that emphasizes its chaotic atmosphere and hails Edwardian intellectuals and writers for their social consciences has become an appealingly "relevant" way to think about Edwardianism in the thirty or so years since Hynes and Tuchman published their studies. Nevertheless, the critical voices, stressing the Edwardians' lack of rigorous thought, persist. Jonathan Rose, in his 1986 study *The Edwardian Temperament 1895-1919,* identifies "six broad intellectual movements" of the age (xii) and thereby suggests that he will present a multivalent account of the era. Yet Rose's book opens on the single note of social disruption that sounds consistently throughout his study: "Of all the philosophical problems that troubled the Edwardians," he begins, "none disturbed so many people as deeply as the decline of Victorian religion" (1). The triad of difficulty, disturbance, and decline forms the defining perspective of Rose's analysis. When the final chapter evaluates the Edwardians' attempts to reconcile opposing forces, to effect inner harmony, they come up short: "The undivided Edwardians achieved inner wholeness by affirming unity everywhere," Rose notes, "but in so doing, they sacrificed philosophical integrity" (210). Rose's Edwardians emerge as "slack" thinkers with "soft center[s]" (210, 211), very much in contrast to the Modernists who came after them, who are praised for their mental complexity and intellectual candor. The Modernist critique of the Edwardians is thereby recovered and reaffirmed by Rose's study.

Recent literary criticism, attempting to broaden the terms of the analysis, has acknowledged the ideological divisions within and between the Edwardians while beginning to credit their artistic aims as well. The Edwardians' patient realism and their adaptations of romance modes are acknowledged (along with their emphases on environmental problems and cultures domestic and exotic) in studies by John Batchelor and Jefferson Hunter. Despite these two treatments, the Edwardian writer continues to be thought of, in intellectual circles, as a monologic, rather boorish sociologist manqué. Such a conception elides one of the most fascinating aspects of Edwardian literature, and one of its most pressing aesthetic claims: the ability to hold in tension competing philosophical positions on contemporary culture. In this way, many Edwardian writers create a complex balance of propositions that the reader must assess as the work moves toward its (often surprising) resolution. By the same token, despite several recent examinations of Edwardian technique—for example, Robert L. Caserio's "The Novel as a Novel Experiment in Statement" addresses the narratological experimentation of Wells—the Edwardians' formal innovations remain largely unexplored. Commentators tend to treat Bennett, Galsworthy, and Wells, as important and influential as they were, as if they alone constituted all Edwardian literature; for the most part, critics ignore the works of other authors of the period, especially women. In university curricula, Edwardian literature is both unread and untaught; the efforts of appreciative historians and sympathetic readers notwithstanding, the Modernist judgment prevails.

What was it about the Edwardians that propelled their younger contemporaries into such a profound repudiation of Edwardian art, one that has proved to be so convincing? Two early manifestos—Virginia Woolf's "Mr. Bennett and Mrs. Brown" (1924) and E. M. Forster's *Aspects of the Novel* (1927)—offer the defining frame for the argument, serving to valorize the literature produced by Modernist writers at the grave expense of the work of their fellow artists. Looking back from the perspective of three quarters of a century later, the major difference between these two groups of writers appears to be not so much the difference in artistic quality both Woolf and Forster claimed, but the difference in their attitudes toward history. The Edwardians responded directly in their fiction to the events of their time; the Modernists né Georgians proclaimed themselves emancipated from history, inhabitants of a world of art governed not by the vagaries of daily events but by timeless aesthetic standards, disinterested creation, and universal human concerns.

"Mr. Bennett and Mrs. Brown" proclaims its rebellious project from the first: the essay will answer the challenge flung down by the older novelist, Bennett (cast here in the role of disapproving father-figure), who had claimed that the younger novelists could not create character. In her rejoinder to this challenge, determined not only to answer back but to best the father, Woolf goes on to show that what Bennett calls character is not character at all—it is materialism: a vulgar, gross concern with the things of the world, especially its products and goods, which she considered the chief failing of the Victorian era. It is from the weight of these goods, ostensibly the products but in actuality the detritus of industrialism, that Woolf wishes to free herself and her literary compatriots. Modernist novelists, Woolf asserts, create character from the inside, with subtlety and complexity. Edwardian novelists, on the other hand, harp on causes: they "preach doctrines [and] sing songs" (324). The Edwardian writers, she continues, depend too heavily on the world outside the book; one leaves their novels dissatisfied, feeling that "in order to complete them it seems necessary to do something—to join a society, or, more desperately, to write a cheque" (326). Clearly Edwardian novels get up to everything except the real task of novels: that is, evoking character, as Woolf defines it.

In his introductory chapter to *Aspects of the Novel,* Forster's attitude is more conciliatory than Woolf's. He would have all the great novelists of the world, from all periods and all cultures, "seated together in a room . . . all writing their novels simultaneously" (9). Gone would be the threat of revolution in Russia that might worry Dostoevsky or Tolstoi and the bloody double legacy of Revolution and Napoleon in France that might trouble Stendhal and Balzac. In Forster's "Great Writer's Club," artists of every time and culture would be scribbling away to produce literature that transcends the pressures of time and culture. In fact, Forster claims to believe that for great artists such pressures do not exist. Not by chance does this cozy artistic haven from history resemble a Bloomsbury meeting of the

Heretics Club or a latter-day version of the Cambridge Midnight Conversazione Society.

Despite their differences in tone, what Forster's and Woolf's influential manifestos have in common is their repudiation of history. Given their overwhelming success in shaping twentieth-century literary opinion, current literary critics must ask two questions. Why their denial of history? Why their power to determine literary taste and judgment for more than sixty years?

Clearly, one central impulse behind the denial of history is Oedipal: the desire and need to free themselves of the looming figures of their Victorian parents and, by extension, the Edwardian artists (positioned variously by the Modernists in parent-substitute and in elder-sibling roles). Although their history-conscious Edwardian contemporaries had serious quarrels with the Victorians, they were willing to engage in those quarrels in the terms their predecessors had taught them. Not only that: they acknowledged their debt to their forebears in a continuity of social concern and literary forms. Not so with their younger and more openly rebellious counterparts, Woolf, Joyce, Eliot, and company—the Modernists who saw as their "mission," Marjorie Perloff notes, "a call for rupture" (154).

Also endemic to filial rebellion and sibling rivalry is a determination to do it better—whatever the "it" refers to. For the Georgians, better meant more difficult, more demanding, more challenging: a higher art for a more discerning and more dedicated, if smaller, readership. No more catering for the middle-brow middle class, as the Victorians and Edwardians had done. If the new generation could not write at greater length, they would write in greater depth. Against the criticism of shallowness, the Edwardians took up a defensive and ultimately self-destructive stance. Quarreling fiercely with Henry James, Wells asserted his impatience with aesthetic self-enclosure and chose to define himself against James as a "journalist" simply and humbly focused on art as a means to an end (Edel and Ray 264). Bennett, who had authored a sideline of unabashedly commercial how-to books on time management, the formation of literary taste, and marital relations, retreated from the slings and arrows of younger rivals into claims for his own lack of pretentiousness: Woolf, he wrote, "is the queen of the high-brows; and I am a low-brow" (Bennett 225). Both Bennett and Wells, in oversimplifying their aims, fueled the Modernists' assessment of them; and although in retrospect we can see at the heart of the behavior the Edwardians' need to renounce the precepts that the Modernists were wielding against them, their misleading self-characterizations contributed to the increasingly marginalized position of Edwardian art.

Above all else, the Modernists, unlike the Edwardians, were dedicated to the idea that would later be memorialized in Ezra Pound's injunction, "Make it new." Thus they searched for and cultivated new literary forms. In this endeavor, they hoped that new style equaled new substance. As artists, they would start afresh—free of the legacy of their Victorian forebears, free of the unfulfilled doctrine of social progress, free of the anxiety and unrest of the beginning of the new century. This hope informs Woolf's brazen proclamation, "In or about December, 1910, human character changed" (320). But as Perry Meisel has tellingly pointed out, underlying this bold assertion of newness was a deep anxiety that in fact all was old, that Woolf and her fellow artists had come belatedly into a tradition—the Romantic tradition, to be precise. But the Romantics, for all their insistence on originality, had not been able to create themselves entirely afresh, either. In back of *them* were their Renaissance forebears. In fact, when examined, the entire cult of originality could not be a more traditional part of English literary history. Behind it, we find the recurrent and unsatisfiable postmedieval quest for the transcendent, for "a realm beyond culture or outside language to which language and culture can appeal" (Meisel 6). This determination to devise an art that would liberate the artist from the confines of his or her culture, a determination that Meisel terms "the will to modernity," is in fact a preeminently historical phenomenon characterized by "the recurrent desire to find origins or ground despite the impossibility of ever doing so for sure." Thus these strenuous Modernist efforts to find "a place outside of the tradition that enables it" (Meisel 4) were doomed to failure. In fact, as we look back from the perspective of more than half a century, we see this search for originality as confirmation of an enmeshment in history similar to the more overtly acknowledged historical engagement of their Edwardian cohorts.

Yet denial is a different strategy from overt anxiety, both in life and in literature. And it results in artistic productions that are stylistically different—that *appear* different—from works whose underlying concerns may in fact be quite similar. In Modernist writing, these stylistic distinctions are often so arresting that the reader does not probe beyond the surface but accepts at face value the liberation from history, the autonomy, and the uniqueness that the work of art proclaims. In general, denial tends to evoke greater admiration than the admission of crisis: for its apparent calm and triumph over adversity, for its apparent self-liberation from cultural blindness and temporal limitation. The ascendancy of Modernist literature over Edwardian literature, we suggest, derived from this advantage. One of our purposes in this present collection of essays is to question the proclamations of artistic detachment made by the Moderns in their art and in their manifestos. We dispute the separation or freedom of Modernist art from history and seek to restore it to a temporal and cultural context, to discover its reflection of historical events and to uncover its ideological assumptions.

All this discussion of Modernism's flight from history is not to suggest an entirely disingenuous position or pose. Rather, this Modernist desire for escape is an index of the intolerable nature of early twentieth-century historical events—particularly of the events of World War I. We locate the traces of this war and of a myriad other distinctly "modern" problems in Modernist literature and find them to be the same problems that concerned their Edwardian elders and contemporaries.

Inevitably, the question arises, why did we for so long accept the Modernists' claims of artistic purity and political neutrality? Given our small but crucial historical distance from these writers, we must look back to the creation of the discipline of English literature itself for an answer to this question. As Terry Eagleton points out, the study of English arose as a response to the desire for education by the working classes combined with a socially ameliorative and class-narrowing impulse on the part of the university-educated middle classes (22-27). Since working men had not enjoyed the privileges of a public-school education with its grounding in Latin and Greek, the education of the working classes would have to be in the only language they knew, that is, English. Thus by its very origin the discipline of English arose as a pragmatic, faute de mieux and apparently lesser discipline, intellectually, to the traditional field of Classics. In order to legitimize the study of English literature or make it acceptable to the educated classes, one would have to demonstrate over time that it was not merely a secondary or compensatory course of education. The new discipline's demand to be taken seriously was most likely to be successful if the objects of its study were difficult, esoteric, not readily accessible even to the recipients of a traditional classical education. The field of English could best justify itself if what it taught was in need of translation or decoding by specialists. Surely the demanding and not easily accessible literary art offered by the Modernists helped to demonstrate the necessity for training a new learned priesthood of professors of English literature. Thus the study of literature written in English became a legitimate and justifiable academic concern.

The rationale for and defense of a new esoteric literature and the establishment of a new branch of the academy that specialized in the interpretation of English literary texts was a case made most eloquently by the younger generation of academics. In advancing this case, they were attempting to elevate themselves from the socially modest origins which many of them shared (Eagleton 30-31). Many early twentieth-century academics turned to the works of Modernist artists precisely because they recognized in the outsider status of many of the Modernists an affinity with their own precarious social positioning.

The Modernist writers' bravado in defining themselves as a new creative and cultural aristocracy was in fact a compensation for their underlying anxiety that they stood outside the culture and audience for which they wrote. Some were anxious about their birth and social placement: D. H. Lawrence, because of his working-class background; James Joyce, because of his Irish birth and culture; T. S. Eliot, because of his American origin. Others, like Forster and Woolf, who were born to the privileges of the upper middle class, the class that had produced most previous British writers, still suffered from dis-ease: Forster felt marginalized by dint of his homosexuality; Woolf felt excluded on the basis of gender. All longed to move from outsider to insider status and hoped to do so by producing the new art. This would be an art for the elite, an elite not of the well born but of the intrinsically worthy—the intelligent, the cultured, or in Forster's terms, "the sensitive, the considerate and the plucky" ("What I Believe" 73).

This aspiration to occupy the position of insider helps to explain the essentially conservative social and political bias of much Modernist literature of the early part of this century, as well as the cautious conservatism of its interpreters. (Conservatism also underscores the Modernists' contempt for the Edwardians, whose politics were generally liberal.) From the vantage point of the 1990s, the wish to be on the inside, with its accompanying denigration of the outside, suggests a hierarchy of value that we can—and do—question, drawing on the insights of contemporary critical theory, particularly deconstruction. As we reconsider the relation of margin to center, noting interdependence rather than opposition, it has become possible to scrutinize the categories and evaluations of early twentieth-century British literature that have prevailed for more than six decades.

And so we come, by this route, to the inception and the purposes of the present volume of essays. Following trails blazed by recent criticism—by feminism, by gender studies, by cultural studies, by New Historicism, and by post-colonial theory—we enter into the current dialog of our discipline. This dialog is complicated and enriched by calling into question traditional literary categories and judgments, by attempting to redefine the concerns and objects of literary analysis, by including formerly marginalized perspectives, and by encouraging previously silenced minorities to cultivate their own voices. All these developments have contributed to our current project. As American women in the academy, we also occupy a dual position in our examinations of insider and outsider roles; for, having come late to the ranks of institutional power, we both enjoy its privileges and know our "difference."

In this volume, we set out to discover and to rediscover literary figures, to question previous categories of major and minor, and to examine "canonical" writers in new ways. Further, from the polyphonic expressions and multiple perspectives of current criticism, we call attention to issues that it is only recently possible to discuss—issues that earlier critics either could not notice or felt obligated to deny, especially as these are embedded in the toxic discourses of sexism, racism, anti-Semitism, class snobbery, and xenophobia in otherwise compelling works by early twentieth-century writers. We aim to underline these prejudices without dismissing works of literature that otherwise make strong artistic claims. Included in the anthology are essays that address such Edwardian and Modernist topics as changing sexual attitudes and practices; evolving roles of women; the growth of consumer culture and of the modern war machine; race, class, and nationhood; and the politics of empire.

Finally, working from the category-breaking and literary inclusiveness of recent treatments of this period—most notably Bonnie Kime Scott's *The Gender of Modernism*—we question the previously posited dichotomy between Edwardian and Modernist works, with the attendant privileging of Modernist over Edwardian. Our reconsideration, which notes the interpenetrations and intersections of Edwardianism and Modernism, helps us to liberate the Edwardians from the ghetto of a second-rate art focused exclusively on social problems; and to enrich our reading of Modernism as embedded in history, infused with culture, and saturated by ideology.

The four sections of this book focus on a spectrum of British writers as they examine issues of self, nation, and global politics. We have chosen the years 1895 to 1920 as the inclusive dates for this study because we trace Edwardian and Modernist concerns back to the concluding years of Victoria's reign and forward to the years immediately following the Armistice. Any such dating, as Jonathan Rose points out, is a somewhat arbitrary enterprise, precisely "because attitudes and movements are things that fade in and out very gradually" (xiii). And yet in the moments surrounding events of national crisis—the Oscar Wilde trials, the morally questionable Boer War, the death of a beloved queen, and the conclusion of a devastating global conflict—the tensions between receding and emergent cultural norms are often most clearly evident. The year 1895, the time of the Wilde scandal, called into question prevailing norms of sexual behavior and focused public attention on the definition of selfhood. We start with this date because we believe that the radical questioning of self is a necessary first step in the larger project of redefining culture and nationhood. We end with 1920 as the year in which, the chaos of World War I having receded, hopefulness returned with the advent of a new decade.

Parts 1 through 3 of this volume contain essays that move outward in widening concentric circles of social awareness and concern; conversely, Part 4 focuses in on works by two representative writers. In Part 1, essays treat evolving conceptions of selfhood, particularly constructions of gender and sexual identity. Part 2 examines social contexts, specifically the relationship of British writers to their cultural milieu and local history. Connecting definitions of British national identity with conceptions of different societies, Part 3 examines both the threats posed by other nations and the attractions offered by diverse cultures. Part 4 considers Forster and Conrad, "canonical" writers of the period, from differing perspectives. Each author is treated in essays by eminent scholars as well as by scholars newly entering the academy, in order to indicate the interest both writers continue to elicit and the variety of approaches they invite. These essays testify to the range of cultural and theoretical concerns that are currently shaping the discipline of literary criticism. Following are brief introductions to each of the four sections of the book.

LOOKING WITHIN: GENDER
CONSTRUCTION AND SEXUAL IDENTITY

This group of essays considers how British writers of the period viewed themselves, particularly how they sought to redefine the nature and boundaries of those most intimate aspects of the self—gender and sexuality. Not surprisingly, the essays that treat this subject deal principally with women. For it was women whose former position was most strenuously being called into question and whose social roles were most rapidly changing, to the enhancement of women's sense of themselves and the accompanying bewilderment, resistance, and tentative support of their male counterparts. Accordingly, Shoshana Milgram Knapp's essay, "Revolutionary Androgyny in the Fiction of 'Victoria Cross,'" charts the course of the literary career of Annie Sophie Cory ("Victoria Cross") in her efforts to create a new character in literature—the androgynous woman—and to find her a place in contemporary society. This essay records both the mixed response of her readership over time—a combination of repugnance, misinterpretation, and qualified admiration—and the author's own ambivalent attitudes toward the challenging literary characters she creates. In her essay "(P)revising Freud: Vernon Lee's Castration Phantasy," Jane Hotchkiss presents the radical work of Cory's contemporary, Violet Paget ("Vernon Lee"), who responded to the late-nineteenth-century debates about the nature of female sexuality by contesting the long-held notion of female lack (lately codified by Freud) with a counternarrative. Her alternative interpretation of women's sexuality as plenitude that elicits male anxiety is deeply embedded in the tale "Prince Alberic and the Snake Lady," as Hotchkiss shows. Anne B. Simpson's essay "Architects of the Erotic: H. G. Wells's 'New Women'" examines the ambivalence of a prominent male writer of the time, H. G. Wells, who endorses the emergence of the newly liberated woman only to reincarcerate her within the confines of traditional male narrative. In his two novels of female emancipation, *Ann Veronica* and *The Wife of Sir Isaac Harman,* Wells positions each of his rebellious heroines on the brink of radical change, but insists finally that a woman's liberation shape itself in the erotic choice of a right-thinking "New Man."

LOOKING AROUND: BRITISH CHARACTER AND SOCIETY

These essays consider British culture and character just after the turn of the century, as British writers interpreted themselves to themselves and for their compatriots. John Lucas's wide-ranging treatment in "The Sunlight on the Garden" of British cultural self-depiction in visual terms shows how country houses and gardens concretized the dominant prewar metaphor of England as Eden. This idealized conception, embedded in the popular imagination, increasingly conflicted with Britain's complex social reality. In his tightly focused account, "Self-Isolation and Self-Advertisement in *The Old Wives' Tale,*" Robert Squillace traces a significant social change that demarcates the Victorian world from the modern, as individuals are compelled to move from egocentrism to involvement in the new consumer-driven culture. This change, documented in a family chronicle, is revealed to be relentless and inexorable; yet characters respond with regression and inconsistency. Finally, Jean-Michel Rabaté's essay "Joyce, the Edwardian" revises the commonplace conception of Joyce's art as divorced from social context and historical events. Joyce, Rabaté points out, is an Edwardian writer not only by virtue of the time in which his fictions are set, but also in his documentation of the minutiae of daily life during the Edwardian period and in his preoccupation with the English king, Edward VII, who figures prominently in his work, from *Dubliners* to *Ulysses.*

LOOKING ELSEWHERE: OTHER CULTURES, OTHER NATIONS

Essays in this section connect self and other in a global context, indicating how the changes in British social history and in its evolving self-conception affected its interpretations, evaluations, and understandings of other cultures. The range of these responses, from idealization to paranoia, is reflected in Carola M. Kaplan's "Totem, Taboo, and *Blutbrüderschaft* in D. H. Lawrence's *Women in Love,*" Marianna Torgovnick's "Discovering Jane Harrison," and Patrick Brantlinger's "'The Bloomsbury Fraction' Versus War and Empire." Kaplan's essay examines *Women in Love* as a "Condition of England" novel, in which Lawrence offers a postwar prescription for a new social order. Taking his inspiration from Freud's *Totem and Taboo,* Lawrence sees in "primitive" cultures a model for cultural regeneration. Yet Lawrence's valuation of the "primitive" is so undermined by ambivalence that non-Western, nonindustrial cultures ultimately prove futile in providing the redemptive social vision he seeks in them. In her consideration of Jane Harrison's life and work, Torgovnick reminds us of the classical scholar's important influence on such modern writers as T. S. Eliot, D. H. Lawrence, H.D., and Virginia Woolf in their literary use of myth and ritual. Noting Harrison's interpretation of ancient Greece as the "irrational primitive," and crediting her with generating interest in Mother Goddess figures, Torgovnick asks why Harrison, a scholar of ritual as famous in her day as Sir James Frazer, has fallen into obscurity. She suggests that Harrison's decline points up inequities, prevalent to this day, in the treatment of female as distinguished from male scholars. Countering conventional critical depictions of the Bloomsbury group as detached intellectuals and aesthetes, Brantlinger argues that many Bloomsburyites went far beyond "the classical values of bourgeois enlightenment" that the prominent Marxist critic Raymond Williams grudgingly concedes to them. Rather, Brantlinger maintains that many members of the group, including Virginia and Leonard Woolf, John Maynard Keynes, and E. M. Forster, constructed important social and political theories in order to oppose the evils of patriarchy, war, and empire.

LOOKING AND LOOKING AGAIN:
TWO VIEWS OF TWO WRITERS

These essays examine two prominent writers of the early twentieth century, offering varying responses to their thematic concerns and technical aims. Wilfred H. Stone's "Forster, the Environmentalist" examines Forster's lament for the death of a green England, as he witnessed rapid industrialization and the defacement of the rural landscape and framed, in response, an ironic protest. Forster critiques the equation of "bigness"—big business, big money, big city, big empire—with progress, suggesting instead that scale can be the measure of a brutality far removed from aesthetic values and moral imperatives. Margaret Goscilo, in "Forster's Italian Comedies: Que[e]rying Heterosexuality Abroad," examines Forster's Italian novels and their recent adaptations into film as coded responses to his personal concerns over the cultural Otherness of the homosexual. Forster's own psychosexual awareness, as Goscilo shows, was imaginatively shaped by mythic ideals of Mediterranean society. Envisioning Italy as a symbolic landscape, Forster presents it as a site in which homoerotic self-discovery and expression, both forbidden in England, can be realized.

The second set of essays, Paul Delany's "*Nostromo:* Economism and Its Discontents" and Michael Mageean's "*The Secret Agent*'s (T)extimacies: A Traumatic Reading Beyond Rhetoric," examine Conrad's fiction from highly divergent perspectives. Delany argues that *Nostromo* tacitly engages with premises of Cobdenite liberal "economism," based on internationalism, open markets, and dislike of aristocratic privilege. Yet Conrad ultimately rejects Cobden's proposal for a peaceful and multilateral world system of trade, dismissing it as both unrealistic and unattainable. As Delany notes, Cobden's economism is at odds with Conrad's vision of a humanity that is never innocent of self-interest and thus is doomed to enact a tragic cycle of idealism and corruption. Mageean credits Conrad with devising a means of indicating, through language, the unrepresentability of violence within language. This verbal construct Mageean calls a "(t)extimacy": a linguistic device that indicates the presence within the symbolic order of that which exceeds it and cannot be named. Unlike tropes, which help to represent an event, Conrad creates, in Mageean's term, "entropes," linguistic blockages serving to demonstrate that violence can never be represented.

From the range of the studies in this collection we are struck by the exciting possibilities for literary criticism to remap what had appeared to be the all too familiar terrain of Edwardian and Modernist literature. These essays have, in some cases, disclosed to us territories previously forgotten or unknown. In other instances, they have defamiliarized spaces that we had come to look at in narrow and prescriptive ways. We call these joint endeavors of discovery a "revisioning," to stress the infinite possibilities for seeing Edwardian and Modernist texts—and indeed all texts—both for the first time and yet again.

WORKS CITED

Batchelor, John. *The Edwardian Novelists*. New York: St. Martin's, 1982.

Bennett, Arnold. "Virginia Woolf's *A Room of One's Own* (1929)." *The Author's Craft and Other Critical Writings of Arnold Bennett*. Ed. Samuel Hynes. Lincoln: U of Nebraska P, 1968, 225-27.

Caserio, Robert L. "The Novel as a Novel Experiment in Statement: The Anticanonical Example of H. G. Wells." *Decolonizing Tradition: New Views of Twentieth-Century "British" Literary Canons*. Ed. Karen R. Lawrence. Urbana: U of Illinois P, 1992, 88-109.

Eagleton, Terry. *Literary Theory: An Introduction*. Minneapolis: U of Minnesota P, 1984.

Edel, Leon, and Gordon N. Ray, eds. *Henry James and H. G. Wells: A Record of their Friendship, their Debate on the Art of Fiction, and their Quarrel*. Urbana: U of Illinois P, 1958.

Forster, E. M. *Aspects of the Novel*. San Diego: Harcourt Brace Jovanovich, 1955.

———. "What I Believe." *Two Cheers for Democracy*. New York: Harcourt, Brace, 1951, 67-76.

Hunter, Jefferson. *Edwardian Fiction*. Cambridge, Mass.: Harvard UP, 1982.

Hynes, Samuel. *The Edwardian Turn of Mind*. Princeton: Princeton UP, 1968.

Jauss, Hans Robert. "Literary History as a Challenge to Literary Theory." *Critical Theory Since 1965*. Ed. Hazard Adams and Leroy Searle. Tallahassee: Florida State UP, 1986, 164-83.

Masterman, C. F. G. *The Condition of England*. 1909. London: Methuen, 1911.

Meisel, Perry. *The Myth of the Modern: A Study in British Literature and Criticism after 1850*. New Haven: Yale UP, 1987.

Minney, R. J. *The Edwardian Age*. Boston: Little, Brown, 1964.

Nowell-Smith, Simon, ed. *Edwardian England 1901-1914*. London: Oxford UP, 1964.

Perloff, Marjorie. "Modernist Studies." *Redrawing the Boundaries: The Transformation of English and American Literary Studies*. Ed. Stephen Greenblatt and Giles Gunn. New York: Modern Language Association, 1992, 154-78.

Rose, Jonathan. *The Edwardian Temperament 1895-1919*. Athens: Ohio UP, 1986.

Scott, Bonnie Kime, ed. *The Gender of Modernism: A Critical Anthology*. Bloomington: Indiana UP, 1990.

Tuchman, Barbara. *The Proud Tower: A Portrait of the World Before the War 1890-1914*. New York: Macmillan, 1966.

Woolf, Virginia. "Mr. Bennett and Mrs. Brown." *Collected Essays*. Vol. 1. London: Hogarth, 1966, 319-37.

Part One

Looking Within: Gender Construction and Sexual Identity

Revolutionary Androgyny in the Fiction of "Victoria Cross"

Shoshana Milgram Knapp

Some are born Edwardian, some become Edwardian, and some have the Edwardian period thrust upon them. When Annie Sophie Cory (1868-1952) began writing, in the late nineteenth century, the response to her early fiction was disheartening: her readers, even those who were enthusiastic, seemed to miss the point. Reviewers typically commended or condemned her treatment of sexual passion without noticing psychological, philosophical, or ethical implications. Understandably intent on achieving popular success and understanding, she attempted to package herself for the contemporary audience. Accordingly, she felt compelled to withhold for a few crucial years the radical visions at which she had hinted in "Theodora" and *The Woman Who Didn't,* both of 1895.

In the first decade of the twentieth century, she published several novels that addressed and attracted a public more prepared to grasp and embrace her purposes—not only three books that were ultimately worldwide best-sellers, in multiple editions and in translation (*Anna Lombard,* 1901; *Life's Shop-Window,* 1907; *Five Nights,* 1908), but *Six Chapters of a Man's Life* (1903), the novel-length continuation of her very first story. These two texts—the fragmentary story of 1895 and the segmented novel of

1903—show her increasingly daring attempts to place at the core of popular fiction a woman who challenged conventions of gender and thought. In her Edwardian fiction, she exposed and explored the figure of the revolutionary androgyne she had introduced, to little effect, in her late Victorian fiction. A full century after Victoria Cross launched her fictional trial balloon, the current study examines the reasons she chose to conclude her story not at once, but at last.

THE VICTORIAN FICTION OF VICTORIA CROSS

In 1895, British readers weary of the angel in the house were invited to confront a profoundly different image of womanhood: the demon on the divan. The charms of Theodora Dudley, the clever, independent heiress who serves as eponymous heroine of a story published in the *Yellow Book,* encompassed not only wit and style but also masculine ease, habits, and even physique. Her character and her story shocked contemporary readers and launched the career of a novelist who wrote under the name Victoria Cross and who has been described as "a veritable Noel Coward of the early Nineties" (Stokes 72). The writer's early notoriety, original literary context, and punning pseudonym have positioned her, to the extent that she figures in literary history, primarily as a "New Woman" novelist and a defender of the rights of women against the wrongs of men (Mix 253-54; Lauterbach and Davis 81; Lucas 202; Harris 114).

This view, however, is at best limited. To interpret Victoria Cross as a late Victorian polemicist is to misread both her fiction and the public that eventually devoured her books. She exemplified, in fact, not only a rejection of the legal restriction of women's freedom and the social constriction of women's biological and emotional identity, but a thorough engagement in what Marjorie Garber has called "category crisis," the disruption and foregrounding of "cultural, social, or aesthetic dissonances" (16), testing and questioning boundaries. Victoria Cross, accordingly, wrote most of her novels, and achieved her largest readership, in the early years of the twentieth century, a time in which a variety of borders, from geography to class, came to be seen as permeable. As Jonathan Rose persuasively claims: "The reconciliation of the sacred and the secular, the rich and the poor, sexuality and spirituality, the child and the adult brought with it an inner reconciliation of the self" (200). Years before Modernist writers (as Gilbert and Gubar have argued) used cross-dressing as a metaphor, Victoria Cross considered what it would mean for women and for men to cross the border of gender construction and identity.

Victoria Cross began her writing career during the period of "New Woman" fiction, exemplified by such figures as Sarah Grand, "George Egerton," and Mona Caird and characterized, as Ann Ardis notes, by such concerns as the reform of marriage laws, the promotion of women's intellectual advancement, the advocacy of women's emotional fulfillment, and altogether a more radical feminism than that of the 1860s. Born in India, where her father was an army officer, she seems to have chosen the pseudonym "Victoria Cross" as a complicated joke: she deserved the Victoria Cross for her military valor, and she expected to cross Queen Victoria, or to make Victoria cross, through her candor. Her name, in other words, identified her as both a hero, displaying courage and enterprise, and an outlaw, violating conventions of manners and morals (Knapp, "Victoria Cross" 76, 78).

"Theodora: A Fragment," her first published work, appeared in the fourth issue of the *Yellow Book*. At a banquet in February 1894, George Moore and Frank Harris had urged John Lane (who, together with C. Elkins Mathews, owned the Bodley Head publishing business) to start "a really first-rate, up-to-date review" (quoted in May 71). With Henry Harland as literary editor and Aubrey Beardsley as art editor, the *Yellow Book* became known as an adventurous journal, new, vital, daring, and significant; early *Yellow Book* contributors included Arthur Symons, Henry James, Ella D'Arcy, Alice Meynell, Francis Thompson, Grant Allen, Kenneth Grahame, Max Beerbohm, Richard Le Gallienne, and H. G. Wells (Harrison 9). In this setting, one might expect a story by "Victoria Cross" to address women's economic, spiritual, and sexual well-being with a dashing, unconventional approach. This expectation was, in part, met.

Cecil Ray, an Egyptologist temporarily in England, is intrigued by Theodora Dudley, a wealthy young woman, "clever" and "peculiar," who would lose her fortune if she married. Although he is indifferent to the "opening-primrose type of woman, the girl who does or wishes to suggest the modest violet unfolding beneath the rural hedge," he finds himself attracted by Theodora, "in whom there was a dash of virility, a hint at dissipation, a suggestion of a certain decorous looseness of morals and fastness of manners" and an "intellectual but careless and independent spirit" (12)—not to mention her boyish figure and her slight mustache, "that curious masculine shade upon the upper lip" (26). She looks, he observes, "like a young fellow of nineteen as she sp[eaks]" (19). Several times, he notes, almost with surprise, that she is very beautiful, while reminding himself that her hips and bosom are unsuited physically to child-bearing and breast-feeding, "a poor if possible mother, and a still poorer nurse" (21). When she visits his chambers, she is wearing a tight velvet jacket and a fez-like hat; she takes her costume a step further when she tries on Eastern dress (a tight Zouave jacket of silk, and a genuine fez).

As they converse, walk, drink, and survey artifacts and sketches from his explorations, she tantalizes him with a pair of glances (the first "tender and appealing," the second "virile and mocking") that signal "a strange mingling of extremes in her. At one moment she seemed will-less, deliciously weak, a thing only made to be taken in one's arms and kissed. The next, she was full of independent uncontrollable determination and opinion" (31). Just as their visit is ending, he yields to the "overwhelming desire to take her in my arms and hold her, control her, assert my will over hers, this exasperating object who had been pleasing and seducing every sense for the last three hours," and kisses her "in a wild, unheeding, unsparing frenzy" (36). He returns to his rooms and opens the windows to let the snow in. The story concludes inconclusively, with an ellipsis.

As an unfinished story narrated by a man's voice yet under a woman's name, "Theodora" permitted readers a variety of interpretations of the writer's goals and attitudes. Although Cecil is clearly overwhelmed by Theodora's daring and sensuality, the lack of resolution in the story makes it possible to see the woman—androgynous in her attire, speech, and sexual aggressiveness—as a phenomenon for study and possibly the target of social and moral criticism, rather than as a moral exemplar or an object of admiration. Cecil himself appears ambivalent, less than clear about the source of Theodora's appeal to him. Although he contrasts her with the conventionally passive "opening-primrose" woman, he notes that Theodora is both passive and aggressive. Does he relish the contrast of Theodora's will-less weakness and resolute determination? Does he tolerate her strength because of her weakness? Is his interest in her affected by his experiences in the East? What significance should one place on the pictures in his sketchbook, which include not only women he has loved, but a young Sikh with a "lovely face" and "beautiful hair" (26), whom Theodora at first assumes to be a woman? Why does Theodora refer to his attachment to his sketchbook as that of Herod for the daughter of Herodias? What, moreover, is the point of Cecil's explicit attack on romantic possessiveness (loving another for one's own sake and pleasure), and to what extent is this the story's moral message?

Victoria Cross presented Theodora without committing herself to a judgment about Theodora's mind, character, or appropriate destiny. The fragment was, like Cecil's anthropological artifacts, a key to an unknown culture—not in the past but in the present and future. The fragment, offered under the double mask of a female pseudonym and a male persona, allowed Victoria

Cross to see if readers were ready for a woman who combined integrity with complexity, "masculine" assertion with "feminine" surrender. The story provoked considerable controversy. Janet E. Hogarth, in "Literary Degenerates," criticizes the "sex mania" of women writers of the nineties: "Few people are without the germs of possible disease; but are the confused and morbid imaginings, which the sane hide deep within their breast, to be offered to the world at large as the discovery of a privileged few? To be silly and sinful is not necessarily to be singular. We commend this consideration to the authoress of *Theodora* " (592). The writer and the story are attacked not for the characterization of Theodora, but for Cecil's "confused and morbid" passion.

Blanche Crackanthorpe, in "Sex in Modern Literature," similarly condemns writers who force readers "down into the stifling charnel-house, where animal decay, with its swarm of loathsome activities, meets us at every turn." It is "revolting," in fact, "that it should be possible for a girl to project herself into the mood of a man at one of his baser moments, faithfully identifying herself with the sequence of his sensation, as was done in a recent notable instance" (614)—a direct reference to "Theodora." The issue, again, is Cecil's sexual attraction to Theodora, rather than the qualities of Theodora herself.

The positive notices, too, stressed the experience of the man involved. The reviewer for *Woman* called the story "a brilliant and penetrating study of the beginning of a passion." The *Birmingham Daily Post* similarly praised it as "a full-blooded fragment of passion." According to *Literary World:* "Victoria Cross sets forth in powerful fashion what we may term desire at first sight." The *Daily Chronicle* noted "a style brutal in its strength" and "an eye which sees the essentials of human motive and passion." Fans and foes of the story responded to the evocation of Cecil's passion rather than to Theodora herself.

A partial exception was Ada Leverson, whose one-page parody "Tooraloora. A Fragment. (By Charing Cross)" appeared in *Punch* within a few weeks of "Theodora." Leverson's Tooraloora flings her long hair about on the floor, boasts of frequent public intoxication, and brawls with her suitor. Although Leverson also addresses the man's incipient passion, the details of the characterization of Tooraloora/Theodora are the main target and source of humor. Yet the parody does not aim to diminish the original, any more than was the case with her parodies of the work of such friends as Max Beerbohm and Oscar Wilde. Leverson had hoped to write a serious review of this issue of the *Yellow Book*, and had told John Lane: "I am *quite* delighted at the story of 'Victoria Cross'. It is brilliant" (Speedie 73). She paid tribute to the brilliance by highlighting the romantic attractiveness of a powerful woman to a man who enjoys seeing and matching her power. "I did not offer her a chair. I flung one at her head." When she responds by punching him in the eye, he is delighted: "Now, this is the moment I had been expecting and dreading, practically, ever since her hand had left my ear the night before" (58). Leverson humorously celebrates the woman's strength.

Most readers, however, seemed oblivious to the innovative character-ization of a woman who was neither the traditional supportive and subser-vient woman nor the crusading or suffering New Woman; they seemed, moreover, indifferent to her destiny and to the clues Victoria Cross had planted. No one seemed to ask if Cecil and Theodora ever moved beyond the ellipsis, if he actually left for Egypt, if she forfeited her inheritance. No one picked up on the hint that Cecil needed a "fellow" to be his companion in Egypt, or that, if a young Sikh could look like a woman, a young woman with a mustache might be able to look like a man. In trying to placate read-ers who might have been shocked or frightened by Theodora, Victoria Cross hid her character so well within the male narrative that the novelty was too subtle to be felt.

Victoria Cross followed "Theodora" with a novel presented from a similarly disguised perspective. John Lane misleadingly marketed *The Woman Who Didn't* (1895) as if it were a rejoinder to Grant Allen's *The Woman Who Did,* which had appeared earlier that year in Lane's Bodley Head "Keynotes" series. Grant Allen's novel, condemned in the company of *Jude the Obscure* as hideous and repulsive, deals with a woman's deci-sion to live with a lover in free union; all married women, by definition, are thus women who didn't do what his heroine did. Victoria Cross's *The Woman Who Didn't* has as its subject a much narrower topic: not the legitimacy of marriage itself but the allegiance to a preexisting tie. Although the novel can hardly be read as an endorsement of the sacredness of legal mar-riage, its title may have led superficial readers to assume that the writer was attempting a latter-day version of *Pamela, or Virtue Rewarded.* Victoria Cross, with the cooperation of her publisher, may have been trying to overcome the resistance aroused by "Theodora" without alien-ating either liberal or conservative readers. The title, however, implies a binary division of women into those who did and those who didn't—an opposition that Victoria Cross typically mocks.

In *The Woman Who Didn't,* Eurydice, a married woman, declines the affections of Evelyn, a distinctly charmless man, and one who, like Cecil Ray, has spent time in the East. Although one might expect him, as the first-person narrator, to emphasize his good qualities, he does not appear to be a tempting romantic partner to any woman, married or single. He seizes on every hint that she tolerates his presence as if she had declared undying love; his unwarranted self-confidence and prolonged self-deception are ludicrous. Eurydice explains that she views marriage as a symbol of self-respect, whatever the merits or defects of her husband; she enjoys Evelyn's company but is not tempted to betray what she regards as her own integrity.

Here, again, was a version of the androgynous woman, a combination of strength and surrender, presented this time in a story that neither violated legal and social rules nor subscribed to them. Eurydice first attracts Evelyn through the "supercilious scepticism" (3) he hears in her voice; he feels admiration when, after repulsing his attempt to embrace her and accepting his apology, she is disinclined to dwell on the matter. "I was rather surprised at her summary dismissal of the subject. It was more a masculine than a feminine way of treating it" (24). He confesses himself "stimulated" by her tone, as contrasted with "the anxious servility which characterises the ordinary young girl's conversation with men" (28). Eurydice, physically graceful and musically gifted, combines conventionally feminine attractions (including a moderate fondness for the man who loves her) with fortitude, serenity, and principled endurance—qualities Evelyn describes, with mixed emotions, as "rather of the heroic order" (135). His passion is fueled by her moral and intellectual power, which he recognizes as superior to his, and which he ultimately aspires to emulate. From a woman he perceives as in part unwomanly, he learns to be more of a man.

The reviews of *The Woman Who Didn't,* while arranged on a spectrum similar to the reviews of "Theodora," uniformly miss the point. Unable to perceive Eurydice as anything but the love object, they ignore her distinctive qualities and displace her from the center of attention. At best, the *Critic* reviewer observes that the events are "weird" and the characterizations "quaint." The reviewer for *Literary World* expresses some surprise at the ease with which Eurydice resists temptation. In effect, the novel is retitled "The Man Who Didn't, Although He Would Have If He Could Have."

Given that readers appeared unable to grasp the nature and appeal of women who were unconventionally attractive, Victoria Cross settled, in her next two novels, for portraying women who were unconventional and attractive. Paula thinks independently and charts a career as a playwright; Katrine lives alone and relishes the freedom to drink, gamble, and protect the helpless with her six-shooter. Although the courage and ambition of the heroines of *Paula* (1896) and *A Girl of the Klondike* (1899) make them unusual, this unusualness is not identified as the reason their respective romantic partners love them, nor are they explicitly described as masculine in physique, speech, or demeanor. (Although the initial description of Paula, in a jacket and a fez-like hat, seems to recall Theodora, Paula does not wear trousers or pass as a man.) Their strength is devoted to rescuing their lovers through self-sacrifice: Paula arranges for her blood to be transfused into her lover's veins, and Katrine of the Klondike stops a bullet aimed at her lover.

During these years, too, Victoria Cross also began a lifelong pattern of travel and increasing seclusion. In the mid-1890s, she was sufficiently known, through her connection with John Lane, to be the subject of one of Oscar Wilde's quips (F. Harris 331). However, she was not one of the regulars in Henry Harland's circle, and she is absent from the reminiscences of such figures as Netta Syrett, Evelyn Sharp, Frederic Whyte, Grant Richards, Maurice Baring, W. Graham Robertson, Ernest Rhys, Vincent O'Sullivan, and Richard Le Gallienne. Living on the Riviera and in Italy and Switzerland, generally with her uncle Heneage Griffin, she continued to write but not to mingle with writers.

ANNA LOMBARD AS A CHALLENGE TO EDWARDIAN READERS

With *Anna Lombard* (1901), Victoria Cross tested her readers by breaking more taboos than in all of her earlier works put together. Anna, an Indian general's daughter educated in England, secretly marries Gaida Khan (a Pathan servant), although she is also devoted to Gerald Ethridge, an intelligent, enlightened Assistant Commissioner. Anna thus not only experiences passion for a man of a different race and class but also simultaneously loves another man she deems more worthy of her esteem and affection. Her infidelity goes both ways: in desiring Gaida, she is untrue to her "higher nature"; in loving Gerald while married to Gaida, she is untrue to her husband. When, not long after Gaida dies of cholera, she learns she is pregnant, Gerald immediately marries her. After the child is born, Anna develops an irresistible obsession with her son, a feeling that partakes of both incest and the persistence of her passion for Gaida. Unable to tolerate this barrier to her marriage, she smothers the child, takes a year to recover, and then joins Gerald in a true (and presumably lasting) marriage.

Given the interracial romance, the complex multiple infidelities, the hint of incest, and the act of infanticide, no one could accuse Victoria Cross of playing it safe. She had placed her protagonist in what the contemporary audience could readily have recognized as a masculine situation: attracted to—and committed to—multiple romantic partners for multiple reasons. She had, moreover, given Anna a variant of her own birth name (Annie).

Although she had exchanged that name for "Vivian" even before she abandoned all her names for her pseudonym, the name—along with the shared background of a father in the Indian army and an education in England—may indicate her special identification with this character. Although Anna is not herself described as possessing the masculine habits and physical traits of Theodora, Victoria Cross tested her audience by crossing most of the other gender boundaries.

The public response included the sneers, snorts, and shrieks that had greeted "Theodora." William L. Alden, for example, saw the novel as "brazen," "nauseating," the sort of book "which no man should read immediately before dinner unless he wishes to lose his appetite" (395).

One prominent reader, however, not only admired the novel's intensity but grasped the significance of its role reversals. William T. Stead featured *Anna Lombard* as a "Book of the Month" in his *Review of Reviews,* with an extended summary and critique of what he deemed a "remarkable novel," for

> never before in English fiction can I remember so clearly cut a representation of an embodiment in a woman of what, alas! is common enough in a man. Ethridge, an almost ideal hero, plays the part which is so normal to women as never to call for remark, while Anna abandoned herself to the force of a passion to which men succumb so often as seldom to call for comment or censure.

Although Stead wishes that the plot could have been resolved without infanticide (and, indeed, he offers several suggestions for alternative possibilities), he concludes by quoting a long description of Anna's passion for Gaida, on which he comments: "There is one passage in the book which sums up the experience of many a man, but is seldom put into the mouth of a woman" (597). A friend of Millicent Garrett Fawcett and Elizabeth Robins, Stead had a strong interest in women's rights and a record of praising women writers, as is displayed here (Knapp, "Stead" 22-23).

Victoria Cross saw that readers would accept a woman whose dilemma and conduct are, in an important sense, manlike. Indeed, *Academy and Literature* noted, not entirely with pleasure, that Anna seemed to think of herself as a man. Other reviewers described Anna as "a striking character in the portrait galleries of fiction" *(Daily News)* and "a pure woman—good, sincere, clean, fit to be admired and beloved" *(Vanity Fair). Anna Lombard* ultimately sold more than six million copies (Stokes 75) and went through more than forty editions; the transgressive elements did not obviate popularity. With the encouragement of enthusiastic reviews and an avid public, Victoria Cross returned to "Theodora," the heroine with a "dash of virility."

"THEODORA" AND SIX CHAPTERS OF A MAN'S LIFE

Her new title, *Six Chapters of a Man's Life,* appears designed to reassure readers that she had no intention of neglecting the male perspective; the name "Victoria Cross," after the triumph of *Anna Lombard,* would catch the attention of readers with a primary interest in a woman's story. In constructing the new narrative, she framed the former fragment. In addition to providing the prehistory of a story that had begun in medias res, she followed it through past the lovers' union. She also assigns the work a clear moral/religious message. She intended the novel, she writes in the preface, as a criticism of self-centered love and as a plea on behalf of an exalted love for another's sake and happiness. Much as she invoked Christian virtues in the preface to *Anna Lombard,* she here portrays *Six Chapters* as a paean to altruism—however peripheral this tribute in fact is to the narrative in question.

The full novel explores further the issue of sexual identity, develops hints and references implied in the fragment, disrupts conventions and expectations in a variety of frameworks, and expands exponentially the possibilities of a man's attraction to a manlike woman. Theodora here has not only a slight mustache but one "so perceptible that you can see it all across the room" (10-11); her face, moreover, has "a male fire in the eyes, and a male curve of the determined lip" (90). To a passage describing Cecil's thoughts regarding Theodora's appeal to him, the novel adds two significant sentences: "I disliked in a mild, theoretical way, women in the general term. I had an aversion, slight and faint it is true, but still an aversion, to everything suggestively, typically feminine; but Theodora, with her peculiarity, her apparent power of mind, her hermaphroditism of looks, stimulated violently that strongest, perhaps, of our feelings—curiosity" (76). Victoria Cross even renames Theodora's sister—Helen Long in the fragment, Hester Strong in the novel—to suggest greater power.

In new introductory chapters of the novel (which precede the events of the fragment), Theodora explains her philosophy of life: a pagan adherence to pleasure and beauty, with an indifference to creeds and systems she sees as arbitrary. She recognizes no "moral law for conduct and action," condemns "restrictions" as "tiresome," and hates "iconoclasts and puritans" alike (32-33). Cecil, as it happens, entirely shares her beliefs (or lack of beliefs), and significantly attributes his own attitude to the years he has spent in the East—as if this is where one learns to cross borders. And this, of course, is where he intends to return.

The novel develops the implications of the fragment. In the earlier text, Cecil had considered Theodora's Eastern outfit "not at all complete without the trousers," and had expressed a wish for a "chum," a "companion," a "fellow" to go with him to Egypt. In the novel, Theodora adopts full male dress, burns her hair, and, passing as a man, joins Cecil on his journey. In the fragment, Cecil observes that Theodora's body appears nonmaternal. In the novel, he discovers with relief and gratitude that she dislikes children, as she asserts: "They bore me unutterably. I should detest the man who made me a mother!" (150) He thinks to himself: "I must get rid of all my old-fashioned ideas of women, that was very clear" (151). Discarding his ideas about women proves an enjoyable, but formidable, challenge.

He finds their relationship more stimulating and satisfying than any romance he has had or any marriage he has imagined:

> We met on equal, easy, broad, pleasant grounds, where the companionship and comradeship and friendship of a man to a man joined and met and merged easily into passionate desire and the pleasure of sense; and I felt—I don't say other men would feel—but I felt an infinitely stronger, more violent passion grow in me for this associate, this fellow-being, this co-thinker, and constant companion than I could possibly have done for any womanly wife. (141-42)

He is, however, jealous of Theodora's interactions with both men and women. During their sea journey, he becomes enraged when she spends half the night drinking and playing cards with a group of men, and seeing her laughing with a pretty young woman "set my brain in a savage whirl" (181). The woman with whom she flirts is one Cecil himself has failed to attract; Theodora competes with him as a man, and wins.

The final crisis, which contrasts Cecil's indecision and inconsistency with Theodora's resolution and power, is ignited by a transgressive dance. In Port Said, they visit a dancing den in the native part of town where, with an all-male audience, they watch the erotic dancing of a white-skinned Levantine boy of seventeen, whom the audience cheers on, as he bends his "smooth boneless body double, backwards till the head rested on the ground" and the dancer faints (217). The slender dancer may be, so to speak, a veiled allusion to Salome (referred to by Theodora, in both the fragment and the novel, to describe Cecil's attachment to his sketchbook of former lovers). And Salome—in Oscar Wilde's play, the most recent version of the story Victoria Cross was likely to have encountered—was, according to Marjorie Garber, "a figure for transvestitism in its power to destabilize and define" (344). The dancer, with or without an implicit connection to Wilde's Salome, marks the crossing of numerous borders, including that between awareness and unconsciousness.

Aroused, Cecil kisses Theodora, thus bringing her to the attention of their Egyptian host, who bars the door with a group of armed men—all presumably drawn to Theodora as a womanlike man, or perhaps as a man-like woman. If Theodora joins them for a week, both she and Cecil will be permitted to live and leave; otherwise, Theodora will be killed. The lie they have been living—lovers passing as companions—has proved a deadly risk in this culture and this setting.

In a remarkable passage, Cecil imagines killing her himself to avoid the dishonor to his property. "I longed to destroy her now . . . to shatter and burst those eyeballs and blot out their light for ever, to lay open the temples and transform them into a shapeless bleeding mass, to keep her mine now" (224). She tells him that their lives are worth more to her than a conventional notion of "honor." She insists that he remember the unique nature of their relationship. "The friend and comrade I have been to you, you will throw away because you are asked to lend the mistress!" (227) He allows her to go, but nurses "a bitter, implacable anger that she had rejected death by our own hands" (237). Although he struggles against his conventional ideas about women and women's "honor," he is trapped.

She returns to him with a face "blotted and covered with sores," expecting him to reject her. Although he is prepared to love her even "when all my senses turned from her, stricken with loathing," this is a change from his earlier position, he now realizes, and he admits, with shame, that he had allowed her to assume that he loved her for her beauty alone (238). Back on the ship, she throws herself over the side, and he is left with regrets for giving her cause to feel that exclusive possession mattered more to him than her well-being, or that his love for her was based on her appearance. Victoria Cross implies that Cecil was unable to experience, much less to communicate, the appropriate response to a woman who wanted to be his equal in a relationship unfettered by the conventional emphases on a woman's beauty and "honor." He has, he admits, murdered her by his failure to appreciate her. There is no place in his sketchbook for her portrait, and his inability to see her in her own (complex) right as more than a chapter in his life has deprived her of her own.

Six Chapters, tragic in its conclusion, seems to imply that there is no place in the world for the androgynous woman—and that this is the fault of that world. Leaving England, and in the company of a man who appeared attracted by her strength, Theodora nonetheless becomes the emotional victim of one man and the physical victim of others. She is threatened on land, she dies at sea, she is nowhere seen and understood. The story implies that no place is safe, no companion is loyal. Theodora cannot endure—except, of course, in fiction, where Victoria Cross was able to publish in 1903 the story she left unfinished in 1895.

Although the novel provoked protest, reviewers commended the writer's "vivid imagination" *(Liverpool Mercury),* intense drama *(Daily News),* "uncommon literary ability" *(Aberdeen Free Press),* and cleverness *(Scotsman, Birmingham Post).* Stead again wrote favorably in his *Review of Reviews,* calling Victoria Cross "a woman of genius" and the novel "a difficult book to forget." He interpreted it, however, as "a vision of lost souls mutually tempting and tempted, with no redeeming gleam from a higher and purer world," "a study of lost souls making their damnation sure." Describing Theodora as "epicene," he appears to have noticed her androgynous qualities, yet he does not regard her as an attractive figure in any sense, or as the victim of Cecil's moral deficiencies. Even a reviewer who consistently admires her work, referring in this later review to *Anna Lombard* as "wonderful" and "powerful and daring," cannot see in Theodora anything more than a "woman who did." Victoria Cross's crossover character remained, to a large degree, invisible.

Within the next few years, Victoria Cross published, among others, two novels that have rivaled *Anna Lombard* in popularity. Both were reprinted many times. *Life's Shop-Window* became, with a tamer ending, a play performed on both sides of the Atlantic, and *Five Nights* was adapted to the screen in 1915 in a notorious film that led some authorities to call for centralized official censorship (Low 128-29). In both, she permits characters guiltlessly to violate legal restrictions and social conventions, and gives full rein to the evocation of sexual passion that had shocked readers since 1895; she does not, however, recreate Theodora.

In *Life's Shop-Window* (1907), Lydia marries a kind, honorable Arizona rancher, leaves him for a cultured British lover of independent means, considers leaving him for a half-Russian, half-English soldier-explorer-writer she meets in Turkey, and ultimately returns to her British lover because one cannot, after all, continue to exchange one's purchases. Although Lydia is capable of a decisiveness characterized as masculine ("with a certain virility of thought and strength that was always hers" [287]), Victoria Cross more often, and at length, contrasts Lydia's qualities and concerns with those of the men in her life, and men in general. The androgyny is muted, and explicitly contravened.

In *Five Nights* (1908), the author situates Trevor, a painter, in Anna Lombard's romantic dilemma: his Gaida is Suzee, a young Eskimo woman, "a toy to caress, to fondle" (253), for whom he feels a "frenzy of hungered, starving love" (227), and his Gerald is Viola, a professional singer (and his cousin), with whom he shares "exquisite mental companionship" (253). Although Victoria Cross has taken a step backward by placing the male protagonist in the typically male situation, she takes the chance of hinting that Viola, who knows mathematics and classical literature better than does Trevor, is not a traditional woman. "In her outlook upon life she was more like a man than a woman, and, never having been to school or mixed much with other girls of her own age, she was free from all those small, petty habits of mind, that littleness of mental vision that so mars and dwarfs the ordinary feminine character" (87-88). Victoria Cross contrasts independent Viola (who sends Trevor away without explanation when she discovers she is pregnant) with clinging Suzee (who tries to become pregnant in order to hold Trevor); Viola is a far less disruptive and disturbing version of Theodora.

Victoria Cross's works appeared at intervals of a year or two; all dealt with erotic adventures, several in exotic settings, and often with ingeniously contrived premises, such as a wife's telepathic communication with her soldier-husband on the African veldt (*The Religion of Evelyn Hastings,* 1905) and a dream-romance between Apollo and a schoolgirl (*The Eternal Fires,* 1910). Several, notably *Life of My Heart* (1905), *Six Women* (1906), and *Self and the Other* (1911), portrayed romances across racial boundaries.

VICTORIA CROSS'S POST-EDWARDIAN FICTION

After 1914, Cross's pace slowed; she returned to publication, for the first time in six years, with a volume of short stories (*Daughters of Heaven,* 1920) and a novel (*Over Life's Edge,* 1921), which centers on a successful writer, suggestively named Violet Cresswell, who abandoned her career and the entire civilized world. Victoria Cross herself continued to flee the spotlight and to avoid literary circles. Although she continued to write, she did not revive Theodora; nor did she, as she had with Viola, assign masculine qualities to her women. At most, she placed a woman in a man's situation (as in *The Girl in the Studio: Her Strange, New Way of Loving,* 1934), as she had with Anna Lombard. Although twentieth-century readers appeared receptive to her romantic fiction, they had not taken an interest in her revolutionary character.

Even the new century, apparently, had no place for androgyny. Although Victoria Cross showed love transcending boundaries of race, religion, culture, and legal sanction, she did not again try to embody in one character the crossing of the gender boundary. She did not, after all, create the newer-than-new woman. At the end of her fictional career, however, she attempted the androgyne one more time. In this novel, the manlike woman, the treasured unique figure of her early fiction, has become the rule. Her heroine is not merely adopting a man's costume (as did Theodora) or experiencing a man's sexual dilemma (as did Anna Lombard), but living as a man-woman in a world that matches her.

Martha Brown, M.P.: A Girl of Tomorrow (1935), a utopian fantasy set in a thirtieth-century England in which women are the dominant sex, further develops the notion that "masculinity" is attractive in a woman; the heroine, who is responsible for major reforms in politics, education, and the arts, flies her own plane from lover to lover. To create a safe place for a Theodora, for the woman with a "dash of virility," Victoria Cross rebuilds the fictional context.

The ending, to be sure, hints again at tragedy. Shortly before agreeing to serve as prime minister, Martha meets Bruce Campbell Campbell [*sic*]— tall, strong, vigorous, and unperfumed—and returns home with him to the United States, where men have remained dominant. She joins him over the (literally) dead body of the husband who could not bear to lose her. Martha appears to flee her own strength, and she herself perceives her departure as a kind of death. And yet she goes.

In spite, though, of the problematic outcomes faced by Victoria Cross's androgynous women, the enduring impression is one of power, energy, and vitality, perhaps best expressed in the opening paragraphs of *Martha Brown:*

> The newcomer walked in with the air of the owner of the house, and flinging the heavy airman's cap down on the hall table walked straight to the dining-room door at one side of the hall and pushed it open. "Hello, darling! Here I am again!"
> And standing there in the doorway the lithe active figure framed in it, hands thrust deep down in the pockets of the leather coat, short pipe held firmly between the straight white teeth, . . . Martha Brown looked, as she stood there, a magnificent specimen of bronzed womanhood. (7-8)

Not in this millennium, not in the beginning of the twentieth century, but some day a thousand years hence, there may be a place for the stalwart figure in airman's uniform, entering the home with the air of an owner—the woman who is more like a man.

WORKS CITED

Alden, William L. "London Literary Letter." *New York Times,* 1 June 1901: 395.

Reviews of *Anna Lombard. Daily News* and *Vanity Fair* quoted on front page of *Anna Lombard,* 39th ed. *Academy and Literature* quoted in Grimes, Janet, and Diva Daims. *Novels in English, 1891-1920: A Preliminary Checklist.* New York: Garland, 1981.

Ardis, Ann. *New Women, New Novels: Feminism and Early Modernism.* New Brunswick: Rutgers UP, 1990.

Crackanthorpe, Blanche A. "Sex in Modern Literature." *Nineteenth Century* 31 (1895): 607-20.

Cross, Victoria. *Anna Lombard.* 1901. 39th ed. London: Laurie, 1930.

———. *Five Nights.* New York: Kennerley, 1908.

———. *Life's Shop-Window.* New York: Macaulay, 1907.

———. *Martha Brown, M.P.: A Girl of Tomorrow.* London: Laurie, 1935.

———. *Six Chapters in a Man's Life.* 1903. New York: Macaulay, 1904.

———. "Theodora: A Fragment." 1895. *Daughters of Decadence: Women Writers of the Fin-de-Siècle.* Ed. Elaine Showalter. London: Virago, 1993, 6-37.

———. *The Woman Who Didn't.* Boston: Roberts, 1895.

Garber, Marjorie. *Vested Interests: Cross-Dressing and Cultural Anxiety.* New York: Routledge, 1992.

Gilbert, Sandra M., and Susan Gubar. "Cross-Dressing and Re-Dressing: Transvestitism as Metaphor." *Sexchanges.* New Haven: Yale UP, 1989. Vol. 2 of *No Man's Land: The Place of the Woman Writer in the Twentieth Century,* 324-76.

Harris, Frank. *Oscar Wilde: His Life and Confessions.* New York: Covici, Friede, 1930.

Harris, Wendell V. *British Short Fiction in the Nineteenth Century: A Literary and Bibliographic Guide.* Detroit: Wayne State UP, 1979.

Harrison, Fraser. Introduction. *The Yellow Book: An anthology selected and introduced by Fraser Harrison.* 1914. Suffolk, Eng.: Boydell, 1982, 7-31.

Hogarth, Janet E. "Literary Degenerates." *Fortnightly Review* ns 57 (1895): 586-92.

Knapp, Shoshana Milgram. "Stead Among the Feminists: From Victoria Cross Onwards." *News-Stead* 2 (1993): 15-25.

———. "Victoria Cross." *British Short-Fiction Writers 1880-1914: The Realist Tradition.* Ed. William B. Thesing. Detroit: Gale, 1994. Vol. 135 of *Dictionary of Literary Biography.* 75-84.

Lauterbach, Edward S., and W. Eugene Davis. *The Transitional Age: British Literature 1880-1920.* Troy, N.Y.: Whitston, 1973.

Leverson, Ada. "Tooraloora. A Fragment. (By Charing Cross)." *Punch* 2 February 1895: 58.

Low, Rachael. *The History of the British Film 1914-1918.* London: BFI, 1973. Vol. 3 of *The History of the British Film.* 5 vols.

Lucas, John. *The Literature of Change: Studies in the Nineteenth-Century Provincial Novel.* Rev. ed. Totowa, N.J.: Barnes and Noble, 1980.

May, J. Lewis. *John Lane and the Nineties.* London: Bodley Head, 1936.

Mix, Katherine Lyon. *A Study in Yellow: The Yellow Book and Its Contributors.* 1960. New York: Greenwood, 1969.

Rose, Jonathan. *The Edwardian Temperament 1895-1919.* Athens: Ohio UP, 1986.

Reviews of *Six Chapters of a Man's Life. Aberdeen Free Press, Birmingham Post, Daily News, Liverpool Mercury, Scotsman.* Quoted on back page of *Paula.* London: Scott, 1907.

Speedie, Julie. *Wonderful Sphinx: The Biography of Ada Leverson.* London: Virago, 1993.

Stead, William T. "Anna Lombard: A Novel of the Ethics of Sex." (Book of the Month) *Review of Reviews* 23 (1901): 595-97.

————. Review of *Six Chapters of a Man's Life. Review of Reviews* 28 (1903): 307.

Stokes, Sewell. "How I Won My Victoria Cross." *Pilloried!* London: Richards, 1928, 71-83.

Reviews of *Theodora. Birmingham Daily Post, Daily Chronicle, Literary World,* and *Woman.* Quoted on back page of *The Woman Who Didn't.* Boston: Roberts, 1895.

Reviews of *The Woman Who Didn't. Critic,* 25 July 1895: 56; *Literary World,* 5 October 1895: 331.

(P)revising Freud: Vernon Lee's Castration Phantasy

Jane Hotchkiss

In 1896, during roughly the same period when Freud was first developing his highly persuasive version of the old story of female lack, Vernon Lee's (Violet Paget's) story, "Prince Alberic and the Snake Lady," appeared in the *Yellow Book.* Her Gothic fairy tale abounds in imagery suggestive of castration: bodiless, Holofernes-like heads with staring eyes are replicated around the walls of the "tomato-colored" Red Palace; a grotto filled with stone statues of animals suggests a *vagina dentata.* In fact the text readily lends itself to the sort of retroactive psychoanalytic reading that Sigmund Freud performed on E. T. A. Hoffman's "The Sandman," which provided confirmation of his theory that castration anxiety is a prime motivator in the masculine psyche. By extension, corroborations of male castration anxiety legitimated (in Freud's eyes, at any rate) his construction of a corresponding theory of penis envy that complicated resolution of the Oedipus complex for girls.

"The little creature without a penis" must come to accept the "fact of her castration" in order to move successfully from her earlier "masculine" sexuality into a "specifically feminine" sexuality that Freud defines as vaginal and as characterized by "marked diminution in the active and an augmentation of the passive sexual impulses" ("Female Sexuality" 207). Calling the "fact of [female] castration" a fiction and refusing to undergo gracefully what amounts to a castration of subjectivity becomes proof of penis envy, or so Freud concluded in his famous footnote (199) in which he creates a Catch-22 that cuts both ways to disarm, specifically, feminist revisions of psychoanalysis.

At the end of Vernon Lee's *Yellow Book* story, the decapitation, which in Freud's view "equals" castration, is the fate of the powerful female figure, surrogate mother, intellectual mentor, and lover to the prince of the story's title: the Snake Lady, really the fairy Oriana, who "cannot die unless her head is severed from her trunk" (57). Freud, had he read this tale, might have interpreted the moment of decapitation as the instance of the youth's deferred perception of the female "lack" that is always already there. I argue that it represents, instead, patriarchy's act of castration of the feminine: one might say, the moment when the fact of the presence of the clitoris becomes the fiction of its absence. The Snake Lady, with her various potencies and her majestic coiled and folded serpent's tail, represents what psychoanalysis calls the "phallic woman" but more accurately might be called the clitoral woman, the woman who has "never already" lacked anything until patriarchal history reified its own parapraxis and claimed, as Freud often did, that there was "nothing" where there was, in fact, the powerful and exclusively erotic (a distinction the male organ lacks) female organ of pleasure.[1]

In her essay "Is Female to Male as Ground Is to Figure?" Barbara Johnson observes that the clitoris can function as a "synecdoche for the possibility that the world could be articulated differently, that resistance is always the sign of a counterstory" (264). This essay will examine and contextualize Vernon Lee's different articulation of the "phallic" woman figure in her tragic fable of castration, which constitutes, albeit unwittingly, a timely "counterstory" to Freud's readings of castration and of female sexuality.

Ironically, a mid-twentieth-century analysis of Lee's story exists that will serve quite well to introduce the gynophobic cultural context that frames Lee's tale. Burdett Gardner's "psychological and critical study" of Lee's oeuvre, reprinted in 1987, was completed in 1954 and declares itself Freudian in its methodology. Gardner "discovers" Lee's lesbian inclinations and takes it upon himself to explore the "effect . . . the neurosis [had] upon her entire literary production" (28). The story he first came upon while browsing through the *Yellow Book,* "Prince Alberic and the Snake Lady," serves as starting point for his investigation of Lee's personal and literary "perversions" and as a touchstone throughout his study; his reading both recognizes and repudiates what I am calling the "clitoral woman" in Lee's Snake Lady figure. Gardner speculates "that [Oriana's] 'enchantment'" is Vernon Lee's own sexual inversion and that she is presenting a fantastic allegory of her own struggle to achieve 'freedom' and mental health" (28); the critic does not say whether the symbolic decapitation at the end constitutes success or failure in this allegorical struggle. Clearly, the tale, with its "overwrought sensuousness," disgusts this male reader, as does the tail of the Snake Lady, that "latter-day re-incarnation of the medieval incubus, or succubus" (27). The story, which "fairly squirms with reptiles," in Gardner's opinion exhibits an "unwholesome weirdness": "The evidence of diseased sensibility is not to be found merely in the perverse and brutal plot. The style is everywhere loaded with an unhealthy excess of color and jewelled ornament" (23, 21).

I cannot determine whether the gynophobia in Gardner's reading is a product of homophobia or vice versa. What interests me is the applicability of his reading to Lee's own time, for Gardner's study is remarkably nineteenth-century in its reading of lesbianism and female eroticism as pathological. In *Sexual Anarchy,* Elaine Showalter shows that the "phallic woman" was already associated with the clitoris and with lesbianism, as well as with the cultural "repudiation of the feminine" that Freud naturalized as biological: "By the late nineteenth century, the clitoris seemed like a threatening organ. Lesbians were rumored to have grossly enlarged clitorises, and in addition to homosexuality, other 'diseases' of the New Woman, such as masturbation, depression, marital dissatisfaction, and nymphomania, were attributed to clitoral overdevelopment" (130).

"Discovered" by medicine in the Renaissance and tamed by the attribution to it of a crucial role in reproduction, the clitoris had become a problematic entity in the nineteenth century, which represented a resistance to the equation of female sexuality with heterosexuality and the desire to mother. It was recognized to be without generative function—an organ with no purpose other than the erotic—by which women could enjoy orgasm with or without penetration, and with or without men: "Joined through the imperative of repression, the clitoris and the 'lesbian' together signify women's erotic potential for a pleasure outside of masculine control" (Traub 82). Thus, rather than representing simply a "female penis," as Freud and others insisted (and feminists often repeat this mistake), the clitoris represents female autonomy and a difference that has no "mirror image" in male physiology (unlike, for instance, the vagina, the birth canal that can "become" a penis through surgical techniques). And as even a "virgin" could enjoy clitoral orgasm, the clitoris eludes patriarchal control as that other distinctively female feature, the hymen, could not.

Nineteenth-century and Decadent perpetuations of the clitoris/phallus equation and the horror of femininity they reify are disturbed, if not unequivocally revised, in Lee's representation of the serpent-woman grotesque as beautiful, wise, erotic, and good. The half-serpent, half-woman form that descends from Milton's Sin (itself looking backward to predecessors in Spenser and in Ovid) was a favorite in the nineteenth century, from Keats's Lamia to George Macdonald's Lilith, one of a panoply of figures—along with vampires, Salomes and Sapphos—that came to embody male fears of the New Woman with her threatening sexuality (Robbins 156). As Ruth Robbins notes, "Given this dishonourable cast of foremothers, it comes as something of a surprise to find that Lee's Snake Lady is unequivocally good" (157).[2]

Moreover, in the course of Lee's tale, the phallic-woman image itself undergoes a subtle metamorphosis that undermines the symmetry Freud seeks to impose by calling the clitoris "homologous to the penis" ("Sexual Theories" 32). It becomes clear that the initial representation of the Snake Lady as a woman whose form "ends in the long, twisting body of a snake" is deliberately hyperbolic. In the scene at the wellspring (discussed in more detail below), the "symbolic" representation of the female genitals becomes almost graphic, at the very moment of the Prince's erotic initiation, in a way that affirms Freud's eventual concession that women have two genital sites—clitoris and vagina—but resists the erotic primacy of the vagina he would attempt to impose as necessary and "normal."

In Lee's story, then, the blatantly "phallic" woman, the representation of Oriana in the tapestry that hangs in the young Prince's room, serves as a sort of litmus test for gynophobia, a test the Duke fails miserably and the Prince passes with flying colors. Ultimately, his reward is full erotic union with the erstwhile "godmother"; Lee's famous "prudery" is not evident in this tale. The first two Alberics, the prince's ancestors and also Oriana's lovers, failed to fulfill their ten-year vows to her and chose instead to marry, in the first instance, and to enter a life of celibacy in the Church, in the second. Both decisions, to follow more conventionally chaste paths, constitute failures of troth; the "good" thing to do in this tale is to love the enchantress on her own terms, and the prince does the good thing.

The unequivocally positive light cast on the erotic in this tale is of interest because it is unusual in Lee's gothic tales.[3] But as important as the Snake Lady's initiation of the prince into an erotic appreciation of female genitality is her mentorship; she educates him in ethics and philosophy, in the arts of war and compassionate government. Under her tutelage, which begins, indirectly, in his earliest infancy, Alberic becomes eminently fit to rule the Duchy of Luna, which the decadent duke has brought to the brink of ruin. Thus Lee's story firmly links to her representation of feminine genital "superiority" the claims for intellectual and moral capacity that Freud (following, of course, a long tradition) made for the possessor of the phallus.

Lee's fable, set in a particular historical period and place—Italy at an earlier time—looks both back and forward. She begins the tale with an epilogue, thus tying directly this feminine mutilation to the exhaustion and extinction of the imperial patriarchal lineage of the Duchy of Luna in 1701. The name suggests the duchy's connection to the Dionysian, but we learn that under the rule of the Ever Young Duke Balthasar Maria the duchy has recently switched its allegiance to "Apollo and his graces," and that the ancient center of the realm, the Castle of Sparkling Waters, has been left to rack and ruin. The court has removed to the Red Palace with its many (and expensive) monuments honoring conquest and domination. The place and time that contain the fictional duchy, Lee referred to elsewhere as "that strange swamp, bog and quagmire of the Italy of the seventeenth century" (Gunn 72). This was an "age of decadence" when the Renaissance had passed its peak, marked by "the efforts of the nobles to outdo one another in the gorgeousness of their entertainments and equipages," where "to startle, to surprise, to impress by any kind of extravagance, above all by lavish and costly display . . . was the ideal." It was also a period of diminished opportunities even for aristocratic women, who had "lost the freedom of the Renaissance. . . . woman play[ed] but a subordinate part even in the social life"; "the brilliant, cultivated women of earlier days" were gone, no longer "shar[ing] the education of the men" (Collison-Morley xii, xiii).

The court of Luna participates in the Renaissance fascination with classical culture, but the duke clearly favors Imperial Rome as a model to emulate; thus the story's situation in a "decadent" age looks back to the period when Empire had replaced Republic, and to the extreme decadence of late Rome (symbolized by all twelve Caesars presiding, as bodiless heads, over the Court of Honor of the Red Palace). Clearly, the tale looks forward as well to another period during which imperial-colonial expansion was changing global history in order to feed the maws of industry and the demands of a consumer culture. The vigorous progress extolled by many suggested to some, and certainly to Vernon Lee, the imminent—and immanent—exhaustion that must follow excess.

Lee's liberal-intellectual politics and her feminist sympathies informed her choice of setting for her fairy tale, with its many images of domination, displacement, and conquest. Lee consistently opposed wars of imperialism; "the only war she could envisage without utter detestation was a revolutionary one," according to her biographer, Peter Gunn (201). Specifically Gunn records, "her outspoken criticism of Italian political adventures in East Africa in the eighties and nineties" (164). Later, in 1911, when Italy ventured into Tripoli, intent on "carv[ing] itself an empire" there, she went vehemently on record against the invasion, although she knew her stance would estrange her from many of her Italian friends (201).[4] She also joined in the "vigorous denunciation of British policy" during the Boer War, adding her voice to the Liberal protests that saw the action in the Transvaal (where gold had recently been discovered), as an unwarranted aggression against a pastoral nation (164). The other great issue of her own period was, of course, the "Woman Question." Lee was no suffragette, but she "wanted a vote" and recognized the treatment of women as one of the "long-organized social evils" ("Economic Dependence" 90). She felt, however, that the problem of "redistribution of wealth" was a "far more important question," to which the status of women was inextricably linked: "The integration of women as *direct* economic, and therefore *direct* moral and civic, factors in the community, is not a more difficult question than the question of the integration of the laboring classes into the real life of nations; and yet the 'social question' will find, some day, its unexpected solution; and the 'Woman Question' will, very likely, have to be settled beforehand" (100). Above all, the idea of the good of community over the interests of the individual prevails in her arguments on social justice and feminism. She joins Charlotte Perkins Gilman in berating women who take on the duty of conspicuous consumption, the "good" housewife who wastes goods to follow fashion so that others will not think "that the husband's *business* was not thriving. 'It is good for trade.' . . . it makes room for more objects (dresses, crockery, furniture, houses, or human beings); but meanwhile you have wasted those that were already there, and all the labor and capital they have cost to produce" (99).

But, clearly, Lee recognizes that the resources of woman herself are not the least of things wasted. In her enthusiastic 1903 review of Gilman's book *Women and Economics,* from which the above statements are taken, Lee concludes that

> the one thing certain about the future of women is, surely, that they ought to be given a chance, by removal of legal and professional disabilities . . . of showing what they really are. For one of the paradoxes of this most paradoxical question is precisely that . . . we do not really know what women *are*. Women, so to speak, as a natural product, as distinguished from women as a creation of men; for women, hitherto, have been as much a creation of men as the grafted fruit tree,

the milch cow, or the gelding who spends six hours in pulling a carriage, and the rest of the twenty-four standing in a stable. (100)

These images of gender constructedness emphasize patriarchy's concentration on woman's role as breeder, and the last, of course, subtly suggests that this very emphasis on her sex "castrates" her.

The representation of the feminine as strong, wise, and sensual also had personal ramifications for Lee, who formed intense "romantic friendships" with women throughout her life. In the nineties, she was deeply into the most intense, and, ultimately, the most emotionally devastating of these relationships with Kit Anstruther-Thomson, an athletically "handsome" young woman with a penchant for nursing weaker spirits and bodies. It is not known whether Lee and Anstruther-Thomson were lovers; the fact that Lee was in love was obvious to her acquaintances of the time. Her friend Dame Ethel Smyth observed that the tragedy of Lee's life was that

> without knowing it she loved the *cultes* humanly and with passion; but being the stateliest, chastest of beings she refused to face the fact, or indulge in the most innocent demonstrations of affection, preferring to create a fiction that these friends were merely *intellectual* necessities. . . . The thought of, say, a good bear-hug would have been, I fancy, as alien and would have seemed as vulgar to her as much mild slang as we all indulge in now and then. (Gunn 167)

That Lee, a preeminently introspective person, capable of remarkable self-honesty, was so out of touch with her own passions, seems unlikely; moreover, the wellspring scene in the Snake Lady tale suggests that she knew a thing or two about cunnilingus. Nonetheless, "the fact of sex," particularly sex between men and women, that "perpetually obtruded on one's consciousness" aroused a good deal of disgust in her. Yet the sexualized female body, powerfully erotic but often linked to tragedy and death, "perpetually obtrudes" in her supernatural stories. A passage Lee wrote in her journal late in life may throw some light on her own ambivalences: "In my present more developed (perhaps a little owing to my *bête noire* Freud!) ways of thought, it strikes me that many—almost all—of our supposed beliefs are emotional states, indeed bodily conditions, movements, urges, attitudes, which some magically fine instrument might show and measure, as our deepest seated organs are shown by the radiographer through *les parois* of our body" (Gunn 230).

The symbolism in "Prince Alberic and the Snake Lady," then, deserves the designation "overdetermined," because it invites multiple levels of interpretation, from the psychosexual to what we might call the psycho-political. Lee's story, like Hoffman's "The Sandman," employs the time-honored technique of the horror tale, repetitions of uncanniness, with a strong emphasis on "seeings" and symbols. Throughout, the young prince's "readings" of these sights and symbols, of feminine and masculine power, contrast with those of the surrounding patriarchy, instructing the attentive reader in a different way of reading female difference.

The story begins with the duke's point of view: his repudiation of the "phallic" feminine and his summary removal and destruction of the "tattered and Gothic" tapestry that the prince has come to love. The narration then moves backward in time to establish the primacy of the tapestry/ Snake Lady in the prince's developmental history; the prince's very different way of seeing repels the duke. Alberic's ardent and unschooled approval of the Snake Lady, in her various manifestations, forms a counterpoint to the duke's overweening narcissism and culturally constructed misogyny.

The opening scene enacts patriarchal usurpation; a representation of female power is replaced by an image more amenable to the "envious powers" that be (51). This is described as "the first act of hostility of old Duke Balthasar toward the Snake Lady, in whose existence he did not, of course, believe" (27), an oxymoronic statement reminiscent of Freud's ambivalent expressions concerning the "thereness" of the clitoris. In the course of a general redecorating spree, wherein everything old is being replaced with the newest fashion, the duke visits for the first time the out-of-the-way wing of the palace to which his grandson has long been relegated. There he discovers the venerable tapestry depicting the prince's ancestor Alberic the Blond in attendance on the Snake Lady Oriana, with her glorious and fearful nether parts. The duke reacts with derision, fear, and loathing. He orders the tapestry removed and replaces it with one of Susannah and the Elders, a scene of patriarchal voyeurism and judgment of the feminine more to his liking. When the young prince discovers the substitution, he slashes the new tapestry "into strips with a knife he had stolen out of the ducal kitchens" (28), an act which leads to his banishment from the Red Palace; as it turns out, a fortunate fall indeed.

The story then takes us back in time, to explain the prince's furious reaction. His relationship to the Snake Lady tapestry is represented as primary in his "remembrance," even "older than that of the Red Palace" (29). The word relationship is appropriate, for the tapestry has constituted the prince's "whole world" from infancy. Lee describes his "seeing" of its details as a slow progression that seems to involve the imaginative as much as the visual faculty; the tapestry literally takes shape under his gaze as he matures.

At first, he can only see the "sorely frayed borders" with their profusion of everyday particulars—the stuff of nature, unknown to the prince in the sterile environment of the Red Palace, with its austere grounds in which vegetation is carefully controlled and no animals live at all. As he gets older, the center of the tapestry begins to stir his interest. Here, Lee's narration of his growing curiosity resembles Freud's account of the "sexual researches" of childhood. The weaving is badly faded in the center, the figures there "like ghosts," ephemeral, "sometimes emerging and then receding again into vagueness" (29). In fact, "it was only as he grew bigger that Alberic began to see any figures at all," and then he seems to fix the fading forms by his very attention so that "little by little, when the light was strong, he could see them always," the figures of his ancestor, the first Alberic, and his magical consort, not yet identified to the prince as the Snake Lady Oriana. The primacy of the feminine figure for the orphan prince is obvious; although he admires the beautiful blond knight who handles his horse so well, he comes "to love the lady most" (30).

She is faded to the color of summer moonbeams, suggesting her connection to the Duchy of Luna and to the season of ripeness. Her image draws Alberic closer and closer. As his curiosity intensifies, he climbs upon a chest of drawers to examine her hair with its threads of gold, then focuses on her "bodice," which is not flagrantly bared like the bosoms of the women who visit the palace at the duke's invitation, but modestly covered, with "that collar like a lily, and a beautiful gold chain, and patterns in gold (Alberic made them out little by little) all over" (30).

A chest of drawers, bearing a large crucifix of ebony and ivory, conceals the figure of the lady below her waist; over time, Alberic "got to want so much to see her skirt" that he tries to move the crucifix, but it proves "a great deal too heavy" (30). His intense desire to see is unexpectedly fulfilled when his nurse decides to appropriate the chest for her own use—he returns from a walk to find "the tapestry entirely uncovered. For where the big crucifix had stood, the lower part of the beautiful pale lady with the gold-thread hair was now exposed" (31). The prince's reaction suggests Freud's description of a boy's first sight of female genitalia; he is "riveted to the ground" and "violently excited" by the sight, not of a veiling skirt, as he expected, but of "a big snake's tail," its coiled and folded length covered with green and golden scales. The sight evokes no horror in the eleven-year-old boy; rather "he loved the beautiful lady . . . only the more because she ended off in the long, twisting body of a snake. And that, no doubt, was why the knight was so very good to her" (31). Clearly, this lady suffers no "lack."

In Freud's account of the castration complex, the boy attaches no horror to an initial sight of female genitalia; only in retrospect, after the fear of becoming "like" the woman—in other words, castrated—does the vulva take on the "Medusa's head" aspect. In Lee's story, the seeing of a "complete" woman, of the fact of the presence and potency of the female genitals, does reassure the boy; and in fact, we learn, the Snake Lady offers the sort of moral protection Freud would attribute to the "good" father in the Oedipal situation. But here the issue is not the father's prohibition of incest (or of "limitless narcissism") with the mother, but rather prohibition (by the strong or "phallic mother" figure) of the murder of the child by a narcissistic, decadent grandfather, already guilty of the death of his own son.

As if to legitimate the boy's castration anxiety without implicating female lack, Lee provides, almost parenthetically, a scene of patriarchal violence in the prince's past. At an unspecified time in Alberic's early life, his father (who, Oriana tells him, was a friend of hers) died with "mysterious suddenness" and, the text clearly implies, at the order of the duke, whose preoccupation with maintaining the appearance of "unfading youth" breeds in him a poisonous resentment of "any comparison" that threatens his vanity. Obviously, the grandson's existence will one day become such a threat; the boy is like the wrong answer that the mirror gives to the Wicked Queen in the Snow White story. In the logic of Lee's counterstory, then, the prince exhibits fears of "castration" not because of his identification with the Snake Lady, but because he perceives the threat—of the "cutting off" of his very life—that emanates from the duke's narcissism. He accurately locates the threat in the duke and in the Red Palace itself; the malignity of the grandfather, the story's *homme fatal,* makes the Red Palace always already *unheimlich* for the prince—an unhomelike, and uncanny, site of once and future violence.

When the duke forcibly removes the representation of the powerful woman and replaces her with the image of conventionally "weak," compromised femininity acceptable to patriarchy, the child's horror of the masculine recurs or is re-cognized, but it is clearly a preexisting condition: the prince "now" becomes "aware" of how much he has always hated the Red Palace and the duke which he "identif[ies] . . . as the personification and visible manifestation of each other" (32). The "rape" of the tapestry, then—I am using the word in its archaic sense, to mean "kidnap," but also to suggest the threat of violent occupation of female body/space—augments Alberic's already established fears. And those fears seem to involve being seen rather than seeing, being under surveillance in the panopticon that is the Red Palace. For example, the bodiless heads of the Twelve Caesars seen from every window, staring, "multiplied over and over again" had "always" seemed "uncanny," but now he more assiduously avoids the gaze of their "stucco eyeballs" (32). In effect, the boy's anxiety, his "feverish" and "diseased fancy," combines the fear of castration/death with horror at the displacement/disempowerment of the feminine, foreshadowing his own fate and the Snake Lady's, inextricably linked. This is represented dramatically in his dream of the grotto.

The "famous grotto of the Court of Honor" had roused "abhorrence" in the child even before the substitution of the Susannah tapestry for his beloved Snake Lady: "a bare glimpse [had] always filled the youthful Prince with terror"; with the loss of the tapestry, the image "kept recurring to his mind like a nightmare" (32). The grotto repeats the motif of obscene voyeurism and threatening surveillance. Studded with marble figures, the grotto also suggests, of course, a *vagina dentata,* but the details of the prince's nightmare suggest a different interpretation for the occupied, watched-over, and artificially wet "womb" or vagina.

The stark white space of the grotto is presided over by "colossal satyrs" inlaid in mosaic on its roof, which "frightened him into fits, particularly when the fountains were playing." The grotto must be moistened artificially, on occasions when, to create a "spectacle," jets of water "spurted about in a gallant fashion," which especially unnerves the child (33). We later learn that these occasions necessitate the construction of "an aqueduct twenty miles long [to] pour perennial streams from a high mountain lake into the grotto of the Red Palace," depleting the natural resources of the duchy (and exhausting its treasury) for the sake of the duke's obscene extravagances (64). The grotto also houses an uncanny "herd of life-size animals all carved out of various precious marbles." Although the prince is an animal lover, these carven creatures—a rhinoceros, a giraffe, the "Verde Antique monkeys"—terrify him; and they differ from the local fauna the tapestry depicts in that they are exotics, like menagerie animals captured on voyages of conquest and brought back for the sake of spectacle. This monument to exploitation and conquest is "associated in [the prince's] mind" with the duke's other monumental project, a "domed chapel" occupied by a single bronze statue of the duke himself; both grotto and dome are "mysteriously connected with Alberic's grandfather, owing to a particularly terrible dream" (33).

The dream took place in Alberic's eighth year, predating the "exposure" of the Snake Lady, after a rare visit to his grandfather in honor of the latter's birthday. At the duke's chambers, the child is "separated from his nurse" and received by the duke's Jesuit confessor, a "gaunt person in a long black robe like a sheath, and a long shovel hat," whose smile "discover[s] a prodigious number of teeth, in a manner which froze the child's blood" (33). To introduce the Jesuit, ultimately one of the Snake Lady's murderers, Lee seems to have invented, *contra* the *vagina dentata,* a toothy phallus. The duke is *en deshabille,* being entertained by a hired "nymph" singing his praises, and as the young prince approaches him he glimpses "a sight so mysterious and terrible that he fled wildly out of the ducal presence." This is the duke's wig, which the boy mistakes to be his grandfather's head, "stuck on a short pole in the light of a window" (34).

Alberic's nightmare combines all these images into a scene of usurpation of feminine place by "decadent" masculine power that results in the extinction of the masculine, thus capitulating the symbolic content of the story as a whole. He dreams of the phallic figure of the duke leaving its niche in the "domed chapel" to "ascend to the empty place at the end of the rockery grotto," the position of the clitoris in relation to the vagina. The duke occupies this artificially created site of "absence" and lifts his "scepter" to receive the obeisance of all the exotic animals. But as he does so, his facial features fade, and "beneath the great curly peruke" of the duke's wig there suddenly appears the "round blank thing a barber's block!" This comic yet uncanny image remarkably resembles Freud's fanciful literalization of the Medusa's head: the "round blank thing" beneath the "curly peruke" is like the "castrated" female genitals, the no-thing "surrounded by hair" that Freud compares to the "horrifying decapitated head of Medusa" ("Medusa" 212). Yet whereas in Freud's fantasy the sight of this horror causes an erection, which he calls "another way of intimidating the Evil spirit" (213), in Lee's fantasy the duke's penetration of the grotto and his lifting of his scepter seem to result in emasculation, signified by the disappearance of his face, his identity. Rather than "intimidating the Evil spirit" of female sexuality, the duke's actions offend the good spirit represented by Lee's "phallic" feminine; the dream image reduces *him* to an "absence" and predicts the extinction of the patriarchy of Luna.

The entire surreal sequence, from grotto to dream, strongly connects patriarchal domination and cultural "decadence" with rape and with colonization of feminine body/space, and Lee underscores this in a subtle aside later in the tale (59). One of the duke's habitual aesthetic extravaganzas is a "ballet called Daphne Transformed" in which he dances the part of Daphne's would-be violator, Phoebus Apollo, who in fact succeeds in effecting the transformation of Daphne from a flesh and blood woman into a shivering tree, an emblem of "nature" subject to male power and imagination.

When the prince's rage and fear culminate in his slashing of the Susannah and the Elders tapestry, he is banished to the old seat of the duchy, the now ruined Castle of Sparkling Waters, where he will be left to rusticate in the company of the peasant family who caretake the place. The story's move from the palace to the castle suggests Freud's analogy of the pre-Oedipal to the "Minoan-Mycenaean civilization behind that of Greece" ("Female Sexuality" 195); here, Lee excavates an older myth of a primary civilization. Rather than the binary opposition of nature/culture with "man on top," she envisions a rich marriage of nature and culture that fertilizes and sustains both, presided over by a wise and beautiful woman who also wields considerable wealth and worldly power.

The castle interlude recapitulates the tapestry sequence; whereas in his early childhood the prince wanted so much to see the tapestry figure in its entirety, now he yearns and fears to know the nature of the relationship between the first Alberic and the Snake Lady. There is someone at the castle he could ask, but he develops a terrible fear of acquiring more knowledge and so he does not put the question to the beautiful woman who appears for an hour at dusk each day, and who makes of his exile a scene of instruction and play. This is Oriana, whose enchantment allows her to assume human form at night; the "reality" behind the tapestry's image is not half-snake, half-woman, but this temporal shifting of forms. In daytime, unbeknownst to the prince, she appears as the little green grass snake, the beloved companion who befriended him near the deep, clear wellspring at the old castle's center that stands in opposition to the dry grotto of the Red Palace.

Ultimately, his desire for knowledge is gratified, in a way that poses another test of his ability to see through the patriarchal version of the Snake Lady. He persuades an elderly bard to sing him the ballad of the legend. The first Alberic, he learns, had discovered, in the perilous course of his return journey from the Crusades, a mysterious palace and a sepulchre on which was carved a description of the Fairy Oriana, doomed through no act of her own to a misery that would satisfy higher powers. Her fate is her enchantment into split serpent/woman form, though the situation is slightly misrepresented to the knight Alberic. He is told that if he will simply kiss the huge, crowned snake that now rises, writhing, before him, Oriana will be released, whereas in fact she will still be obligated to spend her days as a snake, her nights as a woman, until the knight has been faithful to her for a period of ten full years, when she can resume her fairy form without division.

Here Lee brings in a parody of the literary sublime in a comical scene of male revulsion and incapacity at the sight of the "phallic" feminine. Alberic the Blond swears to attempt the task, but he would "rather, a thousand times, confront alone the armed hosts of all the heathen, than put his lips to that cold, creeping beast!" Three times he approaches, three times "a horror takes him, and he falls back, unable." At last he summons all his courage and grasps the snake, kissing it three times—and holds in his arms a damsel "beautiful beyond compare" (52). Young Alberic gets the message, of course, and runs up to the wellspring and fountain where his friend the grass snake lives. The well is "very very deep," lined with "long delicate weeds like pale green hair," and has "a faint briny smell." Three times the prince gently calls "Oriana!" The response is an unveiling of the clitoral image at last; emerging from the grass with a "quiver," the little snake glides toward him "on the well's brink, encircling its central blackness." Aroused by his summons, it "pauses, and st[ands] almost erect" as he leans down and gently "presse[s] his lips on the little flat head of the serpent" (59). The kiss brings on an orgasmic swoon into unconsciousness from which the prince wakes with his head in the lap of his "own dear Godmother."

This new phase of the prince's idyll with Oriana is short-lived, as the duke summons him back to the Red Palace with the idea of marrying him off to some princess wealthy enough to finance the duke's monumental schemes, which have bankrupted the duchy's coffers. The prince returns to the Red Palace with no accoutrements save "two swords, a fowling-piece, a volume of Virgil, a branch of pomegranate blossom, and a tame grass snake" (60). He steadfastly refuses all plans for a marriage and takes an annoying interest in the affairs of the people of the realm, who have never been of the slightest interest to the duke except as sources of revenue. Eventually, as the duke's desperation for a wealthy daughter-in-law becomes acute, the prince ends up under house arrest, confined to increasingly poor quarters where, strangely, he never seems to be as isolated as he should be, being heard to converse with what sounds like a woman in the night hours.

Thus develops the story's climax: the scene of the Snake Lady's demise. The attack upon her—in her grass snake form, "placidly coiled up, sleeping" in a corner of the room—seems at first to be spontaneous. The duke, "his eyeballs starting with terror" like those of the Caesars' heads, jumps up shrieking when he notices the little grass snake, and his three henchmen, the Jesuit, the Jester, and the Dwarf, lunge forward. "With a blow of his harlequin's lath" to the snake's head, the Jester kills it as the other two pierce it with their swords. But the duke suggests as he leaves the scene that the killing was by design, his final act of hostility toward the Snake Lady. He approaches the snake, "look[s] at it for some time . . . kick[s] its mangled head with his ribboned shoe" and says with a laugh: "Who knows whether you were not the Snake Lady?" (71)

The mangled snake is left behind as the prince is dragged away. He dies a few weeks later of self-imposed starvation, intractably loyal to his paramour to the end. When servants return to the cell, they find that the snake's corpse has reverted to its womanly form. The clitoral woman is now the castrated woman, and in place of her magnificent tail, or the grass snake's small head seductively erect on the rim of a briny depth, the duke sees the sign of female "castration" repeated in Oriana's gaping wounds, where his henchmen had pierced her with their swords. The tale's many warnings that patriarchy cannot survive its imposition of castration upon the feminine come to fruition. The duke, haunted by the horrifying visions brought on by the sight of the mutilated Snake Lady, plunges into debauchery (perhaps in an effort to employ what Freud called the "apotropaic" effect of the male organ against the "Evil spirit" of Medusa's head) and dies a few months after the prince. The Duchy of Luna, its ancestral line extinct, lapses to the Empire in 1701.

The prince, we learn, was buried at night, by the duke's orders, under a blank slab, as if to reduce this champion of the Snake Lady to "nothingness" and to remove him from history. The story itself, then, with its narrator's careful reiteration of dates and of the prince's name with its particular history, so integrally connected with the Snake Lady's, becomes a fictionalized act of re-entering this "herstory" into the historical ledger.

My reading of Lee's imagery through a post-Freudian critical lens reveals her pre-Freudian perception of the deep, cultural "repudiation of the feminine" so exacerbated in her era, when women's renewed attempts to become both political and sexual subjects created a backlash of male fear and loathing, a phenomenon we see repeated today. Jessica Benjamin, who has expanded on Dorothy Dinnerstein's meditations on the construction of gender in *The Mermaid and the Minotaur,* makes an observation that seems relevant to Lee's 1896 story: "Quite possibly, the dangerous apparition of women only takes final form in the symbolic unconscious once domination is institutionalized. . . . It may be impossible to say where this cycle of real domination [of women] and the fantasy of maternal omnipotence begins, but this does not mean that we can never break that cycle and restore the balance" (176).

Benjamin's note of optimism is justified by the advances feminism has made in the latter part of this century. Burdett Gardner's 1950s reading of Lee's "perverse and brutal plot" still fantasizes "maternal omnipotence," symbolized in a phallic woman that horrifies and perverts, necessitating drastic measures for the sake of "mental health."[5] Ruth Robbins, reading the same plot in the 1980s, locates the brutality in the dominant institutions. In her view, "the defeat of Oriana and Alberic is one of good by evil, and that represents a reversal of our expectations; the institutions are bad and the hybrid phallic female is good" (157). By reversing her audience's expectations, Lee's highly symbolic story anticipates the psychoanalysis of culture undertaken by feminists and other revisionists in recent decades.

In Lee's chronicle of the Snake Lady's fate, however, the proffered possibility that "the world could be articulated differently" is tragically aborted. In this respect, the story shows its affinity with its period, in which other feminist fictions deliberately refuse an ameliorative "happy ending" and decline to gloss over the grim realities of male hegemony and its effects on female creativity and human desire. From Lee's perspective, perhaps, the restoration of balance that Jessica Benjamin sees as possible would seem too utopian for anything but an idyll in a fairy tale. Nevertheless, as I have argued, Lee saw the need to break the vicious cycle of domination "by removal of legal and professional disabilities" to give women the chance "of showing what they really are" ("Economic Dependence" 100). And her story slyly "shows" the feminine as it "really" is, even as it subtly connects the "long-organized social evil" of the suppression of women to other institutionalized dominations, imperialistic and ideological.

NOTES

1. By the time he wrote his essay "Female Sexuality" in 1931, Freud seems to have accepted the existence of the clitoris as a female genital organ, albeit "secondary" to the "true" female organ, the vagina, and "analogous to the male organ" but inferior to it. In earlier writings, Freud's acknowledgment of the existence of the "permanently stunted" organ itself often seems in doubt. In the Little Hans case history ("Analysis of a Phobia" [1909]), the clitoris has a decidedly now-you-see-it-now-you-don't quality, and Freud waxes indignant about the small boy's recognition that his sister has, indeed, a widdler of her own: "One might well feel horrified at such signs of the premature ruin of a child's intellect. Why did not these young inquirers state what they really saw, namely, that there was no widdler there?" (53) Hans's mother had earlier answered matter of factly his enquiry as to whether she had "got a widdler too" with the nonchalant "Of course," no doubt setting his "intellect" on the road to ruin.

2. Robbins's article considers Lee's claims to the designation of "Decadent woman"; her *Yellow Book* story "Prince Alberic and the Snake Lady" seems to Robbins to make the strongest claim, though her "fairly hostile" essay on

Ruskin and his moral imperative for aesthetics is also cited as support (142-43). Robbins defines Decadence as focused on the marginal and "transgressive," and as fundamentally synecdochal, highlighting the part relative to the whole. In "the appearance of the Snake Lady" and the tapestry that represents her history, Robbins writes, "the due sense of proportion is reassigned to the part rather than the whole [of patriarchal history], and thus it exemplifies the Decadent position" (156). I would add that Lee's deployment of the "synecdoche of the clitoris" is subversive within a subversive artistic movement, because the male Decadents repeated the mainstream culture's representation of female sexuality as frightening and aberrant.

3. Many of Lee's supernatural tales contain powerfully erotic women, but in her earlier tales, published in the collection *Hauntings* in 1890, Lee uses the femme fatale figure in a more typically Decadent manner. In "Amour Dure," for example, the beautiful and brilliant Medea da Carpi has distinctly sadistic traits, although she does effect the liberation of a figure of "winged genius." Dionea, in the story of that title, is Venus returned to earth, an intoxicating girl-woman whose unconscious sensuality creates havoc in the lives of a monk and an artist, resulting ultimately in the death of the artist's wife, sacrificed by her husband on Venus's altar. That Lee's one *Yellow Book* contribution should be a story that revises the erotic femme fatale in her phallic woman form seems to make a statement about Lee's own increasing sensitivity to feminist issues, as well as about the misogyny of the times. A story published along with "Prince Alberic" in a collection of 1902 (*Pope Jacynth*), "A Wedding Chest," repeats the rape theme and portrays a sadistic *homme fatal* who victimizes a young woman Lee compares to Proserpina.

4. Lee's family led a peripatetic expatriate existence for most of her youth. Her mother claimed to have left England because she couldn't abide the stultifying English Sunday. Once she had married Lee's father (her second husband and initially her son Eugene's tutor), the family wandered in order to indulge his passion for hunting and fishing in remote places. Eventually they settled in the country outside of Florence where Lee maintained her home base for the rest of her life.

5. According to Gardner, by the time the prince returns from the castle to the Red Palace, he "has become subtly and perversely initiated" (21) under Oriana's tutelage.

WORKS CITED

Benjamin, Jessica. *The Bonds of Love: Psychoanalysis, Feminism, and the Problem of Domination.* New York: Pantheon, 1988.

Collison-Morley, Lacy. *Italy after the Renaissance.* London: Routledge and Sons, 1930.

Dinnerstein, Dorothy. *The Mermaid and the Minotaur: Sexual Arrangements and Human Malaise.* New York: Harper and Row, 1976.

Freud, Sigmund. "Analysis of a Phobia in a Five-Year-Old Boy." Trans. James Strachey. *The Sexual Enlightenment of Children.* Ed. Philip Rieff. New York: Collier Books, 1963, 47-183.

————. "Female Sexuality." Trans. Joan Riviere. *Sexuality and the Psychology of Love.* Ed. Philip Rieff. New York: Collier Books, 1963, 194-211.

————. "Medusa's Head." Trans. James Strachey. *Sexuality and the Psychology of Love.* Ed. Philip Rieff. New York: Collier Books, 1963, 212-13.

————. "On the Sexual Theories of Children." Trans. Douglas Bryan. *The Sexual Enlightenment of Children.* Ed. Philip Rieff. New York: Collier Books, 1963, 25-40.

Gardner, Burdett. *The Lesbian Imagination (Victorian Style): A Psychological and Critical Study of "Vernon Lee."* New York: Garland, 1987. (Reprint of "Violet Paget," Ph.D. dissertation, Harvard, 1954.)

Gunn, Peter. *Vernon Lee: Violet Paget.* London: Oxford UP, 1964.

Johnson, Barbara. "Is Female to Male as Ground Is to Figure?" *Feminism and Psychoanalysis.* Eds. Richard Feldstein and Judith Roof. Ithaca: Cornell UP, 1989.

Lee, Vernon. "The Economic Dependence of Women." *Critical Essays on Charlotte Perkins Gilman.* Ed. Joanne B. Karpinski. New York: G. K. Hall, 1992, 90-102.

————. "Prince Alberic and the Snake Lady." *The Snake Lady and Other Stories.* Ed. Horace Gregory. New York: Grove, 1954.

Robbins, Ruth. "Vernon Lee: Decadent Woman?" *Fin de Siècle/ Fin du Globe: Fears and Fantasies of the Late Nineteenth Century.* Ed. John Stokes. New York: St. Martin's, 1992, 139-61.

Showalter, Elaine. *Sexual Anarchy: Gender and Culture at the Fin de Siècle.* New York: Penguin, 1990.

Traub, Valerie. "The Psychomorphology of the Clitoris." *GLQ: A Journal of Lesbian and Gay Studies* 2 (1995): 81-113.

Architects of the Erotic: H. G. Wells's "New Women"

Anne B. Simpson

At the locus of his conflicted responses—identification, compassion, terror, and desire—women fascinated H. G. Wells. From the scientific romances he composed in the 1890s to his discussion novels of the early twentieth century to the ruminations in his autobiographical works over his many love affairs, Wells recurrently and deliberately bracketed the feminine. In text after text, he cited the deplorable conditions of women's oppression and exploitation in social life while he also endowed them with privilege, projecting upon them his longing for the retrieval of profound meaning in a moribund cultural landscape. Midcareer, in the Edwardian years between Victoria's reign and the First World War, Wells composed two novels centered specifically on the status of modern women, recording the ambivalences of his position as he attempted to confront the female Others who dominated his cast of mind. In *Ann Veronica* (published in 1909) and *The Wife of Sir Isaac Harman* (1914), the Wellsian woman is fashioned as signifier of distress, evoking the signified of a widespread cultural malaise. Alternatively and sometimes concurrently, she functions as trope for a supreme value—as remedy for the diseased conditions of social life.

A climate of titillation and scandal surrounded Wells's personal attitudes toward women, with his many affairs, extramarital and otherwise, earning him the sometimes disapproving, sometimes admiring rubric of "Don

Juan among the intelligentsia" (quoted in Kemp 108). This behavior, coupled with his numerous statements, often misquoted and overstressed, on the merits of "free love," had a significant impact on the reception given to the novels he wrote at the beginning of the twentieth century that offered a forum for considering the state of women's lives.[1] *Ann Veronica* was among the most shocking and incendiary novels of its day, provoking outraged reviews and, by Wells's own later account, precipitating newly emancipated sexual attitudes in novel-reading British youths *(Experiment* 396). *The Wife of Sir Isaac Harman,* produced five years later, offered even more inflammatory indictments of the abuses of women in the modern world.

Nevertheless, both of these books have fallen, in the late twentieth century, into obscurity; perhaps, in part, due to their aesthetic disappointments for a readership whose conception of the art of the novel has been dominated by the compelling and influential statements of such Modernists as Henry James and Joseph Conrad. Although in early fin de siècle works like *The Time Machine* (1895), Wells was a self-conscious craftsman shaping his narratives economically, for compressed effect, and carefully evoking mood through the manipulation of sense impression, a decade later he had lost patience with what Conrad called the "unremitting never-discouraged care for the shape and ring of sentences . . . the light of magic suggestiveness [that] may be brought to play for an evanescent instant over the commonplace surface of words" (12). Instead, Wells redefined fiction to suit his increasingly urgent sense of social responsibility; enlisting the novel as a vehicle for debate, he used it to examine, in a didactic and insistent manner, a variety of problems within contemporary culture and their possible solutions.[2] This approach has not been congenial to later audiences, and ultimately his own mature assessment, in the *Experiment in Autobiography,* has proved prophetic: the expositions of *Ann Veronica* and *The Wife of Sir Isaac Harman,* as well as his other texts focused on "love and sex-reactions," would be, as he averred, first among his works "to go right out of sight and memory. . . . No one will ever read them for delight" (392). However, in their presentations of the New Woman, that is, the woman seeking political power, intellectual development, and personal emancipation, both novels help to construct a chapter within a greater cultural text; as such, they continue to offer a site of interest for readers of our time.

For influential (male) authors at the dawn of the twentieth century, the New Woman provided attractive subject matter for self-consciously rebellious "new" novels: she functioned as a figure for a state of alienation from Victorian mores and also suggested the potential for dynamic cultural change.

But despite their recurrent and heated renunciations of the values of their parent generation, these writers frequently expressed a concomitant horror of social boundlessness and uncertainty. Art spanning the first two decades of the century often presents conflicted portraits, textured of admiration as well as paranoia, of those individuals who pose the threat of chaos to a morally attenuated culture. Many texts resolve the conflict by recontaining their volatile characters, finding a way to reshape them in consolingly familiar forms; the floating signifiers are ultimately moored. Although they may imply the as yet unthinkable, they come to rest in patterns of predetermined thought, in stable signifieds.

Most particularly, female protagonists who are culturally disruptive are always brought back from where they've been. The feminine has variously occupied, in Western ideology, what Hélène Cixous has called the "dark continent" (the menacing space of the unknowable) and the debased positions in diverse but always hierarchic binary structures ("Laugh" 1091). The apparatus for reclaiming women, which had been solidly constructed by the culture at large, was thus readily available for early twentieth-century British authors to draw upon. The heroine who begins her story as a trope for societal dis-ease and inchoate possibility appears, ultimately, as a vision of passivity as against the activity of man; as lacuna or lack as against his state of repletion; or as simple figure of referentiality as against his self-identical condition.

Characteristically, Wells's fiction is often marked by tensions between a passionately articulated liberalism and a deeply conservative vision—between the wishful fantasy that select individuals might attain more than contemporary culture had to offer and a pronounced fear of how the new might disrupt the foundations of that culture. In this regard *Ann Veronica* is representative of mutually exclusive claims in its author's ideology as well as the intellectual climate of the day. Wells's novel begins by presenting the protagonist's efforts to escape her overbearing family, the repository of prudish norms and anti-life, conformist values. The story traces Ann's discontent to her father's mindless strictures and her own embryonic yearnings for a more satisfying life than that of marriage and obedience to a husband who will replicate the father's role. She is determined to define herself, to assert a freedom that moves her beyond this culture, for within culture she must wear, as Wells puts it, a "mask" (3). Like individuals throughout Edwardian fiction who struggle mightily against the hegemony of the group, Ann Veronica is a bifurcated being, split between inner and outer life, inauthentic because she must address the conflicting demands of psyche and society. But Ann also stands in for a specifically feminine condition, occupying a place of Otherness that Wells's narrator warily suggests: behind her seeming composure, he comments, lurk "her emotions—*whatever they were*" (105; emphasis added). The inaccessibility of the feminine, its location beyond a logocentric discourse that rationally identifies and defines, is signified early in the novel and will cause, ultimately, an authorial act of erasure. Miss Miniver, a caricatured suffragette figure, expresses the menace that women pose as she chillingly wonders how men would react "'if we threw the mask aside—if we really told them what *We* thought of them, really showed them what *We* were'" (30).

On the surface of her story, Ann displays a radical promise by leaving her stuffy father's house and rejecting complacent suburbia; by attempting to support herself as a university student in London; by attending inflammatory meetings of socialist and feminist groups; by joining politicized sisters in militant protest; and ultimately by finding sexual pleasure in the arms of a married lover. But the novel's narrative distancing and lightly comic tone disempower the female protagonist by turning her into a picturesque figure who has been affectionately diminished. She is introduced, for example, sitting "with both her feet on the seat in an attitude that would certainly have distressed her mother to see and horrified her grandmother beyond measure" (1). Later, following a suffragette raid on Parliament and her own imprisonment, Ann's ruminations on what it means to be a woman in a repressive patriarchy are trivialized by the recurrence of a ditty that she finds herself compulsively composing in her head: "For men have reason, women rhyme; / A man scores always, all the time" (200) is followed by thirteen more verses in the same banal, relentless meter. But the one couplet that Ann does not complete, "And children must we women bear—" (201), is worth notation; it prefigures the condition of motherhood and self-restraint that Ann will fulfill at the conclusion of this novel.

Wells's project, as *Ann Veronica* unfolds, is to denude the female characters of potentially uncontrollable power. Most specifically, the women who attempt political action and a selfhood not predicated on the needs of men are viciously satirized. Miss Miniver, champion of Votes for Women, is repeatedly mocked; Wells, who was always, in any case, suspicious of group thinking, belittles her mindless adherence to feminist jargon. Her faith in the importance of direct action is further ridiculed by Wells's insistence on her intellectual unsoundness, her inability to argue any point with either clarity or coherence. But the most damning evidence offered against the suffragettes is that they are all sexual hysterics; Miss Miniver loudly reviles "'Bodies! Bodies! Horrible things'" (144).

As Samuel Hynes and Elaine Showalter have documented, the early New Women *were,* with few exceptions, rigid rather than expansive regarding matters of sex; in advocating feminine purity and chastity for men, they offered a strategy for extricating women from an inevitability of their biological condition—childbearing—which could hamper their attempts at independence (201, 45). Wells chooses the prudery of this movement as a focal point for his presentation as a way to stress the neuroses of feminist organizers and their patent need for a more fulfilling life than political action could offer them. His later comment, in *Experiment in Autobiography,* makes explicit his response to female suffrage; the new feminists, he notes with acerbity, recoiled in horror from the idea of a specifically sexual liberation: "That feminism had anything to do with sexual health and happiness, was repudiated by these ladies with flushed indignation. . . . They were good pure women rightly struggling for a Vote, and that was all they wanted" (407). *Ann Veronica,* which similarly minimizes the significance of women's efforts to achieve the vote, anticipates its own resolution and points to Wells's conception, at this stage in his career, of the feminine domain: women are moved inward from the space of worldly action, to be redeposited in the intimate sphere of domestic life.[3]

The narrative repeatedly insists that Ann Veronica is a palpably physical being who must learn to recognize and applaud her own instincts. Her intellectual work as a serious student of biology points to the primacy of her material existence. It is she who initiates the sexual relation with her curiously passive—or, Morally Blameless—teacher, Capes; and her awakening into self-awareness, when it comes, is a sensual one. It was this aspect of the novel that upset contemporary readers, who pressed for censorship of the "Poisonous Book" (Parrinder 169); for some, the novel clearly offered an outrage to all propriety. E. M. Forster's *A Room with a View,* which had been published a year earlier and which in many respects anticipated the plot of Wells's novel, had not created this kind of stir; the sexuality of Forster's heroine had been romantically blurred and presented only suggestively, in kisses among the violets. In his more explicit insistence on women's rights to their sexual lives, Wells is presenting a serious attack on canons of morality and taste. At the same time he is offering a gesture of appeasement. For in his presentation of Ann as Body, Wells returns woman to a culturally recognizable form. It is this conceptualization—of Ann/the feminine as utter materiality—that comes to dominate the latter half of the text.

Ann and Capes elope to a frozen mountain landscape, which would seem to offer, paradoxically, a symbol of vital new life in contrast with the sterile waste of held-over Victorian mores. However, the frigid scene fittingly represents the narrative's inability to move into a genuinely new framework in its presentation of the heroine's plight. The hills that Ann and Capes climb, in their apparent search for a new world, form a Freudian metaphor of woman's function and place as all-giving mother; Ann becomes the breast that feeds both the body and mind of Capes, thereby achieving, the narrative suggests, her own satisfaction.[4] Ann will evolve into Capes's muse, spurring him to creative undertakings (he becomes a dramatist); and she ultimately settles down in England as the mother of his children—as a woman, the narrative comments without irony, who "loved to be told to do things" (278). Figuratively decapitated, Ann is enclosed in the domestic structure she had once struggled to escape. Although her final speech expresses Wells's insight into what Ann has lost—"'The great time is over,'" she cries, "'and I have to go carefully and bear children'" (295)—this despair is immediately negated by his portrait of a husband who can hold Ann and voice his compassion for the inevitable, material conditions of her existence. Thus the feminine, in the words of Cixous, is ultimately fated to take the shape of "the nonsocial, nonpolitical, nonhuman half of the living structure . . . tirelessly listening to what goes on inside—inside her belly, inside her 'house'" ("Sorties" 66). In its presentation of the New Woman, Wells's text comes full circle.

The author's own fantasy of human relationship, his personal circumstances, and the more general terrors pervasive in Edwardian culture underscore this final depiction of Ann. In the posthumously published *H. G. Wells in Love,* Wells argues that every subject is accompanied through life by a Lover-Shadow, the fantastic embodiment of his ego's dream. Wells unabashedly admits that his own ideal shadow promises "embraces [that are] to be my sure fastness, my ultimate reassurance, the culmination of my realization of myself" (56). As Nancy Steffen-Fluhr has commented, Wells thus attempts to connect his desire for close human companionship with his somewhat less clearly defined wish to comprehend the hidden features of his own psyche ("Women" 158). However, as his fiction demonstrates, Wells cannot fully make the connection. Rarely does he create characters who are complexly imagined individuals; rather, they enact limited roles at two ends of a continuum: as alien, unknowable Others or as projections of the hero's (i.e., Wells's) glamorized self. Wells's women, most particularly, are denied subjectivity under the pressure of the author's powerful need.

In *Ann Veronica* the protagonist becomes, as she wishes, "'a human being'" (24) only by reference to man; as corollary, in other words, to the

Wellsian persona, as it is embodied in the character of Capes. The parallels between Capes's story and Wells's personal history have been repeatedly cited by commentators on the novel and bear noting here. Wells drew on his estrangement from his first wife and elopement with a student (who became his second wife) for the impetus of the affair between Capes and Ann; and at the time of his second marriage, his relationship with the freethinking Amber Reeves, an acolyte in the Fabian circle, inspired his vision of the unbridled sexual passion of Ann and Capes. Throughout his life Wells was reaching for and running away from intimacies with women; his nickname for Amber, "Dusa" (short for Medusa), is most eloquently expressive of his fear of woman's monstrous power.[5] In repeated instances, Wells's fiction suggests that one way to respond to the Medusa's terror is to bind and gag her.

As its closing vision of female achievement, *Ann Veronica* presents a male fantasy in which the conflicted heroine resolves her uncertainties by becoming an architect of the erotic, allied finally and forever with the business of loving. Readers of our own era, in sympathy with Wells's insistent plea for freer sexual expression, nevertheless must witness a presentation of woman that is informed by the needs of a male subject-hero. In this script the female functions as "one of the measures of man, his counterbalance, his salvation, his adventure, his happiness," to cite Simone de Beauvoir (248). It is significant that Ramage, the suburban villain of *Ann Veronica,* frequently insists that women are meant for love alone; although heroine (and author) despise him for his mundane lasciviousness, presumably because he is so blatant in his self-serving attitudes, Ramage gives away a secret at the heart of the text. A darker incarnation of Capes the hero, Ramage grossly expresses the narrative view of woman's lot.

Ann Veronica thus records several powerful Edwardian anxieties, concerning the future of a culture that had dislodged itself from its antecedents; the plight of the individual reacting against societal strictures; and the condition of women, in particular, as the most flagrant example of dislocation and struggle. The fear of the horror that dissatisfied woman *might* express is offered in Arnold Bennett's *Clayhanger,* which introduces Hilda Lessways as a "dangerous and threatening" voice, her face enigmatically obscured "in the dusk" (196). She is the dark potential, the imminent destruction, here. A woman actively fighting on her own behalf is likened, by D. H. Lawrence's Paul Morel in *Sons and Lovers,* to the frightening image of "a dog before a looking-glass, gone into a mad fury with its own shadow" (220). The vision is suggestive, at once, of woman as chaos, as solipsistic obsessiveness, and as grim insubstantiality. However, Lawrence redeposits his "madly furious" suffragette, Clara Dawes, into the arms of her boorish husband by novel's close, thereby resolving the hero's psychic conflicts and not incidentally recuperating an ideal of family life. Bennett's protagonist Edwin ultimately fulfills his own destiny by taking on the "exquisite burden" of Hilda, who finally couples her life to his in a domesticated, knowable world (528).

The Edwardian heroine is ultimately served up to her audience as the bearer of society's oldest standards. As tamed wife, often endowed (like Ann Veronica) with an accompanying maternal function, she is held responsible for reproducing the very culture that denied her needs. This woman is, as Catherine Clément puts it, "double" (7). Doomed to be both anomalous and stabilizing, the feminine is alien and—most reassuringly—conventional.

In 1914, when Wells published *The Wife of Sir Isaac Harman,* the landscape of Europe looked darker, the light seemed harder to find. Wells now recalls the opening of the century as a time of "badly sprained optimism," to suggest a denial at the core of English culture, a willful but not altogether successful effort to avoid the manifest truth of a society in collapse (292). An ominous, brutalizing sense of change is evoked, obsessively, in the text of this novel, which offers recurrent references to the "dissolution of . . . assurances" marking the new age, as it is imagined (125). Characters from all social classes, from the servant Snagsby to the bourgeois Brumley to the elite Lady Harman, are assailed by anxiety over a world that has grown "insecure beneath [their] feet" (235). Accordingly, the Wellsian woman is established even more firmly here than in *Ann Veronica* as a mode of meaning-production. Despite a tale that is fashioned around a heroine's oppression, rebellion, and apparent liberation, Wells enacts another fantasy: of the feminine as emblem of value, as spiritual sustenance, as material essence, all of which will serve to transform a morally bankrupt society of grasping self-seekers into a culture of modern knights empowered by exalted, altruistic ideals.

The novel opens, as if picking up where *Ann Veronica* left off, on a scene suggestive of the petty worries of domestic life. Lady Ellen Harman is first shown in an eminently familial role as she inspects a new house that will, she hopes, snugly enclose herself, her husband, and their four children. As in *Ann Veronica,* Wells's narrator initially establishes a complacent distance from the protagonist, in this case by condescendingly depicting her as a young woman who has, "within her pretty head," a "mind [that] rushed to and fro" (8). Further, she has "a small voice for her size but quite a charming one, a little live bird of a voice, bright and sweet" (10); her powerlessness is very pleasingly evoked.

Nevertheless, Wells does have a project for reformation in mind, and the scene is almost immediately overcast. Like Ann Veronica, this heroine is trapped and thwarted by an overbearing patriarchal figure, in this case her husband. Lord Harman is depicted as a soulless villain who plotted for her hand in marriage when she was an inexperienced schoolgirl and then took advantage of her naiveté to convert her, immediately after wedlock, into a baby-producing machine. She is, the narrator observes, "habitually shut against her husband, as a protection against his continual clumsy mental interferences" (55). But the interferences are clearly physical, too: in addition to the children, there is the prison of a ghastly house that he has built along his own ideal lines; later in the novel he will purchase Brumley's home, ostensibly for his wife, and will proceed to dismantle and disrupt its aesthetic harmonies in favor of his own plodding sense of utility. Here, as elsewhere in Wells's fiction (most notably, his 1909 novel *Tono-Bungay),* the hideous architectural space suggests the defacement of culture itself, with a new tenant in charge who is manifestly unable to replicate the best that English life once had to offer. Ellen Harman, beautiful and glamorous, a princess imprisoned in the castle keep of her husband's foul sensibility, signals the goodness and the vitality that still survive and that must be liberated if meaning is once again to enter the modern world.

In contrast, jealousy and its concomitant, envy, inform Sir Isaac's malevolent actions as he restrains his wife from social intercourse with other women and with her admiring friend, the novelist Brumley. From the turn of the century on, Wells attacked jealousy as the despicable worm that was eating away at the heart of social life. He saw the modern family, in turn, as the residue of this destructive process. The *Autobiography* details his view:

> Continually civilization had been developing, by buying off or generalizing, socializing and legalizing jealousy and possessiveness, in sex as in property. We were debarred from sexual ease, just as we were debarred from economic ease, by this excessive fostering in our institutions of the already sufficiently strong instinct of ownership. The Family . . . was the inseparable correlative of private proprietorship. It embodied jealousy in sexual life as private ownership embodied jealousy in economic life. (400)

The insidious effect of jealousy, in Wells's thought, was that it prevented both intimacy and communication, threatening to disrupt or forestall the development of civilized societies wherein the space between Self and Other might be negotiated reasonably, without fear of aggression and war. For the world of 1914, a world splitting into violent factions and embarking on catastrophic bloodshed, the figure of Sir Isaac offers a particularly resonant nightmare. As a paragon of acquisitiveness, he represents all that Wells despises and has good reason to fear in his vision of the self-involved, treacherous, and rapacious individual who stands poised at the ready as life's destroyer.

Thus Wells records with an apparently generous flow of sympathy Lady Harman's struggles to emerge from her husband's nets. In her first, imitative phase of rebellion, she adopts the conventional suffragette manner of the day by breaking a post office window, which leads to her incarceration. Her action and its consequences offer an effectual, recognizable transmission of her protest, to which her Edwardian husband knows how to respond. When she emerges from prison, Lord Harman presents, as reparation, what seems like a new construction of their marriage contract, allowing her some work—and, by extension, a life—of her own, as overseer for the erection and administration of hostels for single working women. The apparent autonomy she has gained, however, is soon revealed as just another species of spousal control; her husband's overweening need to dominate is again asserted when he hires another woman to manage the daily maintenance of the hostels. She proves to be his surrogate, a regimentarian who seeks to constrain female movement, in this case by enforcing rigid rules for the hostel's tenants. By virtue of this association, Sir Isaac appears even more duplicitous and vile; he has tricked his wife into believing in a power that he has no intention of giving over to her.

The limitations of the villainous-husband conception, and indeed of the allegorical cast of the entire novel, were glaringly apparent to the contemporary press, which faulted Wells for his flat characterizations and simplified depiction of marital disharmony. Walter Lippmann, writing for *New Republic,* went so far as to condemn Wells for having produced "a careless book written with comfortable facility out of the upper layers of his mind" (Parrinder 220), and although subtlety of presentation was never Wells's strong suit in the discussion novels, there does seem a particularly powerful resistance here to detailing the ambiguities and shared responsibility that inhere in human relationship. Wells's easy demarcation of right- and wrong-doers in *The Wife of Sir Isaac Harman* suggests his unwillingness to face the high stakes of interrogating contemporary marriage. And having created such a conventional portrait of wedded discontent, he appears unable to conceive of an original way for his protagonist to free herself. In the latter pages of the book he resorts to the fairy-tale solution of killing off the ogre, Sir Isaac, to allow his heroine an escape. However, as the narrative approaches a presentation of achieved feminine selfhood, it swerves, most tellingly, from this goal: by its closing chapter, the text (like *Ann Veronica)* offers readers the assurance that a specifically female freedom will be delimited, all potential chaos defeated, and the maiden finally imprisoned, again, in the patriarchal tower.

Intimations of the conflicts between Wells's manifest and latent aims are apparent even in the early sections of the novel, where he begins by articulating his conviction that true liberation for women can occur only in the material realm. Lady Harman, as he presents her, is devoid of maternal instinct in spite of her four children: she observes them "with a curious detachment" (73) and, in a more extended discussion, the narrator comments:

> The maternal instinct is not a magic thing, it has to be evoked and developed, and I decline to believe it is indicative of any peculiar unwomanliness in Lady Harman that when at last she beheld her newly-born daughter in the hands of the experts, she moaned druggishly, "Oh! Please take it away. Oh! Take it—away. Anywhere—anywhere." (106)

Her subsequent miscarriage proves to be not in the least traumatic; and after she is counseled by her mother, mother-in-law, the family doctor, and her sister, she turns to birth control to ensure against continuous childbearing.

Wells appears to reverse the position in *Ann Veronica,* which presented woman's highest calling as that of motherhood, and his tone throughout these passages is marked by an explicit sympathy with which his audience is expected to concur. In light of the reality of early-twentieth-century women's lives, he is notably broad-minded and prescient here in his insistence on freeing women from the necessities of pregnancy and on withholding judgment on those who make the choice to control their own reproductive systems. Yet in his decision to define Lady Harman by focusing, now, on *lack* of maternal feeling, Wells is again caught between the poles of a binary structure that serves, ironically, to contain the female—even as he gestures to release her. As the absence of motherly instinct is recurrently made present to the reader's awareness, Wells's heroine is once more tethered to a physical state by virtue of the missing maternal impulse that leaves its traces through the text.

As in *Ann Veronica,* the suffragettes who agitate for a more worldly, politicized construction of gender are scathingly mocked. Here the representatives for the vindictive and petty spirit of the feminist movement are Agatha Alimony, who vibrates with passionate emotions, voicing her hatred of marital restrictions yet insisting that Lady Harman return to her home to fight for her freedoms within its walls; Miss Garradice, "[o]ne of those mute, emotional nervous spinsters who drift detachedly, with quick sudden movements, glittering eyeglasses, and a pent-up imminent look, about our social system" (255); and Ellen's sister Georgina, whose gaze is transfigured by "the light of the Great Insane Movement"—in other words, suffrage, as the narrator scathingly describes it (372-73).

Wells's conviction that the suffrage cause is not only misguided but essentially static is most intriguingly conveyed when he presents his protagonist's violent smashing of the post office window. Chapter 8 pauses for an apparent digression on aesthetics, as the narrator contemplates a distant future when writer and artist are more clearly aligned, their work more symbiotically bound, than in the present moment. In the service of this conception, readers are asked to picture Lady Harman's broken window as an illustration that initially dominates the textual page. Then the picture is to be envisioned as paling slightly, modified on a second page by "a dim sentence or so of explanation." A third page presents an increase in type; on a fourth, full narrative accompanies the pictured window, although, significantly, text is "still darkened and dominated" by illustration (283-84). Wells's meditation suggests a relative ineffectuality of the word, a speechlessness in the face of feminine political agitation; and this inarticulateness is proffered as an appropriate response to the essentially deadening suffrage campaign.

Unwilling to credit certain contemporary social solutions to the issue of women's rights, Wells ultimately turns his attention to the potential that may be realized within the space of personal relations. His deliberation over the prospect of hostels for working women that would liberate them from family limitations is steeped in the atmosphere of charitable do-gooding and is never really worked out fully, or demonstrated to be viable, in the text. Further, the implications of such a scheme do not extend to women of the middle and upper classes, with whom this novel is most centrally concerned. Elsewhere in his writing, Wells did struggle over large-scale provisions for the difficulties faced by women of diverse social classes: his tracts "The Endowment of Motherhood" (1914) and *Socialism and the Family* (1906) offer two examples of his attempts to arrive at collectivist answers to the "Woman Question," as he proposes that the State pay mothers for raising children and thus release them from a position of subordination to their husbands. But Wells's faith in the efficacy of social programs was always complicated by his distaste for bureaucracies and his tendency to valorize the elite few who could heroically, remarkably exert effort on their own behalf. In *The Wife of Sir Isaac Harman,* he enlists an ethic of individual responsibility and interpersonal commitment in order to imagine a better world for his ostensible New Woman. Electing to create a character who is worthy of her—in other words, a New Man—Wells offers, thereby, a new model of intimate relationship.

The writer Brumley, who appears as a target of parodic fun in the text's opening pages, evolves most surprisingly into a heroic figure who articulates Wells's own views about women, love, and life itself as the novel reaches its conclusion. Initially intent on justifying family life and domestic stability in his novels, the buoyant and ridiculous Brumley is accorded the dubious honor of being chosen as the subject for one of Max Beerbohm's caricatures. Wells suggests that this Brumley is very much a man of his time, tenaciously and blindly clinging to the status quo as a response to threatening social change. But in this rendition of the movement of contemporary English history, as the Edwardian epoch darkens, so does Brumley's outlook: his later novels, like the productions of most decadent cultures, prove to be both enervated and forced.

Brumley's state of creative exhaustion serves to bring Lady Harman's character into sharper relief. Her textual role becomes clearer as Brumley loosens his grasp on old, worn-out convictions and is revitalized under the influence of his love for her. Wells now presents a Brumley who, in purging the diseased system of tired cultural beliefs, brings light into the "foetid chamber" of his being and, by implication, presents himself as exemplar to British society at large (340). In his platonic worship of Ellen, the character ascends to a chivalrous state; in insisting on Brumley's growing moral stature, Wells thus recovers a sentimental ideal of knighthood as antidote to the conditions of modern life.

It is at this point in the novel that Brumley, like the biologist Capes before him, begins to stand in for the Wellsian ideal self, the model man. The reading of Sir Isaac's will provides for his wife unless she remarries (at which juncture all of her money will be taken from her), which enables Brumley to rise to his finest hour. First declaring his wish to marry Ellen in spite of her potentially impoverished state, he realizes, when she refuses him, that he is not yet worthy because jealousy, which rules the modern condition, has marked him too. Tortured with his new self-consciousness, Brumley offers an idealizing self-mockery of his divided being: "'I am one of the newer kind of men, one of those men who cannot sit and hug their credit and their honour and their possessions and be content. I have seen the light of better things than that, and because of my vision, because of my vision and for no other reason I am the most ridiculous of men'" (519).

He may not have escaped the nets of jealousy, but in his ability to see them, he is, by strong implication, above the common lot—and worthy of the heroine. Vacillating between his overwhelming desire to marry Ellen, to provide a continuation of the friendship she says she wants, and to renounce all relationship with her, Brumley is the hero par excellence: torn by need, driven by passion, self-abnegating, self-reflective. It is when he attains to this condition that Ellen finally accepts him, offering to become *his* Lady now. The plot approaches resolution on a romantic, wish-fulfilling scene, as an agonized Brumley races through the sunny woods, the green world of Arcadian fantasy, with Ellen in hot pursuit.

The corresponding transformation of the heroine into an (apparently) empowered woman actively seeking out her own happiness can only occur, as Wells makes clear, when the male relinquishes possessive claims and strips himself of power. Lying prone among the bluebells, Brumley symbolically signals the reversal of roles that will make New Womanhood, as Wells envisions it, possible. Looking down at her ardent and supine admirer, Lady Harman is overcome: "she was flooded now with that passion of responsibility, with that wild irrational charity which pours out of the secret depths of a woman's stirred being," the narrator intones (523). He thus effectively takes the sting out of her newly active mode by once more insisting that woman be defined, primarily, as agent of relationship. The comedy of the scene also punctures any concern that the disruption of gender roles be taken too literally; it is suggestive but not insistent and therefore, ultimately, placating.

Further, the relationship, as Wells finally conceives it, is shaped by the erotic choices made by both participants. Brumley, having replaced the acquisitive Lord Harman as the central male figure in the text, requests rather than demands a kiss from Ellen and thereby signals that he has renounced the kind of sexual presumption that characterized her husband's behavior. She, in turn, is free now to achieve the Wellsian ideal of passionate sexual response, as she tumbles Brumley over backward and kisses him avidly. Thus Wells achieves his "solution" to the problem of New Womanhood: aided and abetted by the Wellsian New Man, the right-thinking heroine can blossom into sensuality—and answer his desire. This conception has the paradoxical effect of positioning the feminine in a familiar textual landscape: woman as (only) material being is poised on the brink, but never at the achievement of, full selfhood; her complexity is unimagined and elsewhere.[6]

And so Lady Harman enacts what Cixous has termed "Woman's voyage: as a *body*" ("Sorties" 66). This Other has been successfully harnessed, returned to the place from which she threatened to wander. She is reclaimed as adjunct to the true subject, as enactment of his need. Ultimately, in responding to New Womanhood, Wells makes the old choice—he contains and thus erases. In the face of his efforts to de-problematize the feminine, Wells's titular heroines vanish into the interstices of their texts. Charged with authorial imperatives to reveal his own psychic state; to define, for readers, the disease of the world; and to offer up a blazing hope for its salvation, they simply disappear.

NOTES

1. For an analysis of the misconstructions of Wells's sexual attitudes, both within the Fabian circle and among its conservative opponents, see Brome 133-38; for Wells's own account of the ways in which his views were often misrepresented, see *Experiment* 394-405.

2. In his essay "The Contemporary Novel," Wells presents an extended argument for reconceiving the scope of fiction (Edel and Ray 131-56), and his artistic disagreement with James, in particular, has been well documented (Edel and Ray). I have discussed Wells's aesthetic aims at greater length in "H. G. Wells's *Tono-Bungay:* Individualism and Difference" (75-76).

3. Subsequent to writing this article, I encountered a similar discussion in Sylvia Hardy's introduction to the recent Everyman edition of *Ann Veronica.* Noting Wells's contempt for suffragette thought and impatience with sexual repression, Hardy nonetheless credits Wells with the achievement of a female point of view in this novel (Hardy xxxvi)—an interpretation with which I cannot concur.

4. Peter Kemp offers a thorough and often hilarious overview of the uses of mountain scenery in Wells's work (84-86).

5. The power of the Medusa may have been compounded for Wells by the suggestion of a primal violence. Steffen-Fluhr persuasively argues that the recurrence of Medusa imagery, in the form of the grotesque, bleeding heads found throughout his fiction dating from the fin de siècle, functioned as an evocation of bloody female genitalia and a nightmare of the mutilation that Wells feared men might undergo if they allowed themselves to become too much like the women to whom they were drawn (151).

6. Wells here reinstates a comfortable notion of New Womanhood, one that had been produced by earlier male writers such as George Moore, in "Mildred Lawson" (1895), and Grant Allen, in *The Woman Who Did* (also 1895). As Ann Ardis notes, both of these authors display, albeit in differing ways, "a determination to write the female body so as to master it" (92)—a description that could apply equally to Wells.

WORKS CITED

Ardis, Ann. *New Women, New Novels: Feminism and Early Modernism.* New Brunswick: Rutgers UP, 1990.

Bennett, Arnold. *Clayhanger.* 1910. Harmondsworth: Penguin, 1954.

Brome, Vincent. *H. G. Wells: A Biography.* Freeport, N.Y.: Books for Libraries, 1951.

Cixous, Hélène. "The Laugh of the Medusa." Trans. Keith Cohen and Paula Cohen. *The Critical Tradition: Classic Texts and Contemporary Trends.* Ed. David H. Richter. New York: St. Martin's, 1989. 1090-1102.

———. "Sorties: Out and Out: Attacks/Ways Out/Forays." Hélène Cixous and Catherine Clément. *The Newly Born Woman.* Trans. Betsy Wing. Minneapolis: U of Minnesota P, 1993, 63-132.

Clément, Catherine. "The Guilty One." Hélène Cixous and Catherine Clément. *The Newly Born Woman.* Trans. Betsy Wing. Minneapolis: U of Minnesota P, 1993, 1-59.

Conrad, Joseph. Preface. *The Nigger of the 'Narcissus.'* 1897. New York: Penguin, 1979, 11-14.

de Beauvoir, Simone. *The Second Sex.* Trans. H. M. Parshley. New York: Vintage, 1952.

Edel, Leon, and Gordon N. Ray, eds. *Henry James and H. G. Wells: A Record of their Friendship, their Debate on the Art of Fiction, and their Quarrel.* Urbana: U of Illinois P, 1958.

Forster, E. M. *A Room with a View.* 1908. New York: Vintage, n.d.

Hardy, Sylvia. Introduction. *Ann Veronica.* By H. G. Wells. London: Everyman, 1993, xix-xlv.

Hynes, Samuel. *The Edwardian Turn of Mind.* Princeton: Princeton UP, 1968.

Kemp, Peter. *H. G. Wells and the Culminating Ape.* New York: St. Martin's, 1982.

Lawrence, D. H. *Sons and Lovers.* 1913. New York: New American Library, 1985.

Parrinder, Patrick, ed. *H. G. Wells: The Critical Heritage.* London: Routledge and Kegan Paul, 1972.

Showalter, Elaine. *Sexual Anarchy: Gender and Culture at the Fin de Siècle.* New York: Viking, 1990.

Simpson, Anne B. "H. G. Wells's *Tono-Bungay:* Individualism and Difference." *Essays in Literature* 22.1 (1995): 75-86.

Steffen-Fluhr, Nancy. "Women and H. G. Wells." *Critical Essays on H. G. Wells.*
Ed. John Huntington. Boston: Hall, 1991, 148-69.

Wells, H. G. *Ann Veronica.* 1909. London: Virago, 1980.

———. "The Endowment of Motherhood." *An Englishman Looks at the World:
Being a Series of Unrestrained Remarks Upon Contemporary Matters.* London:
Cassell, 1914, 229-34.

———. *Experiment in Autobiography: Discoveries and Conclusions of a Very
Ordinary Brain (Since 1866).* New York: Macmillan, 1934.

———. *H. G. Wells in Love: Postscript to an Experiment in Autobiography.* Ed.
G. P. Wells. Boston: Little, Brown, 1984.

———. *Socialism and the Family.* 1906. Boston: Ball, 1908.

———. *The Time Machine.* 1895. New York: Random House, 1931.

———. *Tono-Bungay.* 1909. Lincoln: U of Nebraska P, 1978.

———. *The Wife of Sir Isaac Harman.* 1914. New York: Macmillan, 1916.

Part Two

Looking Around: British Character and Society

The Sunlight on the Garden

John Lucas

I.

It is still frequently asserted that when war broke out in August 1914 most people in Britain thought it would soon be over. A cleansing dip in the cold reality of military life, perhaps even a little bloodletting, and the nation could then return to its peaceful ways. "Home for harvest" was a much-used phrase of the time. But some of those who spoke the words were trying to keep their spirits up, and others had a far more apprehensive sense of an ending. Beneath the cheery up-and-at-'em optimism ran an altogether darker current of thought, a fearful sense that the sunlight on the garden of England was about to harden and grow cold. Nobody in that summer of 1914 could have known or even guessed at the horrors to come: of the nine million or so who would die before the war ended, of the wrecked economies of various European nation-states, of the destabilizing and overturning of governments, of the revolutionary changes that would come to Russia and, to a lesser extent, to other nations. But although it was impossible to foresee what would happen in the following years, there were those who had a sure conviction of impending disaster; and in England—which is the subject of this essay—that meant the end of the "record of the long, safe centuries."

The phrase is Henry James's and it comes from an essay he wrote shortly after the outbreak of war. "The first sense of it all to me after the shock and horror was that of a sudden leap back into life of the violence with which the American Civil War broke upon us." That is how James begins and he makes plain that he sees England as having now come, albeit unconsciously, within the rim of tragedy—of history as catastrophe. When "the dark hour" of the announcement of war came, England's genius was in "not being as her tragic sisters were." There was a supreme unawareness of how dark, how tragic the hour in fact was.

> Looking myself more askance at the dark hour (politically speaking I mean) than I after my fashion figured her as doing in the mass, I found it of an extreme, of quite an endless fascination to trace as many as possible of her felt idiosyncrasies back to her settled sea-confidence, and to see this now in turn account for so many other things, the smallest as well as the biggest, that, to give the fewest hints of illustration, the mere spread of the great trees, the mere gathers in the little bluey-white curtains of her cottage windows, the mere curl of the tinted smoke from the old chimneys matching that note, became a sort of exquisite evidence. (25-26)

It might be objected that this vision of pastoral England is very much the outsider's view and that behind the cottage windows there was much more anguished understanding of history than James is willing to concede. Such anguish, and a good deal else beside, can be found in D. H. Lawrence's great story of 1915, "England, My England," with its evocation of wrecked pastoral, of a once "safe" England threatened less by outer forces than by its own loss of energy, of purpose. Yet it is surely significant that Lawrence identifies such enervation with rural circumstance; or rather, he instinctively images England in terms of an unsustainable Edenic garden. (The story turns on the maiming of a child by a sickle her father has thrown down and left half-hidden in deep grass: this Adam won't work for his inheritance.) And in the same year, Lawrence wrote to Lady Cynthia Asquith to tell her that

> [w]hen I drive across this country, with the autumn falling and rustling to pieces, I am so sad, for my country, for this great wave of civilisation, 2,000 years, which is now collapsing, that it is hard to live. So much beauty and pathos of old things passing away ... this England, these shafted windows, the elm-trees, the blue distance— the past, the great past, crumbling down, breaking down, not under the force of the coming buds, but under the weight of many exhausted, lovely yellow leaves, that drift over the lawn and over the pond, like the soldiers, passing away, into winter and the darkness of winter. (431-32)

It is as though the war is a catalyst for breakdown, rather than its specific cause.

Lawrence was by no means alone in grieving for the crumbling away of the great past, and others shared his vision of that past as inseparable from "rootedness"—"these shafted windows, the elm trees, the blue distance." Lawrence has especially in mind Lady Ottoline Morrell's Jacobean house, Garsington Manor, and his vision of England can be linked to the tradition of country-house politics, where the house itself symbolizes settled relationships and mutual responsibility.[1] There is no need here to say anything of a tradition that, despite the attacks mounted on it in the nineteenth century (preeminently by Dickens in *Bleak House*) was clearly unwilling to die. Hence, as we shall see, the different ways in which it is modulated in the prewar fictions of E. M. Forster and Rudyard Kipling. Nor is it merely a literary tradition. It has always held a powerful grip on the English imagination, on how the English like to imagine England. That is why, when war broke out, so many writers and artists felt themselves able to voice both a deep personal and national sense of crisis through imagining England as a lost garden. By no means would all of them have subscribed to the conservative politics implicit in "country-house" values. A garden can, after all, be a place of equal labor: "When Adam delved and Eve span / Who was then the gentleman." Edward Thomas's vision of a lost England in "Adlestrop" is free of any suggestion of hierarchical social relations (25); and in "As the Team's Head-Brass," when he sits "among the boughs of a fallen elm" that has been brought down by a blizzard, he learns from the ploughman to whom he talks that one of the ploughman's "mates is dead. The second day / In France they killed him. It was back in March, / The very night of the blizzard, too" (105). The fallen elm symbolizes not merely a disruption in nature but, brought low as it is by a blizzard, the action of a discreetly hinted-at apocalyptic force that has also destroyed the ploughman's workmate; and "they" who killed the mate testify to the massive impersonality of a war to which men were sent by those who, in earlier days, would have done the fighting themselves. Feudal values, out of which country-house politics emerges and to which it endlessly appeals, took for granted the lord of the manor as armed defender of his serfs/peasants. Thomas knew full well that many of those who "volunteered" to fight in the First World War had in fact no option. Their employers did their volunteering for them. Yet this does not prevent him from glimpsing in "Adlestrop" what feels to be a secret "heart" of England for that minute when "a blackbird sang / Close by and round him mistier, / Farther and farther, all the birds / Of Oxfordshire and Gloucestershire" (25).

II.

That Thomas should locate the deep heart of England in the shires ought not to surprise us. During the period with which I am concerned it is apparent that an England of rooted values has to be associated with all that is unmodern, unindustrial, unchanging: in other words, the "heart" of England has to be essentially non-Northern. It has also to be thought of as a kind of amalgam of "pure" Englishness, not consciously perhaps but perhaps the more powerfully for that very reason. During the last years of the nineteenth century there were debates aplenty about the perceived threat to the purity of stock. English blood was threatened with taint and impurity through miscegenation (blood could be infected by "foreign bodies") or by the corrupting effects of city living. The survival of the fittest might turn out to mean the survival of those making the fewest demands of life—like city rats. "Degeneracy" was in the air, and it might well be passing into the bloodstream of Englishness.[2] All this is well known, but it needs to be mentioned if we are to understand the urgency with which what Forster was to call the "hunt for a home" frequently became a search for the kind of dwelling that could symbolize or even embody uncorrupted Englishness. And any such dwelling had inevitably to be located in the "ancient" England of the shires or south country. Hence, for example, Bateman's.

Kipling discovered the house in 1900 and two years later, when it became vacant, he bought it. It was "a well-built square Jacobean house of stone in a lonely valley, at the foot of a steep lane running down from an unfrequented village," Burwash, in Sussex (Carrington 432). "Behold us lawful owners of a gray stone lichened house," Kipling wrote on November 30, 1902, to his friend Charles Eliot Norton. "A.D. 1634 over the door— beamed, panelled, with old oak staircase, and all untouched and unfaked. . . . It is a good and peaceable place standing in terraced lawns nigh to a walled garden of old red brick"(433). Kipling rejoiced in the house's age and in its being "untouched and unfaked." Bateman's was "authentic." No wonder, then, that he should refuse to have electricity installed. And no wonder that among the works he began to write were *Puck of Pook's Hill* (1906); *Rewards and Fairies* (1910); and "The Glory of the Garden," a poem for inclusion in C. R. L. Fletcher's *History of England,* which also appeared in 1910. In the first of these works, Kipling introduces a tutelary "archetypal" Englishman, "Hobden the Hedger." Hobden is the link figure between the stories of *Puck of Pook's Hill* as he is of those that make up *Rewards and Fairies.* Hobden is Anglo-Saxon in origin. He was born before the imposition of the Norman yoke and his spirit still breathes through those who live where he was born.

His dead are in the churchyard—thirty generations laid.
Their names were old in history when Domesday book was made;
And the passion and the piety and the prowess of his line
Have seeded, rooted, fruited in some land the law calls mine. (x)

The land is that on which Bateman's stands, and Kipling offers himself as the true inheritor of Hobden's gifts—the passion, piety, and prowess that maintain their fruitfulness.

The organicism appealed to here is clearly of the first importance. It speaks both of naturalness and continued vitality, and these qualities are also invoked in "A Charm," the verses that Kipling puts at the front of *Rewards and Fairies*.

> Take of English earth as much
> As either hand may rightly clutch,
> In the taking of it breathe
> Prayer for all who lie beneath—
> Not the great or well bespoke,
> But the more uncounted folk
> Of whose life and death is none
> Report or lamentation.
> Lay that earth upon thy heart,
> And thy sickness shall depart! (ix-x)

What sickness? we may wonder. The answer must be, the malady of modern living, or what Kipling goes on to call "Fevered breath and festered soul / . . . Over-busy hand and brain" (x). England's "folk" offer a corrective to the strains and illnesses of city life. The soil that bred them and that they have rejoined is integral to a life of "useful work."

William Morris coined that phrase in order to contrast such work with what he saw as the horror of "useless toil." Useless toil is intrinsic to the world of industrialized capitalism, in which some men are idle and others waste their lives in labor that gives them no pleasure and denies them any sense of engagement, of "exercising the energies of . . . mind and soul as well as . . . body" (Briggs 118). Hobden the Hedger belongs to a period in English history when work still engaged the whole man. So do the folk whom Kipling invokes in "A Charm." I am by no means the first to remark that Kipling was influenced by the Arts and Crafts movement. Burne-Jones was his uncle and, according to Roderick Gradidge, "Morris and all his set" were around him when he was a child (223). Kipling was undoubtedly drawn to the movement's passion for work with mind and soul as well as body, but he adds to that a conviction of the worth of service that belongs to a political vision not at all in accord with Morris's utopian communism. Hobden is in one sense a free man, but in another he knows his place. He is an image of the feudalistic Toryism that for Kipling, as for others, represented England's ideal. This dream of England creates unlikely bedfellows, and Kipling's might be thought of as a folie à trois shared not merely with natural Tories but with Arts and Crafts socialists. But there is a difference: for while the latter might wish to (re)create a field full of folk, Kipling writes as though it still exists.

> Our England is a garden that is full of stately views,
> Of borders, beds and shrubberies and lawns and avenues,
> With statues on the terraces and peacocks strutting by;
> But the Glory of the Garden lies in more than meets the eye. (132)

The opening stanza of "The Glory of the Garden" takes up the image of England as a garden that had been given primal utterance in *Richard II.* (As soon as war began, John O'Gaunt's famous speech was endlessly used, echoed, paraphrased, and appealed to, even though in the play itself it is steeped in ironic implications.) And as the gardeners of *Richard II* are the emblematic keepers of order, workers in the garden who also clear it of "caterpillars," who willingly maintain its orderliness, so Kipling's "stately" garden embodies a time-honored orderliness which is maintained by invisible yet necessary agents, those "uncounted folk" who do the work.

> Our England is a garden, and such gardens are not made
> By singing: "Oh, how beautiful!" and sitting in the shade,
> While better men than we go out and start their working lives
> At grubbing weeds from gravel-paths with broken dinner knives.
>
> There's not a pair of legs so thin, there's not a head so thick,
> There's not a hand so weak and white, nor yet a heart so sick,
> But it can find some needful job that's crying to be done,
> For the Glory of the Garden glorifieth every one. (132-33)

As Kipling chose to praise Tommy Atkin for his part in holding on to the British Empire, so he praises the workers in the garden as those "better men" who contribute to its and their greater glory.

In its way it is a seductive vision. It is also entirely misleading. Most men in 1910 who had work—many had none—didn't live in rural circumstance. Given the actual hardship of agricultural laborers, this might be thought no bad thing. Who would want to put up with such low wages, such demeaning labor (as it often was), such contemptuous and brutal behavior by farmers and squires who could and often would kick workers out of their tied cottages at a moment's notice? In what possible sense could workers on the land conceivably be called "partners" in its glory? But then the same question could be asked of those millions who worked in industrial cities. In fact, it *was* being asked, and it not surprisingly produced the answer that the only worthwhile partnership for working men lay in the trade unions. For what Kipling's verses choose not to acknowledge is that by the time he was writing them England was not only a fully industrialized nation, it was one in which a few had become rich at the expense of the many.

In the years leading up to the war the gap between the rich and the poor was quite simply huge. And year by year it grew. When in 1899 Thorstein Veblen identified "conspicuous consumption" as a new form of spending, he was concerned specifically with the United States. Yet his diagnosis of such spending as "spending for prestige" applied just as well to England—with one exception. The inequalities in housing were vast. Industrial slums for the poor, country houses for the rich. In America, however, the best as well as the worst of these houses are part of the story of modernism. In England, on the other hand, the houses are deliberately premodern. They pretend to know nothing of new money. Nevertheless pretense is for the most part precisely what it is. Bateman's might have been intended to symbolize the kind of little commonwealth of mutuality that Jonson famously celebrated in "To Penshurst," with its vision of endless hospitality and shared largesse; but in Edwardian England those who owned the big houses had for the most part bought them with money gained from capitalist exploitation. They didn't, however, typically live "over the shop." They kept town houses, of course; but like their eighteenth- and nineteenth-century predecessors they hurried to separate themselves from the cities where their money was made. To settle on a country estate, to "put down roots," was to identify with an England and politics conceived in terms of tradition, continuity, hierarchical orderliness, while in truth the real work of England—the hand-hardening, back-aching labor of millions—was done elsewhere, in factories, down mines, and in conditions that could in no sense be thought of as gardenlike. Out of such conditions a very different politics might develop and a very different vision of England, too.

E. M. Forster attempts to explore these rival visions in *Howards End*. As the Schlegel sisters lie looking out over the English Channel, musing over the implications of Margaret's announcement of her engagement to the city businessman, Henry Wilcox, Forster launches into a kind of aria for England:

> England was alive, throbbing through all her estuaries, crying for joy through the mouths of gulls, and the north wind, with contrary motion, blew stronger against her rising seas. What did it mean? For what end are her fair complexities, her changes of soil, her sinuous coast? Does she belong to those who have moulded and made her feared by other lands, or to those who have added nothing to her power, but have somehow seen her, seen the whole island at once,

lying as a jewel in a silver sea, sailing as a ship of souls, with all the
brave world's fleet accompanying her towards eternity? (138)

Land of Hope and Glory. It is momentarily threatened, maybe, by the contrary North Wind, which I take to be a vague allusion to Germany, but Forster
is more concerned with the question of who owns England: those who belong to the outer world of what Helen Schlegel calls "'telegrams and anger,'" or those who live by the "inner world" of personal relationships, art,
imagination. John O'Gaunt's speech and therefore Shakespeare are predict-
ably recruited for the latter. As to the former, the putative owners must include Wilcox himself and probably his soldier-son, Charles. England in this
sense is the heart of Empire.

Forster intends his vision of England to be problematic. There can be
no objection to that. But it is reasonable to object that the vision isn't
problematic enough. For the contest for "ownership" leaves entirely out
of account those whom Kipling had realized needed to be included: the
workers in the garden. In *Howards End* little if any attention is paid to
work. Leonard Bast is poised on the edge of the abyss. He is a clerk,
struggling to make do on thirty bob a week. The reader's acceptance of
Bast's position—rather than protest against it—is the result of Forster's
persuasive language. Its seductive appeal echoes that of Jack London's
The People of the Abyss (1903) and John Davidson's "Thirty Bob a
Week," a much-favored ballad of the period, in which the clerk who
speaks the poem considers it his inevitable position to be the one who is
bossed rather than the one who does the bossing.

Forster echoes this glum acceptance in the extraordinary opening to
chapter 6 of *Howards End,* where he claims that "The very poor . . . are
unthinkable, and only to be approached by the statistician and poet" (34).
The uneasy irony of this draws far more attention to Forster's failure of
imagination than he can have intended. Here, glumness becomes mere glib-
ness. The episode where Leonard dies of a heart attack brought on by Charles
Wilcox's brandishing a sword at him is more telling, and that the bookcase
should fall on him is a masterstroke. All that culture, all those words are not
for the likes of Bast. Yet we are surely to infer from the manner of Bast's
death that he is in a sense one on whom nurture will never stick; or at least
nurture will never become an enabling agent in changing his life. But then
nothing will change his life. London, where he lives, is a city from which
the sensitive retreat. It isn't there that England is alive. (And the industrial
North, like the very poor, is unthinkable.) London, as James Thomson had
said in "The City of Dreadful Night," simply grinds out death like a mill.
And so, at the beginning of chapter 13, when Forster speaks of London, he

speaks against it, although, he says, "to do so is no longer fashionable. The Earth as an artistic cult has had its day, and the literature of the near future will probably ignore the country and seek inspiration from the town" (84). Against this it has surely to be said that at the moment Forster was writing it was entirely fashionable to speak against London or at least to imagine England in terms of rural circumstance. And this is precisely what Forster, in common with Kipling, does. For though London fascinates, or so Forster says, it is "as a tract of quivering grey" (84), a purposeless, always changing miasma. Its crowds provide for no community: it cannot support a home. The future true owners of England will therefore have to look to the country to provide the rooted dwelling they need. Hence the significance of Howards End.

The house, which is situated in Hertfordshire, is owned by Mrs. Wilcox, whose husband and sons suffer from hay fever when they stay there. They prefer their town house. Mrs. Wilcox recognizes in Margaret Schlegel her true successor and plans that Howards End shall in due course pass to her. Margaret first catches a glimpse of her future home in rainy spring weather:

> Down by the dell-hole more vivid colours were awakening, and Lent lilies stood sentinel on its margin, or advanced in battalions over the grass. Tulips were a tray of jewels. She could not see the wych-elm tree, but a branch of the celebrated vine, studded with velvet knobs, had covered the porch. She was struck by the fertility of the soil; she had seldom been in a garden where the flowers looked so well, and even the weeds she was idly plucking out of the porch were intensely green. (157)

It is a dreadfully inept piece of writing. I don't believe Forster has any ironic implications in mind when he compares lilies to an invading army or tulips to material riches. (Jewels? What jewels?) And what color apart from green does he expect weeds to be? But while the awkwardness of the prose betrays how little at ease Forster is with the rural England he seeks to praise, his insistence on its fertility reveals its importance to his scheme of locating Margaret Schlegel there. She is the fit inheritor of this fit heart of England and Forster spells this out in the following passage, where we are told that "starting from Howards End," Margaret attempts to "visualize England" and

> an unexpected love of the island awoke in her, connecting on this side with the joys of the flesh, on that with the inconceivable. Helen and her father had known this love, poor Leonard Bast was groping after it, but it had been hidden from Margaret till this afternoon. It had certainly come through the house and Miss Avery. Through them: the notion of "through" persisted; her mind trembled towards a

Figure 1. Rook's Nest House, the house upon which Howards End was based. Photo courtesy of the author.

conclusion which only the unwise have put into words. Then, veer-
ing back into warmth, it dwelt on ruddy bricks, flowering plum trees,
and all the tangible joys of spring. (161)

Margaret's spring awakening is to an England of the old house (those
ruddy bricks) with its willing servitor, Miss Avery, who belongs to the
adjoining farm ("And all come in, the farmer and the clown," Jonson
had written of Penshurst) and "natural" fertility ("The early cherry, with
the later plum / Fig, grape, and quince, each in his time doth come": so
Jonson [76]). And we must not forget the wych-elm. "It was a comrade,
bending over the house, strength and adventure in its roots, but in its
utmost fingers tenderness, and the girth, that a dozen men could not
have spanned, became in the end evanescent, till pale bud clusters seemed
to float in the air" (162).[3]

Howards End is not a great country house. It is scaled down to a far
more modest size than those houses that had been celebrated by Jonson,
Carew, Marvell, Pope, and others; but its "naturalness" echoes theirs, the
implication that it was built with no man's ruin, no man's groan (see Fig.1).
Like Donwell Abbey, that "rambling and irregular" house, it is continuous
with rural circumstance, not imposed on it.[4] Moreover, the future of England's
health is bound up with its survival.

At the end of *Howards End,* Forster has so arranged his connective
plotting that Helen Schlegel's illegitimate son by Leonard Bast shall inherit
the house after his aunt's death. The ownership of England will pass to the
fruitful union of the artistic, idealistic woman and the ardent working-class
man. England's future is assured. "'The field's cut!' Helen cried excitedly—
'the big meadow! We've seen to the end, it'll be such a crop of hay as
never!'" (271). But the insistence on coming fruitfulness feels to be a wish-
ing it might be so, and this is at one with the forced plotting that the novel's
famous epigraph-cum-motto "Only connect . . ." entails. *Howards End* may
be about connectedness, but underlying it are very real fears of disconnec-
tion. These undoubtedly have to do with strained relations between England and Germany. It is notable that Forster's characters are forever talking
about the "old" ideal Germany but have nothing to say about the modern
state. Imperialist, militant Germany is, we have to conclude, like the very
poor, "unthinkable." But what cannot be thought may nevertheless exercise
a fearful fascination; and in *Howards End* much that isn't mentioned is, to
use a modish term, an absent presence. Above all, I would say, the fear that
England isn't at all as he tries to account for it conditions Forster's almost
hectic insistence on the nation-as-fruitful garden. And it is after all rather
remarkable that in this garden nobody seems to be doing any work. Wilcox's

money isn't in the end needed: Forster sets up the clash between the
mystificatory account of the "natural/rooted" country house and the actuality of city finance only to evade its implications. At least real work got done
in Kipling's garden. Of course, that too was mystificatory or evasive. As I
have noted, the kind of toil needed to sustain prewar England had nothing
to do with the Arts and Crafts work which Kipling evokes. (I might also
remark that England as a garden would have meant precious little to the
millions who lived without a garden of any sort.) But those who will inherit
Howards End and its fertile garden are imagined as living a kind of radiant
idyll which as good as spells idleness.

This is why Wells's *Tono-Bungay,* which had appeared the previous
year, is so bracing a corrective to both Kipling and Forster. Wells's novel is
also about the condition of England—indeed, *Tono-Bungay* was a key text
for C. F. G. Masterman's study *The Condition of England*—but unlike the
others, Wells will have nothing to do with the search for and then the locating of a heart of England in rural circumstance. His protagonist, who is
brought up as the son of a maidservant in a country house, can't wait to get
to the city:

> I didn't like those young countrymen, and I'm no believer in the
> English countryside under the Bladesover system as a breeding-
> ground for honourable men. One hears a frightful lot of nonsense
> about the Rural Exodus and the degeneration wrought by town
> life upon our population. To my mind, the English townsman even
> in the slums is infinitely better spiritually, more courageous, more
> imaginative and cleaner, than his agricultural cousin. (59-60)

When George becomes a London student, his "apprehension of spaces and
places," which is "reinforced by a quickened apprehension of persons" (87),
is at once more vivid and exact than Forster's cloudy generalities.

Most importantly, Wells shows that the "old" England of country-
house values is dying of a poverty that is as much inner as it is material.
George accompanies his uncle Ponderevo, who has by now moved up
from humble chemist to wealthy chemical manufacturer, to look at Lady
Grove, a stately country house in the Kentish weald. "An old Catholic
family had died out of it, century by century, and was now altogether
dead. Portions of the fabric are the thirteenth century, and its last architectural revision was tudor" (203). They meet the vicar of the nearby
village. "We were pill vendors, he knew, and no doubt horribly vulgar in
soul; but then it might have been some polygamous Indian rajah, a great
strain on a good man's tact, or some Jew with an inherited expression of
contempt" (205). Such "types," as Wells defines them, were certainly

buying up country houses. They were also having them built. After he has grown tired of Lady Grove, this is what George's uncle himself decides to do. As the vast pile called Crest Hill begins to take shape, George reflects: "It is curious how many of these modern financiers of chance and bluff have ended their careers by building. It was not merely my uncle. Sooner or later they all seem to bring their luck to the test of realization, try to make their fluid opulence coagulate out as bricks and mortar" (222). But Edward Ponderevo's financial empire crashes before Crest Hill can be completed, leaving only "that despoiled hillside, that colossal litter of bricks and mortar, and crude roads and paths, the scaffolding and sheds" (222-23). There is nothing particularly modern about "financiers of chance and bluff" wanting to build houses that would at once reflect and validate their opulence. That is simply a fact of history. It is, however, curious that Edward Ponderevo should wish to build so distinctively "modern" a house; for most of those who commissioned big houses during the period with which I am concerned wanted to suggest that they were part of that cultural, political, and social continuum identified with the country house. The houses they had built for themselves were typically situated in the shires, as Crest Hill is, but unlike Edward Ponderevo's dream house most of the houses actually constructed were built "old." That this should be so is largely due to the genius of one man, Edward Lutyens.

III.

This is not the place to speak at length about Lutyens's achievements. Monographs on his work abound.[5] I want here merely to note that what characterizes his work is its eclecticism. A Lutyens house is, in the best sense of the word, a pastiche. Lutyens skillfully mixes styles to suggest that the newest house is part of English architectural history: a touch of Gothic here, a hint of pre-Norman there, elsewhere some Tudor or Jacobean, perhaps a touch of Queen Anne. He blends materials—brick, wood, mullioned glass—and from the blend creates a house that seems not so much out of time as seemingly able to bear the traces of centuries-old longevity. Here, then, we should note the terms in which Gertrude Jekyll in 1900 wrote her warmly appreciative account of the house that Lutyens had built for her four years earlier (see Fig. 2). Munstead Wood, Jekyll says,

> does not stare with newness; it is not new that is in any way disquieting to the eye; it is neither raw nor callow. On the contrary, it gives the impression of a comfortable maturity of something like a couple of hundred years. And yet there is nothing sham-old about it; it is

Figure 2. Munstead Wood.
Photo courtesy of the Country Life Picture Library, London.

not trumped-up with any specious or fashionable devices of spuri-
ous antiquity; there is no pretending to be anything that it is not—no
affectation whatever.

But it is designed and built in the thorough and honest spirit of
the good work of old days, and the body of it, so fashioned and
feared, has, as it were, taken to itself the soul of a more ancient
dwelling-place. The house is not in any way a copy of an old building, though it embodies the general characteristics of the older structures of its own district. (Quoted in Gradidge 116)

Munstead Wood is a triumph of eclecticism. It combines Arts and Crafts
concerns for "good work" with "rootedness"—that comfortable maturity—
and a sense of belonging, taking its place naturally among the "older structures." Like Penshurst and unlike Crest Hill, it is not built "to envious show."
It was sited so as to be glimpsed rather than seen full on. (At the front, that
is: the rear has a little formal garden.)

Jekyll oversaw the building of the house from inception to completion.
She was therefore in crucial ways a part creator of Munstead Wood. As an
already famous designer and creator of gardens, as well as a much older
person—she was fifty in 1826, whereas Lutyens was a mere twenty-seven—
she had a right to be closely involved in planning it. Munstead Wood was

not merely her house, it was an expression of her values, of her own genius. When she wrote about it in the opening chapter of *Home and Garden,* she was for all intents and purposes reestablishing her own credentials. And as she collaborated with Lutyens on many of his most important achievements, she has to be seen as integral to his creation of the Edwardian English country house. For her, as for those eighteenth-century forerunners she so admired, nature was a garden and so a garden ought to be natural. As David Ottewell remarks, at Munstead Wood

> [r]estraint was maintained throughout, planting being carried out only where it seemed called for: 'I thought where the copse looked well and complete in itself it was better left alone.' It must have given the impression of being spontaneous, as though the woodland had been coaxed and encouraged to reveal its intrinsic beauty, had 'happened' rather than been planned. (64)

From this it is easy to see why between them Lutyens and Jekyll embodied in their work the yearning for England as a garden that ministered to the anxieties of the time and offered a consoling and would-be reassuring image of an essentially preindustrial, precapitalist, even prelapsarian nation.

The reality was, of course, very different. Even the gardens at Munstead Wood had eventually to be maintained by no fewer than eleven full-time gardeners. More significantly, Lutyens and Jekyll built for captains of industry, for the nouveaux riches who had gained their money from the world of city finance or commercial exploitation. So did other architects. In his study *The Last Country Houses,* Clive Aslet points out that by the end of the nineteenth century

> [t]extiles were no longer financing country houses, and would not do so again until the development of synthetics after the First World War. . . . Ashby St. Ledgers seems to have been the only house in the period built from a steel fortune, though even there at least part of the money came from banking and an inherited estate. Shipping and shipbuilding were more active (Pangbourne Towers, Coldharbour, Abbey House) and so was the new chemical industry through the Tennant family (Great Maytham, Lympne Castle, Wilsford Hall). The Nobles (Ardkinglas, Besford Court, Wretham Hall) also had interest in chemicals, although the bulk of their fortune came from Sir Andrew's connection with the armaments firm of Armstrong Whitworth and Co. (34)

With the occasional exception, all these houses were built in the south or in "old" England: Coldharbour is in Hampshire, Besford Court in Worcestershire, Wretham in Norfolk, Wilsford Hall in Wiltshire. And although Lutyens was by no means the only architect put to work to turn

Figure 3. Wilsford Manor.
Photo courtesy of the Country Life Picture Library, London.

wealth into bricks and mortar, most of his rivals sought to emulate his style. Detmar Blow, the architect of Wilsford (see Fig. 3), was Lutyens's friend as well as his rival; and the farm steadings and cottages Blow built in York-shire and Leicestershire "honestly attempt to give the impression of a hand-crafted building of any period." This is especially true of Stoneywell Cottage, which Blow built for his fellow architect Sydney Gimson in Charnwood Forest, Leicestershire; and of Lea Cottage, also in the Forest. Both testify to the vitality of the Arts and Crafts movement, but in both cases the sugges-tion of solid partisan dwellings is a charade.[6]

And here is the crux of the matter. The prewar country house, whether in fiction or fact, provides an image that is diametrically at odds with the truth. For all that Lutyens made Munstead Wood the symbol of rural sweet-ness and strength, and despite his building, for the editor of *Country Life,* Deanery Gardens in Berkshire, which is certainly one of his most perfect designs—"its theme, a romantic bachelor's idyllic afternoons beside a Thames backwater" (Hussey 95)—he and other architects of the time were funded by money from the very industries that challenged and had indeed supplanted the country house of developing industrial capitalism. For those who had made a fortune from such industries, to want to escape from the pollution, noise, and slum dwellings they had caused might be understandable. But for them to image themselves as rooted in country values, identified with "old" England, was as inauthentic as the fake Tudor gables to be found on many of their houses. There is a further point. It is not merely that the industries on which country houses were built were contributing to the destruction of country-house values. They were also actively involved in bringing to an end the record of the long, safe centuries. The money for Besford Court and Wretham Hall came from armaments; so for that matter did that used for Abbey House, built by Lutyens in 1913 for Messrs. Vickers Ltd. And many of the largest shipbuilders, including those who in the prewar period had country houses built for them, owed at least some part of their fortunes to naval contracts. Others were inevitably partly linked to the aggressive imperialism that characterizes European energies of the period. In other words, those who chose to present themselves as cherishing and upholding the deep peace of the countryside were among those most directly responsible for bringing that peace to an end.

An anthology published during the war for the enjoyment of English soldiers, *The Old Country,* carried an introduction by Sir Arthur Yapp, who was convinced that the anthology would bring pleasure to every Tommy who read it, for each "in imagination . . . can see his village home" (v). The vast majority of those who volunteered for military life in August 1914 came, of course, from industrial cities. They or their forebears had been ousted from village homes by those now claiming to uphold England as a green and pleasant land, England as a garden.

NOTES

1. There is an exquisite irony in the fact that although Lawrence hymns the house for its quintessential Englishness, the Morrells wanted it, the grounds especially, to look Italianate. Lady Ottoline had herself proclaimed that Garsington "is more Italian than any other place in England that I have known" (quoted in Ottewell 185).

2. The fullest and most sophisticated study of the preoccupation with degeneracy is to be found in Greenslade.

3. Forster may wish to stress the girth, ancientness, and indestructibility of the wych-elm, but I can report that when I visited Rook's Nest House in 1960, the original of Howards End, all that was left of the elm was the base of the trunk. The tree had been recently blown down in gales. But it had clearly been of no great size. Quite why the elm should have been adopted in the latter half of the nineteenth century as the unofficial symbol of England I do not fully

understand, although I have attempted to say more in my study *Modern English Poetry: From Hardy to Hughes,* especially 53-55.

4. The account of Donwell Abbey is to be found in Jane Austen's *Emma* 323-27.

5. The essential introduction is still Christopher Hussey, *The Life of Sir Edwin Lutyens.* There are also good studies by Roderick Gradidge and Daniel O'Neill.

6. For a useful account of Blow as an architect, see Gradidge, especially 165-72.

WORKS CITED

Aslet, Clive. *The Last Country Houses.* London: Yale UP, 1982.

Austen, Jane. *Emma.* Ed. David Lodge. London: Oxford UP, 1971.

Briggs, Asa, ed. *William Morris: Selected Writings and Designs.* Harmondsworth: Penguin, 1962.

Carrington, Charles. *Rudyard Kipling: His Life and Work.* Harmondsworth: Penguin, 1970.

Forster, E. M. *Howards End.* 1910. New York: Bantam, 1985.

Gradidge, Roderick. *Dream Houses: The Edwardian Ideal.* London: Constable, 1980.

Greenslade, William. *Degeneracy and the Fin de Siècle.* London: Cambridge UP, 1993.

Hussey, Christopher. *The Life of Sir Edwin Lutyens.* London: Country Life, 1950.

James, Henry. *Within the Rim and Other Essays.* London: Collins, n.d.

Jonson, Ben. "To Penshurst." *Poems.* Ed. George Burke Johnston. Cambridge, Mass.: Harvard UP, 1962, 76.

Kipling, Rudyard. "The Glory of the Garden." 1910. *The Definitive Edition of Rudyard Kipling's Verse.* London: Hodder and Stoughton, 1969, 132-33.

———. *Puck of Pook's Hill.* London: Macmillan, 1906.

———. *Rewards and Fairies.* London: Macmillan, 1910.

Lawrence, D. H. *The Letters of D. H. Lawrence.* Ed. George J. Zytaruk and James T. Boulton. Vol. 2. Cambridge, Eng.: Cambridge UP, 1981.

Lucas, John. *Modern English Poetry: From Hardy to Hughes.* London: Batsford, 1985.

O'Neill, Daniel. *Lutyens: Country Houses.* London: Lund Humphries, 1980.

Ottewell, David. *The Edwardian Garden.* London: Yale UP, 1989.

Thomas, Edward. *The Collected Poems of Edward Thomas.* Ed. R. George Thomas. Oxford: Oxford UP, 1981.

Wells, H. G. *Tono-Bungay*. 1909. Lincoln: U of Nebraska P, 1986.

Yapp, Sir Arthur. "Introduction: At the Sign of the Red Triangle." *The Old Country: A Book of Love and Praise of England*. Ed. Ernest Rhys. London: J. M. Dent, 1917, v-vii.

Self-Isolation and Self-Advertisement in The Old Wives' Tale

Robert Squillace

That *The Old Wives' Tale* is a novel about time has always seemed clear; indeed, E. M. Forster declares in *Aspects of the Novel* that "it misses greatness" because it concerns nothing but the obvious effects of growing old, and "a great book must rest on something more than an 'of course'" (38). More expansive readings of the work, such as James Hepburn's analysis in *The Art of Arnold Bennett* and Gloria Fromm's in "Re-mythologizing Arnold Bennett," draw attention to its depiction of time's impact, not only on arteries and bones but on the self that must confront the changing world and the fact of its own imminent end. But *The Old Wives' Tale* concerns more than universal human reactions to the eternal fact of the passage of years. Bennett does not merely deal with some patch of time long enough to show the effects of aging but otherwise indifferent; his novel construes the specific period from the early 1860s to 1907 as a revolutionary epoch during which the various repressions of ambition that had supported patriarchal authority slowly yielded to an open expression of desire, an unprecedented valorization of individual autonomy.

The revolution is not an unrelieved success; while Bennett's depiction of the death of John Baines suggests a triumphant assertion of individual desire, the marriage of his daughter Constance and Samuel Povey shows the tenacity of patriarchal privilege. As his fulminations against English conservatism in his column for *The New Age* show, Bennett knew that the transformation from a society based on "self-isolation" to one based on "self-advertisement," to use the novel's terminology, was hardly complete by the time of Edward VII's ascension to the throne. But *The Old Wives' Tale* clearly promulgates an idea of progress as movement toward individual self-possession.

Bennett begins his account of the declining belief in patriarchal rectitude with the death of a patriarch: John Baines, founder of a prosperous draper's shop. On the night of Baines's stroke, Bennett writes, the town of Bursley learned "that the active member of the Local Board, the orator, the religious worker, the very life of the town's life, was permanently done for" (81). The town's life is more literally done for than it recognizes; not only is the heyday of the Wesleyan connection, of Christian oratory, and of Christianity itself essentially over, but the commercial life of the town—particularly St. Luke's Square—has begun a long decline parallel to John Baines's. The great principle of "self-isolation" (40), on which the dignity of both the town and the man's career have depended, will prove suicidal for St. Luke's Square, its retail trade ultimately siphoned off by "arrogant and pushing Hanbridge, with its electric light and its theaters and its big, advertising shops" (511). That Hanbridge achieves its position by advertisement is particularly telling; the self-isolation of mid-Victorian England gradually yields to "the modern craze for unscrupulous self-advertisement" (41). This transformation is at once a commercial and a psychological phenomenon, individual desires repressed in a strict patriarchy coming to the fore as its authority begins to diminish. Just as the Potteries are "lost in the central labyrinth of England" (49), so the words of the stricken John Baines issue from him "as if the sense had to travel miles by labyrinthine passages" (81)—the whole region, like the self-isolating draper, suffers a paralysis that is the emblem of its suppression of desire, of motion, of change. John Baines, a sort of madman in the attic, imposes on himself what is at once a security "from women and fools generally" (59) and a fatal detachment from the desires that constitute and create life. The madness that signifies repressed rebellion in *Jane Eyre* is transferred to the repressive authority himself; the patriarch is the one most confined by clinging to his patriarchy.

Not only does Bennett treat Mr. Baines as a superannuated relic; so, if more politely, do virtually all his surviving fellow characters. At the titanic funeral tea that Mrs. Baines organizes to mark her husband's passing, assembled mourners struggle "to be lugubrious and inconsolable, but the secret relief resulting from the death would not be entirely hidden" (117). Indeed, the whole ethos of self-isolating secrecy that John Baines represents seems to crumble after his death. His obituary, the narrator reports, "did not omit a eulogy of his steady adherence to the wise old English maxims of commerce and his avoidance of dangerous modern methods. Even in the sixties the modern had reared its shameless head" (114). "Shameless" is an inspired choice of adjective, capturing both the voice of the earlier generation, for which it is a pejorative term, and of the later one, for which it is an honorific.

The first words after the funeral chapter has concluded are "'Exquisite, 1s. 11d.'" (118)—the text of an advertisement composed by Samuel Povey, soon to marry Constance and take possession of the shop. Mrs. Baines suppresses this initial outbreak of the language of pleasure and desire, of "the modern spirit" (121) that would "outrage the decency of trade" (120)— the term "decency" continuing the sexual metaphor. But after Constance and Samuel have married, Mrs. Baines secretly takes satisfaction in the defeat of her husband's ideals. Mr. Povey has raised a sign, "thirty-five feet long and two feet in depth," that reads, "'John Baines' in gold letters a foot and a half high, on a green ground" (183), an advertisement of self that Baines explicitly refused to countenance in his own day. On Mrs. Baines's first visit after its installation, Constance "comprehended that her mother had adopted a silently disapproving attitude" (187). But later that day, Mrs. Baines walks (by a circuitous route so that her destination cannot be guessed) to the top of the Square to gaze on the sign. Bennett notes, "She returned to her daughter's by the same extraordinary route, and said not a word on entering. But she was markedly cheerful" (187). When she had departed on this expedition, Constance speculated, "'I expect she has gone to look at father's grave'" (187). And so she has.

Bennett was not so sanguine as to the inevitability of progress as the death of John Baines makes it appear; in John's successor, he shows how stubbornly privilege resists its extinction. Samuel Povey establishes himself early in *The Old Wives' Tale* as a revolutionary in the public acknowledgment of private desires—a comic revolutionary whose acts of rebellion consist of marrying above his class and attaching a ticket that reads "exquisite" to a bolt of fabric, but a revolutionary nonetheless. As soon as he assumes a position of authority, however, his progressive tendencies diminish. Marriage, property, and fatherhood develop habits of secrecy in him antithetical to the exposure of desires. Fearing a feminized world of public emotion, he increasingly assumes a posture of impenetrable masculine authority. He is at last unable to cope with all that self-advertisement reveals, going half-mad from the revelation of his cousin Daniel's secrets. He dies, in effect, of exposure.

Samuel's ascension to head of household begins, right after the honeymoon, with the exclusion of Constance from the shop. The title of the chapter in which this occurs, "Revolution," applies most obviously to Samuel's novel business practices but also to the inversion of power that occurs in the relation between Samuel and Constance as marriage succeeds courtship. Formerly beholden to Constance both as shop assistant and suitor,[1] Samuel now assumes control over both shop and wife: "Mr. Povey came in to supper, laden with ledgers and similar works which Constance had never even pretended to understand. It was a sign from him that the honeymoon was over. He was proprietor now" (175). On their first night in the bedroom once occupied by Con's parents, Samuel feels obliged to disguise feelings too uncomfortably close to Constance's womanly perspective, which would expose more than he would admit. Bennett voices Samuel's judgment, then undercuts it thoroughly:

> 'Doesn't it give you a funny feeling, sleeping in this room? It does me,' said Constance. Women, even experienced women, are so foolishly frank. They have no decency, no self-respect.
> 'Really?' replied Mr. Povey, with loftiness, as who should say: 'What an extraordinary thing that a reasonable creature can have such fancies! Now to me this room is exactly like any other room.' And he added aloud, glancing away from the glass, where he was unfastening his necktie: 'It's not a bad room at all.' This, with the judicial air of an auctioneer.
> Not for an instant did he deceive Constance, who read his real sensations with accuracy. (176-77)

Samuel, who had no qualms about outraging "the decency of trade" (120), must regard the exposure of his wife's feelings as indecent in order to separate his province from hers in the psychic realm, just as he has separated shop from home.[2]

When Constance's honesty disturbs Samuel's image of himself—she objects "impulsively," though in a "perfectly gentle" tone (177), to his abandoning the linen collars he had worn on their honeymoon for paper—an argument nearly ensues. Each quickly relents; Constance lets Samuel choose his collars and he chooses linen. But compromise almost immediately becomes Constance's job. In the small talk that follows the quarrel, Constance can only murmur "'Oh!'" to Samuel's announcement of the impending signboard, "the episode of the paper collar having weakened her self-confidence" (178). Samuel imposes his own individuality on the house in a series of unilateral decisions. His actions particularly reinforce his sense of masculine freedom: he buys a dog (though not the bulldog he desires, as it would cost at least 100 sovereigns) and takes up cigars. Sometimes a cigar is not just a cigar. Constance does not challenge these masculine displays; she even enjoys them, finding the odor of the cigars "titillating" and crying "an instant, while admiring her husband's firmness" when he punishes the dog (182). But she fleetingly recognizes something dangerous in her situation; the arrival of the dog breeder leaves her "full of fear for the future" (180). Secrecy has reclaimed the household; Bennett writes of Samuel's first hidden forays into the world of tobacco: "Each was deceiving the other: Mr. Povey hid his crime, and Constance hid her knowledge of his crime. . . . But this is what marriage is" (182). The stream of novelties with which the marriage begins, the series of "Revolutions," soon freezes into habit; having honeymooned in Buxton, Sam and Constance go back on holiday every year. Samuel, installed as the authority in his house, no longer acknowledges the open expression of desire.

But Samuel only fully achieves the self-isolation of John Baines when he too becomes a father; at the same time, the Poveys' creation of a child begins the end of Samuel's reign. Bennett ingeniously associates the birth of Cyril Povey with the eruption of secret desires. Cyril's advent is curiously connected with a ride that Dick Povey, Samuel's first cousin once removed, takes on a primitive bicycle appropriately termed a "boneshaker." The ride shakes many bones; Dick barrels "straight for the church [a bastion of mystification and repressed desire in the novel], as though he meant to disestablish it and perish" (200). Dick's novel mode of transportation, one of a series of innovations that leads from trains to boneshakers to bicycles to automobiles to balloons, itself symbolizes motion, the approaching future, which Bennett suggests will have no place for Samuel's brand of patriarchal suppression. Further, Dick Povey's ride shakes Samuel from "the deep groove of [his] habits" (198), initiating a more intimate friendship with his cousin, Daniel, a Regency survival, a "worshipper of the god Pan" (202), than ever before. Soon Constance has missed her period and proves to be pregnant. This peculiar concatenation of events suggests that the Poveys cannot have children, cannot make the future, until cycles are broken; habitual action, after all, is action unconnected with desire; habit is the fortress that secrecy erects to preserve itself. But desire breaches its walls; Cyril, "the incredible, incomprehensible future," symbolically the result of Samuel's "initiation into the cult [of Pan]," is the "secret [who] refuses to be kept" (202-3).

The birth of Cyril establishes an Oedipal triangle that Bennett portrays chiefly from the perspective of Laius (and, perhaps uniquely for his time,

Jocasta; see 21-23). Cyril's birth completes Samuel's transformation into a doomed and jealous, if consciously benevolent, autocrat; the man who earlier pursued the "shameless" modern now learns shame at the exposure of "the unconscious primitive savagery of a young mother" (209): Constance breast-feeding Cyril before the unmarried shop assistant, Miss Insull. Civilization itself has thus come to mean secrecy to Samuel; exposure is savagery. His reaction originates in exclusion from the quasi-erotic bond between mother and son, for which he compensates by an inflated sense of possession: "*his* wife feeding *his* baby" (209).

In the face of a revolution that leaves him the displaced rather than the displacer—"the whole house was inverted and disorganized, hopelessly," thinks Constance during labor (210)—Samuel reconceives of himself as "the seat of government and of Constance and Cyril as a sort of permanent opposition" (236). In a dispute over punishment for Cyril's misbehavior at his birthday party, Samuel uses the excuse of disciplining Cyril to deny Constance the pleasure of contact with him. That Bennett sets this fight on Cyril's birthday indicates its origin in jealousy of the newcomer. When, after some unspecified "punishment" determined and inflicted in secret by Samuel, Constance demands to see her sleeping son: "For a brief instant Cyril did not exist for Constance. Samuel alone obsessed her, and yet Samuel seemed a strange, unknown man. It was in Constance's life one of those crises when the human soul seems to be on the very brink of mysterious and disconcerting cognitions, and then the wave recedes as inexplicably as it surged up" (223). Although the wave of Constance's recognition recedes, the conflict itself remains, its Oedipal nature becoming more and more apparent. Cyril, of course, must ultimately win the contest with his father, despite his apparent powerlessness. Before he has reached the age of thirteen, he has engineered the purchase of a bulldog—a desire that Samuel had expressed, but had never possessed the boldness to fulfill—and broken the tradition of spending family holidays in Buxton.

Like John Baines, Samuel gradually renders himself irrelevant by a retreat into privacy. He dies in a hopeless struggle to maintain secrets that he cannot hide from himself, a psychic conflict from which Bennett characteristically diverts attention by means of an attractively conventional, moralistic cover plot: the rebounding of Daniel's licentiousness upon his own head (or, more accurately, neck). Daniel, the worshiper of Pan, hangs for the murder of a wife whose fondness for liquor (and whose probable infidelity) he cannot stomach. Contemplating the murder, Samuel recoils from the last vestiges of his progressive past: "For many years he, Samuel, had seen in Daniel a living refutation of the old Hebrew menaces. But he had been wrong, after all! God is not mocked! And Samuel was aware of a revulsion in himself towards that strict codified godliness from which, in thought, he had perhaps been slipping away" (250-51). Sam not only takes up his cousin's defense with such abandon that he works himself to death; in the process he becomes that against which he ostensibly revolts: "He became Daniel's defending angel, rescuing Daniel from Daniel's own weakness and apathy. He became, indeed, Daniel" (257). Furthermore, Samuel descends into his own fundamental being more deeply than ever before by "becoming" his cousin; Constance recognizes that "she could do nothing; she had come to the bedrock of Samuel's character" (258). While readers may surmise that they have unearthed the text's secret by noting the undermining irony of Samuel's simultaneous support for Daniel and the Ten Commandments, Bennett adds an even more challenging complication. Despite the insinuation of Samuel's madness, the narrator declares after his death that "destiny took hold of him and displayed, to the observant, the vein of greatness which runs through every soul without exception" (275).

To detect any greatness in Samuel Povey, one must consider him against the backdrop of his community, particularly in its reaction to the exposure of Daniel's secrets. The responses of Bennett's fictitious Bursley to Daniel's crime, trial, and execution were closely based, as Louis Tillier has shown, on the furious protest mounted by the actual town of Burslem against the hanging of William Frederick Horry for the murder of Jane Horry, his wife. However, Bennett made an enormous change in his source—whereas a drunken Frederick Horry acted with repulsive premeditation, tracking his wife to Lincolnshire and there shooting her, Daniel returns home one night to find his inebriated wife ignoring the cries of their son, who has broken his leg on the stairs, and throttles her to death almost before realizing it.

According to Tillier, Bennett's revisions were meant to justify the town's impassioned defense of the murderer:

> He [Daniel] is worthy of the efforts his cousin Samuel and his fellow-citizens make to save him; he deserves sympathy and even respect. In this way Bennett transformed a demonstration of bad taste into a collective rising against injustice: the petition to the Home Secretary does honour to its sponsors; and the posthumous procession in memory of the hanged man becomes the symbol of a grim fidelity to lost causes. (52)

Tillier has succumbed to a common affliction—the misidentification of Bennett's values with those of the Five Towns he portrays. The notion that the "grim fidelity" of Bursley's devotion to Daniel Povey represents "a collective rising against injustice" is continually undermined. Even the most sentimental descriptions of Bursley's mourning at Daniel's memorial service are compromised by irony: "The boom of the drum, desolating the interruptions of the melody, made sick the heart, but with a lofty grief; and the dirge seemed to be weaving a purple pall that covered every meanness" (269-70). The pall, parodically reflected in the purpleness of the prose, covers a multiplicity of meannesses. As Mr. Critchlow, always unpleasant but never wrong, announces in identifying Bursley's self-delusion: "'I'm told as she was a gallivanting woman and no housekeeper, and as often drunk as sober. I'd no call to be told that. If strangling is a right punishment for a wife as spends her time in drinking brandy instead of sweeping floors and airing sheets, then Dan's safe. But I don't seem to see Judge Lindley telling the jury as it is'" (262). He doesn't: "As Judge Lindley remarked in his confidential report, the sole arguments in favour of Daniel were provocation and his previous high character; and these were no sort of an argument" (269).

Later, Bennett describes the sudden shift in Bursley's opinion—from a conviction of Daniel's absolute innocence to one of his mere fitness for clemency—in unmistakably ironic terms: "Without any sense of any inconsistency or of shame, they took up an absolutely new position. The structure of blind faith had once again crumbled at the assault of realities, and unhealthy, un-English truths, the statement of which would have meant ostracism twenty-four hours earlier, became suddenly the platitudes of the Square and the market-place" (266). "Un-English" is invariably an adjective of approval in Bennett's lexicon. Even the procession that Tillier cites with such regard is motivated more by provincial jealousy that a seat of power outside the Five Towns has the power to condemn a Bursleyite than by a belief in Daniel's innocence. It is difficult to accept that the town's emotions well from a devotion to justice when one reads that "[s]ince the execution of the elephant, nothing had so profoundly agitated Bursley" (271). Bursley seems even less laudable when Bennett continues: "Constance . . . reflected that the death and burial of Cyril's honoured grandfather, though a resounding event, had not caused one-tenth of the stir which she beheld. But then John Baines had killed nobody" (271). The hypocrisy of Victorian self-isolation could hardly be plainer; the men of Bursley keep their real interest in Daniel's case a deep secret even from themselves.

The citizens of Bursley leap to Daniel's defense not in the interests of justice, but from loyalty to a member of the club—which is ultimately loyalty to themselves, to a social structure that yields them control (the funeral procession is strictly male). It is crucial, then, that Bennett make Daniel, unlike Frederick Horry, essentially a respectable burgher. Bursley uses the opportunity of the murder to indulge itself vicariously in the same violent passions it collectively denies could possess any of its leaders. Identification with Daniel comes in two forms. For the poor, Daniel's case holds the same appeal as indulgence in a religion based on human sacrifice (of Jesus), worship of a God who "declined to say whether or not he would require more bloodshed" (124). When Daniel is arraigned for the murder, Bennett portrays him as a sacrificial outlet for the mob's passions: "For the captive is more sacred even than a messiah. . . . It was as though the crowd had yelled for Daniel's blood and bones, and the faithful constables had saved him from their lust" (255). Both criminals and messiahs—particularly the messiah who was executed as a criminal—are excluded as alien to society and simultaneously designated as its surrogate sufferers.

On the other hand, as another stroke of deadpan irony establishes, the wealthy identify with Daniel Povey even more duplicitously: "Why! Dan Povey had actually once been Chairman of the Bursley Society for the Prosecution of Felons, that association for annual eating and drinking, whose members humorously called each other 'felons'! Impossible, monstrous, that an ex-chairman of the 'Felons' should be a sentenced criminal!" (266). Faced with the reality of its own sublimated desires, with a "felon" who has committed a real murder, Bursley chooses denial. Its crusade to save Daniel aims both to preserve the ancient customs of male privilege and to disguise the violence inherent to such privilege. Not surprisingly, this campaign develops a religious veneer, the chief promulgators of unreasoning custom and convention being religious institutions; petitions for clemency are "exposed in the porches of Churches and chapels" (267).

Samuel Povey, though, witnesses the exposure, both in his own and his cousin's life, of the very secrets that Bursley denies. The self-advertisement he once embraced becomes nightmarish in his present position, where his authority depends on his refusal to acknowledge before his wife and son that his commands originate in personal desire, not unquestionable right. Even before learning of the murder, Samuel hears more about his cousin's domestic life than he would like; he finds the revelation of Mrs. Daniel Povey's drinking and the idea of her adultery to be a "brutal rending of the cloak of decency" (245). The phenomenon of self-advertisement outrages more than the decency of trade. Images of nudity haunt the scene of Samuel's discovery of the body. When Samuel enters the living quarters behind the bakery shop-front of his cousin's home, he feels that:

> Never before had he penetrated so far into his cousin's secrets. On the left, within the doorway, were the stairs, dark; on the right a shut door; and in front an open door giving on to a yard. At the extremity of the yard he discerned a building, vaguely lit, and naked figures

strangely moving in it. . . . [The building turns out to be Daniel's bakehouse.] Never, during the brief remainder of his life, did Samuel eat a mouthful of common bread without recalling that midnight apparition. (246-47)

The vision of naked figures laboring at night to create daily bread suggests all the secret desires that are denied in the daily course of things and yet are their foundation. Further, it implies the instability of the shopkeeper's own domestic kingdom. When Samuel has entered the shut door in his cousin's life and discovered the corpse of Mrs. Daniel Povey, filthy from self-neglect, he is shocked less by the squalor itself than by its association with a woman. That the role of angel in the house might not exhaust the character of woman has apparently never occurred to Samuel, despite his own resentment over Constance's too lively affections for their son. Images of nudity and insecurity recur when he contrasts Daniel's house with his own:

He thought of *his* wife and child, innocently asleep in the cleanly pureness of *his* home. And he felt the roughness of his coat-collar round his neck and the insecurity of his trousers. He passed out of the room, shutting the door. And across the yard he had a momentary glimpse of those nude nocturnal forms, unconsciously attitudinizing in the bakehouse. (249)

Samuel Povey directs his crusade against this vision, attempting to stuff the genie of self-exposure back in the bottle by strict obedience to God—surrender to a greater patriarch than himself.

But the forces that destroy Daniel's household maintain a secret presence in the "cleanly pureness" of Samuel's own home. The emphatic *"his"* recalls Sam's attempt to take refuge in his status as putative head of house when Constance's breast-feeding of Cyril had offended him. No exposure of the secrets of the feminine body, whether slatternly or domestic, can be truly decent for Samuel; it finally seems that Daniel's Mrs. Povey is "vile" less because of her difference from Samuel's Mrs. Povey than because she apotheosizes Samuel's fears concerning his own wife. Indeed, Samuel's defense of his cousin threatens the domestic peace that ostensibly inspires it. When Constance objects to her husband's overwork, she is described much as Daniel's wife had been: "She deliberately gave way to hysteria; she was no longer soft and gentle; she flung bitterness at him like vitriol; she shrieked like a common shrew. . . . She accused him, amid sobs, of putting his cousin before his wife and son" (258).

Bennett establishes numerous other equivalences between the two houses of Povey. The chapter in which Daniel murders his wife, with her treatment of their son Dick as his immediate excuse, follows a chapter in which Samuel has quarreled with his wife over Cyril. The chapters are titled "Crime" and "Another Crime," respectively. That Bennett invented Dick Povey's role in provoking his mother's murder—Jane Horry's children played no part in hers—further suggests a deliberate parallel. Nor are the titular crimes of these chapters—Cyril's theft of a few shillings from the shop's till and Daniel's murder of his wife—so ironically distant, at least to Samuel, as one might surmise. Cyril, who reasonably asserts that his motive was his father's failure to provide him with any discretionary funds whatsoever, has not merely stolen, but stolen money, thus striking at a symbol: "a till was not a cupboard or a larder. A till was a till. Cyril had struck at the very basis of society" (241). It is particularly significant that Cyril steals money to provide himself with smoking apparatus. While punishing Cyril for his "crime," Samuel already casts himself as a surrogate of his cousin: "But deep down in his heart a little voice was telling him, as regards the smoking, that *he* had set the example. Mr. Baines had never smoked. Mr. Critchlow never smoked. Only men like Daniel smoked" (240). For Cyril to enter this fellowship of freely expressed desire is, in Samuel's eyes, for freedom to go too far—he begins to see how self-advertisement threatens his own position. Indeed, he re-envisions the goal of commercial revolution as greater protection, rather than freer circulation, blaming himself for continuing to leave the till unlocked: "The fact was that the functioning of that till was a patriarchal survival, which he ought to have revolutionized" (238). Samuel has it precisely backward; for the patriarchy to survive, the till must be secured, the flow of money controlled like the flow of desires.

In becoming Daniel, then, Samuel Povey simultaneously reaches his own bedrock, for Daniel represents the illicit desires that underlie the calm surface of his life. The end of the chapter in which Samuel and Daniel die, unique in the novel for Bennett's use of the first person, insists that

> I have often laughed at Samuel Povey. But I liked and respected him. He was a very honest man. I have always been glad to think that, at the end of his life, destiny took hold of him and displayed, to the observant, the vein of greatness which runs through every soul without exception. He embraced a cause, lost it, and died of it. (275)

As André Gide wrote of this passage in a letter to Bennett: "L'unique instant de tout le livre où vous, l'auteur, intervenez, est d'un effet prodigieux [The only time in the book when you, the author, intervene, has a prodigious effect]" (Bennett and Gide 106). The effect owes its prodigiousness to surprise; Bennett has been encouraging, if not laughter, a sense of the misguidedness of Samuel's behavior throughout the chapter almost without exception. The narrator's sudden intrusion challenges readers to detect Samuel's strain of greatness, which he establishes by identifying himself with a murderer, by the honesty and profundity of his disturbance among townspeople of shallower loyalties. While Samuel's townsmen may stare at his cousin's house, "hypnotized by this face of bricks and mortar . . . determined to stare at it till the house fell down or otherwise rendered up its secret" (252), only Samuel has been inside, only Samuel has been possessed of the secret behind the stolid façade of Bursley itself. Samuel, that is, and his readers, who have observed secrets unknown even to Samuel himself. While the town of Bursley hardly notices Samuel's death, if readers are "observant," they may distinguish themselves from the townspeople by understanding the significance of his crusade.

The threat of change that terrifies Samuel Povey and paralyzes John Baines is emphasized through the relentlessness of time's passage and leads both men into a defensive, self-isolating mode. Women suffer a different sort of self-isolation, however; John's older daughter endures a confinement that has no basis in temporal change, nor does she have a choice. Briefly empowered by the rituals of courtship, Constance finds the interiors in which romance ultimately installs her becoming more and more restrictive.[3] Excluded from the exterior world of change, she increasingly invests identity in location, who in where, until emergence from the domestic shell, the familial hearth celebrated in the days of high Victorianism, is so disorienting as to be deadly. Bennett argues that the restriction of women's freedom of movement equally represses their desires, leaving them as incapable of self-advertisement as the patriarchs who initiate their confinement. Desire kept secret, of course, finds other channels of expression; Bennett especially turns the ideal of motherhood on its head in his presentation of Constance's Jocasta complex.

The constancy of Constance Baines is rooted in her identification with the values of a Bursley that has less and less relevance to her shrinking domestic space. She belongs so emphatically to the Baines stock that she marries "the surrogate of bedridden Mr Baines [Samuel Povey]" (50), and soon transfers her fondest affections from her husband, a Baines by acclamation, to her son, a Baines by blood: "Without depreciating Samuel in her faithful heart, Constance saw plainly the singular differences between Samuel and the boy. . . . Cyril had now scarcely any obvious resemblance to his father. He was a Baines" (226-27). The phrase "her faithful heart" at once accurately transcribes the language Constance would use of herself and ironically hints that in this matter Constance's heart is the opposite of faithful. Constance's preference for her graceful son has unmistakable sexual origins: "Samuel was inimical to [Cyril's] tastes for sports and his triumphs therein. But Constance had pride in all that. She liked to feel him and to gaze at him, and to smell that faint, uncleanly odour of sweat that hung in his clothes" (235). Later, Constance observes that Cyril "was a far more brilliant, more advanced, more complicated, more seductive being than his homely father" (303).

After Cyril is caught stealing and is duly punished by his father, Bennett offers, in summation, a double entendre: "During the remainder of existence this unspeakable horror would lift its obscene form between them" (242). That Constance's desire is "unspeakable" makes it particularly dangerous to her husband; as Michel Foucault argues in *The History of Sexuality*, the Victorian enterprise is not so much to repress sexuality as to transform it into a discourse, to subject it to the disciplines of language (22).[4] "Obscene form" is at once an ironic overstatement of the theft's outlandish importance in the eyes of Samuel and Constance and an appropriate reading of secrets the characters do not recognize. Through the "obscenity" of her Jocasta complex, Constance maintains herself in the only location allowed her since her exclusion from the shop: the fastness of her family. A woman who symbolically marries her father and substitutes her son for her husband is locked in a fantasy of changelessness. After Samuel dies, Constance "want[s] the impossible: that matters should proceed in the future as in the past, that Samuel's death should change nothing save in her heart" (278). Soon she determines to yield to Cyril in all things, being afraid to lose him— "and there was ecstasy in her yielding," the narrator reports (287), stressing Constance's deep, erotic attachment to Cyril after the death of her husband.

Cyril, however, swiftly becomes Samuel all over again—he adopts cigar smoking, keeps secrets, and generally cultivates a "triumphant masculinity, content with itself, and needing nothing" (471)—with the important exception that he does not love Constance as Samuel had, does not court her good opinion nor fear her bad. Samuel found Constance's attention to his preferences "astoundingly feminine" (197) and attractive; Cyril finds it suffocating. When he wins a scholarship to study in London, "[h]is joy in the prospect of departure from the Five Towns, from her, though he masked it, was more manifest than she could bear" (306-7). The morning of Cyril's departure from the provinces, the sort of moment so often brimming with hope when narrated from the young son's perspective, becomes intensely sad when narrated from the mother's point of view. As her son's departure suggests, Constance's confinement to stasis offers her no emotional security in a world constructed by male activity.

Cyril's conflation of his mother with the Five Towns indicates the degree to which her identity is founded in location. Indeed, Constance and Bursley both suffer an isolation from the dynamism of commercial life that ultimately hardens them in identities that belong irremediably to the past. Bursley, set like John Baines against self-advertisement, loses its business to the more progressive town of Hanbridge. John's daughter loses more. When Mr. Critchlow obtains the mortgage on the lot beneath her feet, she finds herself irreversibly isolated from the draper's shop into which she had been born. Critchlow, offering to buy the draper's business for his wife (formerly Maria Insull) to run, suggests to Constance, "'Suppose I brick ye this up'"(296), thereby sealing Constance in her domicile by erecting walls between shop and house. In finally agreeing, Constance finds that the process of restriction begun by her marriage has confined her to an intolerably narrow space.

But it is a space Constance cannot leave, despite efforts extended on her behalf. When Sophia returns after thirty-one years in France, she arrogates to herself the role of surrogate husband that Cyril has refused.[5] Rather than confining Constance, however, Sophia makes an equally imperious attempt to liberate her, spiriting her away from Bursley on what is ostensibly a vacation but is in fact planned as the first maneuver in a campaign to divide Constance from the cramped ancestral home permanently. Sophia initiates this operation on the advice of Constance's doctor, who affirms that, in consequence of a freer, more active life, the elder sister "'wouldn't be the same woman'" (532)—which is precisely why the decampment cannot succeed. Sophia ultimately suggests that she and Constance settle in a resort hotel rather than return to St. Luke's Square, pointing out to her sister that "'[i]nstead of the house existing for you, you exist for the house'" (553). Constance displays a willful incomprehension, deflecting criticism of her house by retorting, "'It's a great deal better built than a lot of those new houses by the Park'" (553), a reply that reveals how strictly she limits her frame of reference to Bursley itself. While Sophia correctly informs her sister that "'You can't see yourself'" (554), neither can she see her older sister; not only does Constance exist for the house, her existence is the house. To alter her is simply to unmake her; Constance bests her sharper sister by breaking down and sobbing, "'You mustn't kill me. . . . I'm like that—you can't alter me'" (556).

The next nine years at St. Luke's Square bring England into the twentieth century, but not the house of Baines, which, with Constance as its genial spirit, has not altered a bit. "The buried question of domicile" (561) remains a source of silent resentment between the sisters. Sophia is secretly appalled at how "vast and ruthless an egotism" (560) Constance exhibits in her refusal to quit the Square. Ego, however, is precisely what Constance preserves by remaining where she is (and, so, who she is). Without this protection, she would be dominated by her younger sister as she was at Buxton; in the house, by contrast, Constance holds sway, as the narrator reports of Sophia's failure to modernize the premises: "She did bully Constance, but the house defied her" (560). Indeed, Sophia's death, "though . . . the cause of a most genuine and durable sorrow . . . had been a relief to her [Constance]. . . . [I]t had been only by a wearying expenditure of nervous force that Constance had succeeded in holding a small part of her own against the unconscious domination of Sophia" (590-91).

Constance cannot escape her limited perspective sufficiently even to imagine Sophia's inner life, as she pacifies herself after her sister's death with the preposterous thought that she "had never even had a true home till, in all her sterile splendour, she came to Bursley. . . . Hers had not been a life at all" (585). She projects her own need for stasis onto a sister who she knew hated the cramped domicile in which she was forced to spend her last decade. Focusing particularly on the indifference with which Cyril succeeds to the childless Sophia's fortune, Constance is content to reduce her sister's life to a Victorian moral fable: "Headstrong Sophia had deceived her mother, and for the deception had paid with thirty years of melancholy and the entire frustration of her proper destiny" (589). But as Constance herself reported in her first letter reestablishing contact with Sophia, her sister's old mentor in teaching has ended life penniless; it seems unlikely, then, that had Sophia indeed become a teacher her end would have been any happier. Rather, Constance is projecting her own anxieties regarding Cyril's indifference to her (he will in fact miss her funeral) onto her sister, compensating for her own mistreatment as a mother by asserting the inevitable tragic consequences of offending the matriarch. As the narrator reports, "Constance, under the various influences of destiny, had remained essentially what her father had been" (586). In addition to being an icon of Victorian solidity, her father had been an invalid, rooted to one spot, movement from which would cause death. His oldest daughter imitates him in this reduction to a vegetative existence as well.

The geographic basis of Constance's identity is most apparent at the hour of her death. Bennett prepares for this event by recital of the tragedy of Maria Critchlow, which repeats the long arc of Constance's decline in compressed fashion. Maria, who has assumed charge of "Baines'," begins to behave oddly in frustration at the deepening (and, to her, incomprehensible) red ink into which the shop falls as St. Luke's Square steadily loses its business to Hanbridge. For her, too, imminent exile from her place of business is death. The threat of isolation issues in the exposure of long-repressed desires; Maria gravely confesses to imaginary sexual encounters with Samuel Povey, which shock the assistant in whom she confides.[6] By claiming possession of Mr. Povey and the shop, Maria transforms herself into Constance; certainly, the fates of the two women are one. After a suicide attempt, Maria is committed to an asylum and the draper's shop closes, never to open again.

The end of "Baines'" foretells the end of Constance. Although she had never liked Maria, Constance sees her demise as another insult to St. Luke's Square (she is not told of the sexual allegations). When the topic of Bursley's proposed federation with the other Potteries towns intrudes on a conversation regarding Maria, Constance, who hates the idea of so great a change as federation, makes an immediate connection between the two events: "Did they [supporters of federation] know that poor Maria Critchlow was in a lunatic asylum because Hanbridge was so grasping? Ah, poor Maria was already forgotten!" (608). Just as the imminent collapse of her business drives Maria to attempted suicide, so the threat of expulsion from her home when the Midland Clothiers Company swallows all of Critchlow's holdings in St. Luke's Square initiates Constance's final, self-inflicted illness: "The enterprise of finding a new house and moving into it loomed before her gigantic, terrible; the idea of it was alone sufficient to make her ill" (603). Bennett does see the danger of the free expression of desire becoming commercial exploitation of it; the company that displaces Constance extends Samuel's modest revolution in advertisement to monstrous lengths, "[l]oudly and coarsely" (601) hawking overcoats on the front page of the *Signal.* Midland is not the property of any particular citizen of any particular community, but a sprawling conglomeration of branch stores—a foretaste of the increasing anonymity that incorporation was to inflict on the new century. Its identity is not invested in place; indeed, the identity of a particular instance of a franchise store is difficult to define. But Bennett also recognized that the tendency to incorporate both businesses and communities arose from a social and physical mobility never before available to the provinces.

Of course, mobility is precisely what Constance fears. Bursley's hopeless fight against federation is Constance's hopeless fight against the transformation of her familiar world. The anti-federationists continually wrap their cause in the mantle of motherhood, referring to Bursley as "the old Mother of the Five Towns" (604); Constance locates her own identity in motherhood and age. While "the mere blind, deaf, inert forces of reaction, with faulty organization, and quite deprived of the aid of logic" (610) win the first plebiscite, the ultimate defeat of the anti-federationists is clearly indicated in the novel. Attempting to preserve the isolation long imposed on her, Constance provokes her final illness by walking in cold, damp weather to cast her vote against federation, the symbol of the new style of self-advertisement. Constance never rises from her bed again: "Her experiences of the night had given her a dread of the slightest movement; anything was better than movement" (610). The last clause might serve as her epitaph. On her deathbed, Constance is at times suspended over the same inchoate consciousness she possessed when she was an unmolded child: "In all her delirium she was invariably wandering to and fro, lost, in the long underground passage leading from the scullery past the coal-cellar and the cinder-cellar to the backyard. And she was afraid of the vast-obscure of those regions, as she had been in her infancy" (614). To be lost in the backwash of time is to lose the bearings by which one has oriented oneself, and so to lose the self one has built; physical death is a metaphor for the descent into history. Reviewing her life, Constance takes pride in the idea that "she had a position" (613). It would be more accurate to say that she was a position.

By assimilating Constance to a lost Victorian age, Bennett pursues the general strategy of *The Old Wives' Tale:* to claim progress toward personal autonomy as the soul of Edwardianism by continually identifying the modern with the anti-authoritarian and the patriarchal with the past. Constance, isolated from her own desires by patriarchal usages, comes to symbolize the superannuation of the values of patriarchy (as do her father and husband). Rather than merely observing the effects of the passage of time, then, Arnold Bennett simultaneously constructs and dismantles the Victorian era by encyclopedically depicting it as past; he consigns innumerable paternalisms and repressions that he knew well endured into his own time to a Victorian England that he portrays as dim and dead. When Virginia Woolf consigned the Edwardian trinity of Bennett, Wells, and Galsworthy to irrelevance with the observation that human character changed "in or about December, 1910" (320), she ironically resorted to the very tactic that her chief target had employed.

NOTES

1. Recall that the Baines sisters treat Mr. Povey in the opening scenes of the novel merely as an object of curiosity, Sophia drawing his tooth after they

have given him laudanum, rather than as a fully human individual, let alone a superior power.

2. At Christmas, Samuel rushes from the room when the arrival of an unsigned postcard from Sophia produces "a dangerous lump in his own throat," the emotions evoked by the memory of Sophia having "made even him a woman too!" (192).

3. I am indebted both to Angela Jane Weisl's *Conquering the Reign of Femeny* for the suggestion that the brief empowerment of women in courtship leads ultimately to their confinement to (and identification with) a particular bounded space and more generally to Luce Irigaray's work on the identification of women as locations.

4. Bennett's general reading of Victorian repression, of course, does not square with Foucault's idea that the true representative of Victorian sexuality is not the modest Queen but the author of *My Secret Life* (21-23). Indeed, it would be impossible for a disciple of self-advertisement like Bennett to perceive the continuity between Victorian and modern attitudes toward sexuality that Foucault sees.

5. Sophia almost instantly claims the sitting-room chair formerly occupied by Samuel Povey and John Baines; Bennett later reports that the regular guests at the hotel in Buxton to which Sophia carries off her sister observe that Constance's "gestures were timid and nervous; evidently she relied upon her tall companion to shield her in the first trying contacts of hotel life" (545).

6. Despite the narrator's unambiguous affirmation at the time of the suicide attempt that the affair with Samuel is Maria's invention, Bennett offers a tantalizing hint of another possibility, noting when Constance prepares Sophia's room that "it had never been occupied since the era when Maria Insull used occasionally to sleep in the house" (494).

WORKS CITED

Bennett, Arnold. *Books and Persons.* London: Chatto and Windus, 1917.

———. *The Old Wives' Tale.* 1911. Ed. John Wain. Harmondsworth: Penguin, 1983.

Bennett, Arnold, and André Gide. *Correspondance André Gide-Arnold Bennett.* Ed. Linette Brugmans. Geneva: Librairie Droz, 1964.

Forster, E. M. *Aspects of the Novel.* New York: Harcourt, Brace and World, 1927.

Foucault, Michel. *The History of Sexuality. Vol. 1: An Introduction.* Trans. Robert Hurley. New York: Vintage, 1988.

Fromm, Gloria. "Re-mythologizing Arnold Bennett," *Novel* 16 (Fall 1982): 19-34.

Hepburn, James. *The Art of Arnold Bennett.* Bloomington: Indiana UP, 1963.

Marks, Elaine, and Isabelle de Courtivron, eds. *New French Feminisms: An Anthology.* New York: Schocken, 1981.

Tillier, Louis. *Studies in the Sources of Arnold Bennett's Novels.* Paris: Didier, 1967.

Weisl, Angela Jane. *Conquering the Reign of Femeny: Gender and Genre in Chaucer's Romance.* Cambridge, Eng.: D. S. Brewer, 1995.

Woolf, Virginia. "Mr. Bennett and Mrs. Brown." *Collected Essays.* Vol. 1. London: Hogarth, 1966, 319-37.

Joyce, the Edwardian

Jean-Michel Rabaté

I would like to begin enthymemically—by making use of the trope that figures so prominently in the "Aeolus" episode of *Ulysses,* and that imitates the structure of the syllogism but presents a sophism, or a questionable half-truth. According to Virginia Woolf and historical common sense, Joyce should be defined as a "Georgian" writer (major). However, according to Wyndham Lewis and a number of recent critics who find their inspiration in the field of "cultural studies," Joyce is best categorized as a late "Victorian" (minor). Therefore the conclusion is that we must find truth in the middle ground, and can safely call Joyce an "Edwardian." To qualify this pseudo-syllogism, my main contention is that Joyce appears as an Edwardian indeed, but in a very literal sense, in a sense that bridges the gap between his personal biography, his specific Irish origins, and his link with the spirit of the times. Joyce will appear as a literal Edwardian insofar as his major works testify to a personal link with the English king—a link that cannot but remain strangely symptomatic and, of course, less problematic than critical.

If we follow Woolf's famous remarks on the "new" spirit which has been born just at the end of 1910, then Joyce has to be a Georgian: "I will suggest that we range Edwardians and Georgians into two camps; Mr. Wells, Mr. Bennett and Mr. Galsworthy I will call the Edwardians; Mr. Forster, Mr. Lawrence, Mr. Strachey, Mr. Joyce, and Mr. Eliot I will call the Georgians." The ironical cascade of "Mr.'s" corresponds to the fictional framework suggested by the title: a real Edwardian writer—Arnold Bennett, whose main writings were published before 1911—faces a feminine character who embodies the spirit of the age. This age drastically changed in 1910: "In or about December, 1910, human character changed" (320). If we take Woolf's date a little more seriously than she probably wishes her reader to do, it cannot refer to the death of King Edward in May 1910—a fact that has been noted by most commentators. However, it can neither strictly be assumed to allude to the famous Post-Impressionist exhibition that started in November 1910 at the Grafton Galleries. The first of the two exhibitions organized by Roger Fry in London at the Grafton Galleries started on November 8, 1910, and ended on January 15, 1911. It is true that Virginia Woolf visited the first exhibition, "Manet and the Post-Impressionists," in December. December 1910 nevertheless seems to evoke the eight months that elapsed between the replacement of King Edward by King George and the beginning of a new decade—eight months that are indeed quite sufficient for the half-aborted or at least premature birth of the "modern" spirit in early 1911.

Woolf wishes to identify the change in mentality by which we usually define "Modernism" with the Georgian period, while the first decade of this century (1901-1910), so conveniently identified with the reign of Edward VII, would merely have seen the stammering of a new generation, still caught up in the antiquated ideas and ideals of the Victorian age. Joyce, Eliot, and Lawrence stand on one side of the divide, and smile with the wide, aggressive grin of *Les Jeunes,* whereas Wells, Bennett, and Galsworthy still wave at us coyly from behind the fence separating us from the Victorian era. But what of Conrad and Hardy, Yeats and Shaw? Most commentators are prone to underline the artificiality of these distinctions, to the point that one of the best recent studies of the Edwardian age has it end in 1919 (Rose xiii-xiv). And it now seems that Modernism recedes further back into the endings of the Victorian age.

Another version of "High Modernism," however, has often defined it as a male reaction to a Victorian literature that was highly feminized. If one situates Joyce from the point of view of the very vocal proponents of a "male" and "hard" Modernism, then Joyce is less a Georgian—a term that would already sound negative for Pound and Lewis—than a very late Victorian. Pound and Lewis often oppose the "men of 1914" to the "Georgians"— by which they generally mean the difference between parochial British writers and the internationalism, cosmopolitanism, and radicalism of their avant-garde, limited to the "Vorticists" and the group of artists and writers gathered in *Blast.* The attack on Joyce published in the first issue of *The Enemy* in January 1927 contains the most coherent argument in favor of Joyce's belated Victorianism:

The nineteenth-century naturalism of that obsessional, fanatical order is what you find on the one hand in *Ulysses*. On the other, you
have a great variety of recent influences enabling Mr. Joyce to use it
in the way that he did. . . . It is like a gigantic victorian [*sic*] quilt or
antimacassar. Or it is the voluminous curtain that fell, belated (with
the alarming momentum of a ton or two of personally organized
rubbish), upon the victorian [*sic*] scene. So rich was its delivery, its
pent-up outpouring so vehement, that it will remain, eternally ca-
thartic, a monument like a record diarrhoea. No one who looks *at* it
will ever want to look *behind* it. It is the sardonic catafalque of the
victorian [*sic*] world. (Lewis 90)

Such a view had also been voiced in a milder tone by Pound, a tone
that became more and more rabid with the thirties. Pound sees in *Ulysses* a
similar catharsis, a purge (following Joyce's own metaphor in his "Holy
Office" poem) that somehow erases an ancient and corrupted state of civilization. And even when Pound praised *Ulysses* for the readers of *The Dial,*
he took pains to point out that Bloom's mind is made up of the remnants
of a dead culture: "Bloom . . . is the man in the street, the next man, the
public, not our public, but Mr. Wells's public" (403). I shall return to
Wells's ideas, to suggest that this public was not after all so wrong when
asserting its values.

This aspect of *Ulysses* has recently been stressed by such critics as
Cheryl Herr, who in her *Joyce's Anatomy of Culture* shows how much Joyce's
mind is indeed full of the trivia of a culture that can be called Victorian in a
broad sense. This has obviously to do with the surface realism of *Ulysses,*
its naturalism even, its extensive use of newspaper cuttings, advertisements,
local and topical gossip, which in the end recreates so convincingly the
Dublin of 1904. This world had already disappeared when Joyce was busy
reconstructing it from memory but also with the aid of maps and of Thom's
Directory in Trieste, Zurich, and Paris. A retrospective referential illusion
would have us take this world for a given, whereas it is indeed a construct—
which makes it all the more interesting. In this sense, *Ulysses* remains indeed an Edwardian text, since it presents us with one of the most systematic
explorations of the world of 1904 that are available. A comparable time lag
between the moment of the publication of *Ulysses* (1922) and of the historical period evoked (1904) applies in the case of *Finnegans Wake:* published
in 1939, this nightmare of a universal history is nevertheless situated in
Ireland and refers to the Dublin Easter Rising of 1916 as much as to the
Civil War that marked Ireland's independence (1921-23).

Can Joyce thus be called an "Edwardian" just because of the massive
presence of the Edwardian world and mentality in *Ulysses?* If Joyce had

died in 1911, on the other hand, he would probably be classified as a minor Irish poet, critic, and wit, the author of some excellent short stories evincing the influence of naturalism, a disciple of Flaubert, Maupassant, and Ibsen, whose untimely death prevented the completion of what should have been his masterpiece: a complete system of aesthetics based on Aristotelian definitions. As we know, Joyce never completed his treatise, nor found fame as a poet (although he tried with some obstinacy). But if an historical category such as Edwardianism has some sense, it cannot merely serve to oppose an "early Joyce" and a "later Joyce" in terms of publication dates. Following from these, one would posit that *A Portrait of the Artist as a Young Man* is entirely Edwardian, while *Ulysses* would be entirely Georgian. My contention is that on the contrary, if there is a fracture, it appears later, within *Ulysses,* and that the greater part of *Ulysses* can be called Edwardian—and not merely because the time of the action is June 1904.

Let us return to Woolf's sense that "human character" had changed in 1910. If this is true, it is indeed the old "ego" that has died and been replaced with a new "self." Modernism can be defined as the age of egoism—an egoism that unites writers as varied as Dorothy Richardson (who opposes feminine "egoism" to masculine "selfishness" [412]), Pound, and Joyce. Woolf notes shrewdly that one of the worst defects of the male Modernists is their "egotism": "The first-class carriage that takes you to the best hotel in Brighton—that's true of Arnold B[ennett] though not quite true of Wells. Still, there's a worldliness about them both. What's it all for?—as Henry James said. But the worst of Joyce &c. is their egotism—no generosity or comprehensiveness" ("Modern" 642-43). The historical link between this defect—or quality, according to one's sense of personal ethics—and the birth of Modernism lies in the curious coincidence that both *Portrait* and three early chapters of *Ulysses* were published (in 1914 and in 1918) in the magazine called *The Egoist.* The renaming of the "Freewoman" as the "Egoist" revealed a shift in emphasis from an earlier feminism, closer to active Suffragism, to a more cultural critique, which looked back to one of the most interesting Victorian writers, Meredith, as a tutelary figure. Thus, his major novel, *The Egoist,* would have spelled out both the fate of the condemned Victorian man (Sir Willoughby Patterne) and the rise of the new Edwardian woman, Clara Middleton, the feminine Egoist who has finally learned from a male society how to achieve her own sexual, moral, and political independence.

From a simple perusal of any biography, Joyce stands out clearly as the prince—or king—of the "Egoists." But Woolf has technique in mind as much as personal attitude. The only praise she reserves in "Mr. Bennett and Mrs. Brown" for the triumvirate of Wells, Bennett, and Galsworthy is for the way they seem to respect the decorum required by their medium, which is not the case of Joyce: "Mr. Joyce's indecency in *Ulysses* seems to me the conscious and calculated indecency of a desperate man who feels that in order to breathe he must break the windows" (334). Here, artistic "egoism" is combined with the radicalism of a "Modernism" that has no patience with the conventions of an older generation, and that is too confident in the pedagogical quality of the new work. The Modernist seems to say: if you cannot teach yourself how to become the book's or poem's contemporary, then you are not fit to be a contemporary!

This lack of compassion for the "common reader" among the Modernists struck contemporaries (and Woolf) as the main sign of their being "modern": the shock of the new was indeed to provoke a society in its fundamental institutions. This is why Joyce had so many difficulties with censorship. I do not want to tell once more the long and infuriating history of the delayed and thwarted publication of *Dubliners,* whose "scrupulous meanness" implied for Joyce the use of a few "bloody's"—already a great sin for the British censor—and of some political allusions. I shall simply quote Joyce's own account, primarily because it situates the debate where he saw it: between the English king and the Irish writer. When in 1911, exasperated by the hesitations of his publishers, Joyce sent a letter to the king, hoping that George V would admit that the stories of *Dubliners* could not be accused of slandering the previous king, George's secretary simply wrote back to acknowledge this: "The private secretary is commanded to acknowledge the receipt of Mr. James Joyce's letter of the 1 instant and to inform him that it is inconsistent with rule for His Majesty to express his opinion in such cases." Even more outraged, Joyce then addressed the general public, recounting the story in an open letter to the press:

> In December 1909 Messrs Maunsel's manager begged me to alter a passage in one of the stories, *Ivy Day in the Committee Room,* wherein some reference was made to Edward VII. I agreed to do so, much against my will, and altered one or two phrases. Messrs Maunsel continually postponed the date of publication and in the end wrote, asking me to omit the passage or to change it radically. I declined to do either, pointing out that Mr. Grant Richards of London had raised no objection to the passage when Edward VII was alive and that I could not see why any Irish publisher should raise an objection to it when Edward VII had passed into history. (*Selected* 198)

The offensive passage is the discussion in "Ivy Day" in which Mr. Henchy "buries" Parnell and extols the British king for being "'just an ordinary knockabout like you and me.'" Edward VII is described as "'fond of his glass of grog'" and "'a bit of a rake, perhaps,'" but all in all "'a good sportsman'" (*Dubliners* 132). The English king is the "'jolly fine decent fellow'" who reappears in the "Circe" episode dancing and singing: "'On coronation day, on coronation day, / O, won't we have a merry time, / Drinking whisky, beer and wine!'" (*Ulysses* 485). The political satire seems rather mild, and aimed more at the Irish politicians who capitalize on Parnell's name while welcoming British capital. The king's visit to Ireland becomes emblematic of a general betrayal and loss of values, while being connected with Joyce's personal saga. Edward VII visited Ireland between July 21 and August 2, 1903, whereas Joyce's mother died on August 13, 1903. Her cancer had forced her son to come back hurriedly from Paris, and he spent the last weeks of her sickness, during which she was comatose, reading the newspapers with anger and frustration and participating in the meetings of the Irish Republican Socialist party (Costello 214-16).

The king's name remains as the key symbol of an empire that has reduced Ireland to a secondary nation. As Joyce noted in the 1907 article he wrote in Italian for the Triestine *Piccolo della Sera,* Ireland had not only always betrayed leaders like Parnell, but had willingly submitted itself to a double oppression: "Ireland, weighed down by multiple duties, has fulfilled what has hitherto been considered an impossible task—serving both God and Mammon, letting herself be milked by England and yet increasing Peter's pence (perhaps in memory of Pope Adrian IV, who made a gift of the island to the English King Henry II about 800 years ago, in a moment of generosity)" (*Critical* 190-91).

This defines the essential impetus of the politics of the "Artist," both in *A Portrait of the Artist as a Young Man* and in *Ulysses.* Stephen rejects the "old sow that eats her farrow" (*Portrait* 203.) This is why a writer intent upon "forg[ing] . . . the conscience of [his] race" (253) must first fight against the ghosts that paralyze any initiative and prevent a durable liberation. Thus in "Circe," Stephen echoes this idea when, pointing to his head, he says: "'But in here it is I must kill the priest and the king.'" At this point, a passably drunk Private Carr overhears the remark and waxes patriotic: "'What's that you're saying about my king?'" (*Ulysses* 481), which later degenerates into: "'I'll wring the neck of any fucking bastard says a word against my bleeding fucking king'" (488)—a clear escalation in linguistic outrage after the mild oaths of *Dubliners.* And then, the king appears in person:

> *(Edward the Seventh appears in an archway. He wears a white jersey on which an image of the Sacred Heart is stitched with the insignia of Garter and Thistle, Golden Fleece, Elephant of Denmark. . . . He is robed as a grand elect perfect and sublime mason with trowel and apron, marked* made in Germany. *In his*

left hand he holds a plasterer's bucket on which is printed Defense d'uriner. *A roar of welcome greets him.)*
EDWARD THE SEVENTH
(slowly, solemnly but indistinctly) Peace, perfect peace. For identification, bucket in my hand. Cheerio, boys. *(he turns to his subjects)* We have come here to witness a clean straight fight and we heartily wish both men the best of good luck. Mahak makar a bak. *(he shakes hands with Private Carr, Private Compton, Stephen, Bloom and Lynch*
General applause. Edward the Seventh lifts his bucket graciously in acknowledgment.) (482)

Stephen makes it plain that he does not acknowledge this king as his king. He replies to Private Carr's more and more menacing entreaties: "'I understand your point of view though I have no king myself at the moment'" (482). However, Stephen reverses both the ideology of nationalism and the Christian model of self-sacrifice when he explains that he does not want to die for his country, and prefers to let his country die for him. This is repeated in front of Bloom, who expounds his political opinion, flaunting a strange "'patriotism,'" asserting that he is "'as good an Irishman'" as the nationalist Citizen, since he has plans according to which "'all creeds and classes'" would have a "'comfortable tidysized income'" of around "'£ 300 per annum'" (526). The Stephen one meets until late at night in *Ulysses* is still the same; he does not seem to have progressed or learned much since his first flight away from Dublin at the end of *Portrait.* But *Ulysses,* while apparently gently mocking Bloom's utopian hopes, has radically dethroned the young Artist and replaced him with a more responsible "citizen." This is the real outcome of Stephen's decision to kill the priest and the king in his own mind: it amounts to a textual suicide. Such a suicide corresponds to the major shift in the novel that makes it abandon the structure of the *Bildungsroman* or of the *Künstlerroman.* If the second half of *Ulysses* does not merely announce the death of the priest and of the king, but the death of the Artist, it is in the name of the birth of language (not yet of the reader, as Roland Barthes would have it). Thus the entire period from the first "Portrait of the Artist," Joyce's juvenile confession rejected in 1904 by the editors of *Dana* because they found it too opaque, to the strange disappearance of Stephen who fades away in the night of Dublin, leaving Molly and Leopold Bloom facing each other, can be called Edwardian. But the new *Ulysses* that starts rereading itself, thanks to the page proofs first of the *Little Review* and *The Egoist,* then thanks to Darantière's wonderfully large placards, has to be seen in a different light, opening a new space of writing that, for want of a better word, we can identify with "Modernity." The elimination of the

Artist from the general composition of *Ulysses* does not prevent a return of the same theme in *Finnegans Wake;* but it recurs here in a purely parodic mode.

This parodic mode dominates in "Circe": the king has become a clown, a jovial and moronic simpleton, whereas the offensive insults are put in the mouth of his staunchest supporter. Joyce pays off an old debt from Zurich with "Private Carr"—the British official whose fateful intervention makes him such an amusing character in Stoppard's *Travesties*—while opening up the recurrent scene in which a man writes to the king in order to correct some wrongdoing or mistake. This archetypal fantasy returns with alarming frequency in the letters Lucia wrote to her father in the early thirties, but this can be attributed to her paranoid state. However, *Finnegans Wake* uses the incident in itself and gives it a central function. The Earwicker family seems to distinguish itself by an urge to write or carry letters. What kind of letters? One answer among many is given by the childish language of the "Nightlessons" of II, 2:

> All the world's in want and is writing a letters. A letters from a person to a place about a thing. And all the world's on wish to be carrying a letters. A letters to a king about a treasure from a cat. When men want to write a letters. Ten men, ton men, pen men, pun men, wont to rise a ladder. And den men, dun men, fen men, fun men, hen men, hun men wend to raze a leader. Is then any lettersday from many peoples, Daganasanavitch? Empire, your outermost. (278)

The allegorical letter that is being written by A. L. P. in order to defend H. C. E. from numerous false accusations and slanders is sent to a king (whatever the letter says, it always begins with "Dear Majesty"), and this king controls an "Empire." At times, the speaker or speakers identify with the king's concerns, at times they seem more eager to "raze a leader" who will kill the king. The transformation of the incident in various sorts of comedy should not have us conclude, like Lewis and Pound, that the Joyce who was writing his *Work in Progress* between the wars was radically apolitical. If on the one hand, Joyce refuses to take a political position as a writer—which would be, for him, out of character with what is expected of a "clerk"—he knows how deeply subversive any "true" writing can be.

One could compare the attitude of H. G. Wells reviewing *A Portrait of the Artist as a Young Man* in 1917 to Joyce's attitude in response to Hardy a decade later. Wells saw immediately in the novel a classic and he wrote that its claims to literature were "as good as . . . *Gulliver's Travels*" (330). At the same time, he was struck by its political orientation, by the evocation of the "political atmosphere in which Stephen Dedalus grows up." Noting a little naively that the treatment of religion as a repressive force would not apply to a "boy's experience who has been trained under modern conditions," he also stresses the general anti-English feeling that dominates in Joyce's novel: "everyone in this Dublin story, every human being, accepts as a matter of course . . . that the English are to be hated. There is no discrimination in that hatred, there is no gleam of recognition that a considerable number of Englishmen have displayed a very earnest disposition to put matters right with Ireland" (332). This testimony to the political power of Joyce's quasi-autobiography is blind to the fact that Stephen seems to reject any political commitment and asserts his artistic career above the rest. In a way, Wells reads the novel more correctly than readers who conclude with a complete identification of the author with the "hero."

When asked to write a tribute to Thomas Hardy, who had just died, in 1928, Joyce declined to send a contribution to a special issue of the *Revue Nouvelle* in February 1928, citing his incompetence and his ignorance, but praising Hardy's integrity "in a period when the reader seems to content himself with less and less of the poor written word and when, in consequence, the writer tends to concern himself more and more with the great questions which, for all that, are settled very well without his aid" (originally written in French; I have slightly modified the translation of *"qui, du reste, se règlent très bien sans son aide"*). This is the apolitical Joyce who restricts his domain of competence to his language and even more his nation; he leaves Hardy's encomium "to critics of his own country" (*Selected* 329)—and Wells did not fail to write one.

This would be the picture presented by Lewis in *Time and Western Man* when he describes how Joyce turns into a "writing specialist" who is only interested in problems of literary technique. In love with his own "enjoyable virtuosity," he never tries to express any idea, since he is only interested in how to present ideas. To this artistic indifference, Lewis opposes the "creative intelligence" which "today" is "political" (88). However, this attitude is based on a misunderstanding of what appears as the political nature of *Finnegans Wake,* a text that situates both the Irish civil war and its emancipation from the British rule and the end of colonialism in a worldwide context. The problems posed by the birth of the Irish Free State are compared with the return to a Babelian situation, while the archetypal family that Joyce posits in order to organize his linguistic germinations functions as a structural grid upon which he embroiders endlessly. This universe is indeed a post-colonial world in which English is taken as the dominant vehicular language, while a Britain that loses its colonies one after the other is superimposed on the fate of the ancient Irish kings slowly divested of their power by successive waves of invaders. Indeed, in presenting this linguistic philosophy as his own brand of Modernism, Joyce can be inscribed among those who believe in a "time-philosophy" and who affirm the typically Edwardian value of "Life" as opposed to "Art." But Lewis's perspective, with its ambiguous political position (he condemns Futurism and Fascism as applied Bergsonism just a few years before praising Hitler's classical genius) leaves him alone against all the other "Modernists."

In a sense, Joyce's Edwardian stance leaves him poised between two worlds, the old Victorian world that has never completely died away, and the shadowy world of the future which he hopes can be "ear-open" more than "European," to use a recurrent pun of the *Wake*. Joyce believed that his book was prophetic, and thought that the Finno-Russian war of 1940 was a confirmation that the "Finn again Wakes" (*Selected* 403). In 1940 as in 1909, Joyce never doubted the importance of his own work (more than his own importance). Thus when he was jotting down the sentence "The Irish provinces not England and her tradition stand between me and Edward VII" (Scholes and Kain 100) some time in 1909, after one of his two visits to Dublin that year, only one year before the death of the English king, Joyce was aware of his own status in the European world of letters. Agreeing with Pound, Joyce proclaimed his opposition to provincialism, recognizing simultaneously that tradition, provided it be rethought, was still the best ally a Modernist could dispose of.

If, indeed, the preparatory notes to *Exiles* show that Joyce was entertaining dreams of making Dublin a capital just like Ibsen's Christiana, he never believed he would be the king or even an "acknowledged legislator" of his world—a world defined by exile rather than sovereignty. Joyce was satisfied with being a "producer" working with lots of "anticollaborators," an "engineer" who devises the software necessary to make the universal word-machine function hypertextually (Rabaté, *Void* 112). Like Shem, Joyce could boast that "'he would wipe alley english spooker, multaphoniaksically speaking, off the face of the erse'" (*Finnegans* 178)—but in order to invent a new Anglo-Irish language, which speaks in and out of seventy or so different idioms in order to radically abolish the "King's English."

Works Cited

Costello, Peter. *James Joyce: The Years of Growth 1882-1915.* London: Kyle Cathie, 1992.

Herr, Cheryl. *Joyce's Anatomy of Culture.* Urbana: U of Illinois P, 1986.

Joyce, James. *Critical Writings*. Ed. Ellsworth Mason and Richard Ellmann. New York: Viking, 1964.

————. *Dubliners*. 1914. Harmondsworth: Penguin, 1985.

————. *Finnegans Wake*. London: Faber, 1939.

————. *A Portrait of the Artist as a Young Man*. 1916. Ed. Chester Anderson. New York: Penguin, 1978.

————. *Selected Letters*. Ed. Richard Ellmann. London: Faber, 1975.

————. *Ulysses*. 1922. Ed. H. W. Gabler. London: Penguin, 1986.

Lewis, Wyndham. *Time and Western Man*. Ed. Paul Edwards. Santa Rosa, Calif.: Black Sparrow, 1993.

Pound, Ezra. *Literary Essays*. Ed. T. S. Eliot. London: Faber, 1964.

Rabaté, Jean-Michel. *Joyce Upon the Void: The Genesis of Doubt*. London: Macmillan, 1991.

Richardson, Dorothy. "Women and the Future." *The Gender of Modernism*. Ed. Bonnie Kime Scott. Bloomington: Indiana UP, 1990, 411-14.

Rose, Jonathan. *The Edwardian Temperament 1895-1919*. Athens: Ohio UP, 1986.

Scholes, Robert, and Richard M. Kain, eds. *The Workshop of Daedalus*. Evanston: Northwestern UP, 1965.

Wells, H. G. "James Joyce." *The New Republic* (March 10, 1917): 158-60. Reprinted in *A Portrait of the Artist as a Young Man*. Ed. Chester Anderson. 329-33.

Woolf, Virginia. "Mr. Bennett and Mrs. Brown." *Collected Essays*. Vol. 1. London: Hogarth, 1966, 319-37.

————. "Modern Novels (Joyce)." *The Gender of Modernism*. Ed. Bonnie Kime Scott. Bloomington: Indiana UP, 1990, 642-45.

Part Three

Looking Elsewhere:
Other Cultures,
Other Nations

Totem, Taboo, and Blutbrüderschaft in D. H. Lawrence's Women in Love

Carola M. Kaplan

On the surface, D. H. Lawrence's *The Rainbow* and *Women in Love,* although they originated as a single fictional work, "The Sisters," appear to be two distinctly different kinds of novels: the first, a generational narrative, its roots in the nineteenth century; the second, an end-of-the-world vision, its nihilism forged by the nightmare of the Great War. Yet for all the apparent differences between the two books, their author insisted that they form "an organic, artistic whole." While conceding that the two novels are "very different," Lawrence maintained that *Women in Love* is a "sequel" to *The Rainbow* (quoted in Ford, *Double* 164).

However divergent in tone and form, the two works are indeed united by a common purpose: that of diagnosing the ills of a culture and of proposing a new direction for men and women in the modern world. In this shared impulse, the novels are examples of a familiar Victorian and Edwardian fictional genre: the "Condition of England novel" (Lodge 113). Accordingly, *Women in Love* continues the diagnosis of England's ills begun in *The Rainbow.* Further, unlike such literary antecedents as C. F. G. Masterman's

The Condition of England and H. G. Wells's *Tono-Bungay*, Lawrence's text
is not content with mere diagnosis but offers a prescription as well for a new
social order. This utopian vision of the England that might be is inspired by
non-Western, nonindustrial cultures. Lawrence, like other artists of his
generation, looked to "primitive" cultures,[1] in whose difference he saw both
warning and blueprint for the West. His bifurcated conception of the primitive
gave Lawrence a model for cultural regeneration through a new male-centered social order; but it also conjured up for him a nightmare vision of
degeneration and eventual destruction through a female-dominated world
of sensation seeking and unbridled sensuality. Thus Lawrence's primitivism was riddled with contradiction and his valuation of primitive cultures
was undermined by ambivalence. As projection of both his deepest longings
and his greatest fears, the primitive remained deeply troubling to Lawrence
and proved ultimately futile in providing him with the sustained artistic
purpose and redemptive social vision he had sought in it.

The purpose of this paper is to show how Lawrence proposes in *Women
in Love* to furnish a cure for the otherwise terminal condition of England by
way of entry into the primitive, but fails, through his cultural assumptions,
historical placement, and unresolved psychosexual conflicts, to find in primitivism either instruction or corrective for modern ills. I will argue further
that one specific primitivist text—Sigmund Freud's *Totem and Taboo*
(1913)—provides both underlying meaning and narrative direction for the
first half of Lawrence's novel. But Lawrence's vision is ultimately overrid-
den by a powerful primitivist nightmare that triumphs in the last part of the
book and destroys the earlier promise of social regeneration.

Continuing *The Rainbow*'s narrative of the unraveling of English culture over three generations, *Women in Love* begins with a diagnosis of
early twentieth-century malaise as proceeding from the loss of communal life and values. From the first, the text explores the possibility of
forging a new community centered around a shared core of meaning.
First it explores one counterculture community of artists in Bohemian
London. Then, rejecting this world as a false alternative, the novel sets
forth a utopian vision of a new social order, designed to compensate for
the deficiencies of the modern world.

Early in the novel, the two central male characters, Rupert Birkin
and Gerald Crich, discuss their longing for meaning in life but conclude
that life "'just doesn't centre'" (58). Rupert expresses the hope that love
for one woman may provide his life with "'one *really* pure single activity'" (57), but quickly adds the somber qualifier, "'seeing there's no God'"
(58). The elegiac tone of this conversation is illustrative of Fredric

Jameson's observation that "the very idea of value comes into being at the moment of its own disappearance . . . which is to say that . . . the study of value is at one with nihilism, or the experience of its absence" (251). *Women in Love* vividly illustrates Jameson's paradox that "it is only in the most humanized environment, the one most fully and obviously the end product of human labor, production, and transformation, that life becomes meaningless, and that existential despair first appears as such in direct proportion to the elimination of nature and the prospect of a well-nigh limitless control over the external universe" (251). Birkin epitomizes this dilemma when he enters London with only negative anticipations: "'I feel such a despair, so hopeless, as if it were the end of the world'" (53). London, to an even greater extent than the mining town of Beldover, exemplifies an overindustrialized society that, while apparently exerting a "well-nigh limitless control" over nature, makes its inhabitants feel that they are trapped and that their lives are devoid of meaning.

The theme of ennui and disaffection so extensively explored in the early part of the novel comes to a head in two interconnected scenes set in London, one in a café and the other in an artist's flat. The sequential chapters "Crème de Menthe" and "Fetish" paint a diagnostic picture of contemporary social malaise. In particular, they foreground the problems of class, race, and sexuality that Rupert and Gerald must confront. These problems, in turn, have their roots in the last half-century of British history, whose major events, trends, and intellectual currents appear in traces in these scenes. In particular, objects and events in Halliday's flat point to problems of England at home and abroad: class differences; the emergence of the New Woman; the intensification of imperialism and its by-product, racism; fin-de-siècle decadence, and Bloomsbury rebellion. In its symbolic contents, Halliday's flat is crowded, indeed.

At first glance, Halliday's lodgings and the London demi-monde he and his fellow artists inhabit are sites of freedom and unconventionality—classless, creative, sexually liberated. Yet Lawrence satirically demonstrates that these characters are more enslaved by conventions than the bourgeoisie they seek to defy. Appearances to the contrary, this Bohemian world is not an alternative space that repudiates the surrounding culture, but rather a microcosm of British society. The events and imagery of the scene suggest that this is but a particular rung in the general social hell of the modern world. The effect of Birkin and Gerald's sojourn in London Bohemia is to demonstrate the need to establish a radically different social order in contradistinction to a mere veneer of freedom that masks the underlying chaos.

If an alternative social structure is to offer real freedom, it must be based on solidarity, shared vision, loyalty, and friendship. The novel proposes that this alliance start with Birkin and Gerald. But there is an obstacle that the book must resolve in order to make their alliance possible: that of class difference. Existing class divisions would ordinarily make close friendship between Gerald and Birkin highly problematic, if not impossible. The novel—as exemplified in this London scene—works to resolve or deflect this problem with a variety of unconvincing and contradictory responses.

The text shows its anxiety about class in a number of ways: it places characters in a social hierarchy yet omits Birkin from this placement, it seeks to establish a new hierarchy based on innate superiority rather than birth, and finally it displaces class difference onto racial difference.

Clearly, Gerald and Birkin occupy different steps on the social ladder. Gerald, the heir to a mining fortune, belongs to a distinctly higher social stratum than Birkin, the school inspector (despite the fact that Birkin's social position is somewhat obscured by his enjoying additional income from an undesignated source). The class difference between them would be even more pronounced if Birkin, who otherwise shares a great many characteristics with D. H. Lawrence, were also to share Lawrence's working-class background as a miner's son who by dint of cleverness has worked his way up in the world. But the narrative is careful to avoid any social placement for Birkin: he is uniquely without family or social background, unlike all the other characters in the text.

The novel goes even further in removing from Birkin any hint of class placement. He is "not to be defined" (79) and, as Gerald puts it, "'above the world'" (209). Throughout the text, Birkin keeps his distance from the working classes; downplays the importance of breadwinning; and, more than Gerald, disparages the value of mere material comfort. Further, Birkin views manual labor with distaste, associating it with dirt and excrement. (Later, he will make a similar association between excrement and Africans, the manual laborers of empire.) Birkin protests, "'we cover the earth with foulness; life is a blotch of labour, like insects scurrying in filth'" (55).

Throughout, the text is irresolvably ambivalent about class. On the one hand, the text faults Gerald for his class-consciousness. When Gerald shows displeasure at learning that Ursula's father is a handicrafts instructor, Birkin jeers at him, "'Class-barriers are breaking down!'" (94). When Gerald later patronizes Will Brangwen at the Crich family's water-party, the narrator comments: "Gerald was so obvious in his demeanour" (160).

Further, the novel takes pains to demonstrate the superficiality of class distinctions in showing how easy it is to be fooled about class, as Gerald is by the aristocratic-looking Hindu servant: "He made Gerald uncertain, because, being tall and slender and reticent, he looked like a gentleman." When Gerald asserts, "'He looks a swell,'" Halliday counters, "'He's anything but a swell, really'" (73).

Having gone to the trouble of showing that the conventional class hierarchy is based on flimsy criteria, the book works to prove that the important differences between people are intrinsic. According to this revised standard of class, Birkin tells Gerald, "'Gudrun Brangwen . . . is your equal like anything, probably your superior'" (209). As for Birkin himself, he is distinguished throughout the narrative by his innate superiority. In fact, in the scene in Halliday's flat, Birkin shows himself to be Gerald's superior in discernment and cultivation. Gerald acknowledges Birkin's superiority in these crucial respects when he asks him how to interpret the African statue in Halliday's flat. Without any specific knowledge of the culture that produced the work, Birkin is somehow equipped to pronounce, "'It is art,'" and to understand intuitively the "complete truth" (78-79) it expresses.

Finally, the text resolves the problem of class difference by displacing it onto racial difference. Thus Gerald and Birkin band together as exponents of English culture, asserting its social and racial superiority to all other cultures. After all, when Englishmen deal with the racial Other, class differences between them and within British culture become so minimal as virtually to disappear. Unlike the uncertain and equivocal hierarchy of class, the racial hierarchy in the room is reassuringly clear. At the top are the white males; below them, the Hindu servant; at the bottom, the black female as represented in the African statue.

In this scene, all the white men band together to establish this racial hierarchy. Collectively, they disparage the Arab, relying solely on stereotypes in their assessment of him. In this way, the narrator, Halliday, Maxim, Gerald, and Birkin describe him as inscrutable (80), "'very dirty'" (73), static (80), dishonest (74), "half a savage" (73), sporting a borrowed veneer of civilization (a gentleman's cast-off clothing) but lacking underwear (showing that underneath, he is a naked savage). He exists only to serve (conveniently disappearing and reappearing to perform his job) and is abused for his efforts. Yet this treatment is to be seen as his salvation, since Halliday boasts that he picked the Hindu up by the roadside and thus kept him from starving (73).

The ideas, actions, and dialog of this scene reproduce the racist discourse of the late Victorian and Edwardian eras[2] during which the intensification of the imperial enterprise in Arab countries, in the West Pacific, and in Africa was justified by a British-produced colonial view of natives as childish, savage, debauched, in need of moral betterment and of useful work (to be specific, the menial work of empire—serving its builders and maintainers). In reciting Gerald's credentials, Birkin makes clear the connection between social ascendancy at home in England and racial ascendancy abroad: "'He's a soldier, and an explorer, and a Napoleon of industry'" (64). Gerald's attributes—his status as a gentleman, his patriotism as a soldier, his courage as an explorer, and his power as an industrial magnate—all make evident his fitness to rule. The description of Gerald, who "'explored the Amazon . . . and now . . . is ruling over coal-mines'" (64), recalls the nineteenth-century discourse about qualifications for empire building.

Gerald's fitness to rule at home and abroad is further confirmed by his response to Pussum's question, "'Were you ever vewy much afwaid of the savages?'" Gerald declares: "'On the whole they're harmless—they're not born yet, you can't feel really afraid of them. You know you can manage them'" (66). In these words, Gerald asserts his inherent superiority over the people of the Amazon, the site of his explorations. This scene overtly sets forth overlapping assumptions about race, class, and nationality that confirm an Englishman's qualifications to rule at home and abroad.

Birkin shares with Gerald this assumption of cultural and racial superiority, as evidenced in his assessment of the Hindu. "Birkin felt a slight sickness, looking at him, and feeling the slight greyness an ash of corruption, the aristocratic inscrutability of expression a nauseating, bestial stupidity" (80). Birkin associates the gray tone that underlies the Arab's dark skin with death and "corruption." By contrast, in this scene, Birkin is twice described as "white." Thus common cultural and racial assumptions cement the friendship between Gerald and Birkin, taking precedence over the issue of class differences within British culture, and the two men close ranks. Just as Englishmen abroad are above all else Englishmen who must stick together when engaged in the imperial enterprise, class differences between Birkin and Gerald at home in England do not count when compared with the abyss of difference that separates Britons racially, culturally, morally, and—as we shall consider—sexually, from other and lesser cultures.

These same assumptions aid the two men in declaring their ascendancy over women. Their shared sense of racial and cultural superiority assists them in asserting their sexual superiority as well. They enact both their anxiety and their need to achieve mastery over the female in their symbolic encounter with the African statue of a woman in childbirth. In their detailed analysis of the meaning of the fetish, which they find both attractive and repugnant, they temporarily resolve their sexual conflicts and achieve a solidarity that will buttress them, for a time, in dealing with the two assertive

and independent women with whom they are newly forming intimate relationships: Birkin with Ursula, Gerald with Gudrun. Their symbolic triumph
over the female fetish does much to reassure them, at least temporarily, of
their gender superiority and sexual ascendancy.

At first, the two men seem to disagree in their assessment of the meaning and value of the statue. In his role as art critic and cultural interpreter,
Birkin praises the sculpture and attempts to allay Gerald's misgivings that it
may be obscene. But Birkin's praise of the figure is so ambivalent and qualified that it seems as much criticism as admiration. He asserts of the statue,
"'It contains the whole truth of that state, whatever you feel about it'" (79),
thereby suggesting his own underlying negative feelings. Answering Gerald's
objections that it cannot be high art because it does not come from a highly
developed culture, Birkin maintains that there are "'hundreds of centuries
of development, in a straight line, behind that carving . . . it is an awful pitch
of culture, of a definite sort'" (79). His choice of words—"'awful pitch'"—
suggests that this culture has developed in excessive and frightening ways.³
Clearly, Birkin is both attracted and repelled by the instinctual and uninhib-
ited sexual gratification the statue represents. As Hal Foster notes, "In this
way the phantasmatic figure of the savage elicits an oscillation between
esteem and disgust" (73-74).

At best, Birkin's admiration for the statue is double-edged. He praises
it as representing "'culture in the physical consciousness, really ultimate
physical consciousness, mindless, utterly sensual'" (79). Yet in applauding
the woman's sensuality, he points out her lack of intelligence. By contrast,
Birkin displays his exemplary intelligence throughout the scene: he triumphs
through conscious knowledge; through his ability to describe, place, and
judge the statue; to account for her through language. The fetish, voiceless
and inert, is pure sensation as distinct from male cognition. The scene demonstrates that male cognition has the greater power.

Even the statue's sensuality has its disagreeable side. At first, she seems
to embody the sensual knowledge for which Birkin has expressed longing:
"'It is a fulfillment—the great dark knowledge you can't have in your head—
the dark involuntary being. It is death to one's self—but it is the coming into
being of another'" (43). Of course, this association of sensuality with death
lends it an ominous as well as desirable quality. In addition, the fetish, while
"rather wonderful, conveying the suggestion of the extreme of physical sensation, beyond the limits of mental consciousness," is also "strange and
disturbing," and "looked almost like the foetus of a human being" (74).
This description suggests that if she is highly developed in her sensuality,
she is undeveloped in other important human characteristics. Further, since

she comes from an ancient culture, she seems not so much to embody an early stage of human development but rather to be arrested in development. But there is a yet more disturbing quality to her sensuality. The statue is linked with Pussum—and Pussum, with sexual corruption. Both the statue and Pussum are pregnant; the statue resembles a foetus and Pussum a child; the statue looks "tortured" (74) and Pussum's face is "masked with unwilling suffering" (80); the statue is characterized by extreme sensation and Pussum by sensation seeking; and Pussum's face, like the statue's, is "a small, fine mask, sinister too" (80). Gerald makes explicit the resemblance between Pussum and the statue: "It was a terrible face, void, peaked, abstracted almost into meaninglessness by the weight of sensation beneath. He saw Pussum in it. As in a dream, he knew her" (71). To the extent that the statue and Pussum resemble each other, the statue in her sensuality represents not sensual innocence but sexual dissoluteness.

The connection between Pussum and the African female has powerful historical antecedents in the nineteenth-century linking, noted by Sander Gilman, of two seemingly unrelated female icons—the Hottentot female and the prostitute (231). As in Manet's famous painting *Olympia,* the presence of the black female (the servant) points to the sexualized essence of the white female, whose apparent beauty masks her underlying uncleanliness and even disease. The utter Otherness of the black female, who is the antithesis of European sexual mores and beauty (Gilman 231), and the traditional association of blacks with concupiscence—an association going all the way back to the Middle Ages (228)—enable us to spot the Other in our midst—in the debased if apparently beautiful Pussum. This linkage between the prostitute and the Hottentot connects the sexualized female with deviancy and even disease, a yoking that reflects lingering traces of "the nineteenth-century understanding of female sexuality as pathological" (Gilman 235). In fact, *Women in Love* reveals an anxiety that all women are potentially prostitutes, as in the later scene in which two miners joke about purchasing Gudrun, one of them asserting that he would plunk down a week's wages for five minutes with her. Similarities between these two scenes—the scene in which Birkin and Gerald comment on the statue and the scene in which the miners comment on Gudrun—point out the novel's anxiety that an overt and aggressive female sexuality is essentially degenerate.

What makes Pussum and the statue so frightening to the men is the female sexual power they embody and its potential for destruction. As Birkin complains, "Woman was always so horrible and clutching, she had such a lust for possession. . . . She wanted to have, to own, to control, to be dominant. Everything must be referred back to her, to Woman, the Great Mother of everything" (192). Thus Gerald and Birkin fear that Woman, the Magna Mater, may gain control of them. And, in fact, Pussum as Magna Mater does take possession of Halliday, the father of her child: "She had got her Halliday whom she wanted. She wanted him completely in her power. Then she would marry him" (74). Thus, women are threatening not only because they literally have a power, reproductive power, that men do not have; but also because they can use their power as the givers of life to take life back, to recall men to the womb or tomb.

How are men to deal with such a threat? They must do as Birkin and Gerald do: unite to contain it. Thus, in their encounter with the fetish, Birkin's declaration of her aesthetic value is followed by Gerald's warning, "'You like the wrong things, Rupert . . . things against yourself.'" Birkin heeds this warning by minimizing the statue's importance: "'Oh, I know this isn't everything'" (79). Whereupon Birkin turns away from her. Thus the discussion has come full circle. Birkin, having contained through language the power of the statue, joins Gerald in repudiation of her power over them and, by extension, of the power of all women over men. They forge an alliance to contain female force: This homosocial bond levels all differences between them, both of class and of ideology. As Eve Sedgwick describes such an enabling moment: "The spectacle of the ruin of a woman—apparently almost regardless of what counts as 'ruin' or what counts as 'woman'—is just the right lubricant for an adjustment of differentials of power between landlord and tenant, master and servant, tradesman and customer, or even king and subject" (76). In this instance, the adjustment of differentials of power serves to level the class differences between Gerald and Rupert. This scene prepares them to take the next step which the novel will go on to propose: to form a new, small, utopian community, centered on male power and brotherhood, that contains and controls women.

This scene raises the question whether another culture—especially a non-Western culture, as represented by the African artifact—can assume any importance or even serve an instructive function in the lives of men who are entrenched in the power structure of the West and deeply invested in retaining their position within it. Further, the reactions of the two men suggest that the female statue is too tainted by their Western cultural assumptions about power, race, and sexuality to enrich their lives.

Yet after the novel in this scene denies the value of the primitive as centered on female power, it turns its search for redemption to a primitivist society based on male authority. This vision of a male-centered community takes its inspiration from one specific primitivist text—Sigmund Freud's *Totem and Taboo.* In the first half of the novel, Freud's work provides both narrative direction and underlying thematic meaning (but in the second half of the novel, the denied and problematic side of the primitive resurfaces to doom Lawrence's project for social salvation).

Freud's account of the formation of society through patricide, fraternal alliance, and self-imposed sexual restrictions serves as protonarrative for Lawrence's vision of a new social order, expressed in Rupert Birkin's rebellion against modern life, in his proposed alliance with Gerald Crich, and in his hope for a new community and a new form of marriage. To read Lawrence's text in light of Freud's helps to explain some of the more puzzling aspects of the novel: to understand what Lawrence means by the carbon of character (Moore, 2:183), an essential self that exists distinctly but relates communally; to see male-male relationship as central to the formation of social structure (and thus to understand the meaning of *blutbrüderschaft*); and, finally, to conclude that without a community centered on male alliance, marriage is unstable and incomplete (as is Ursula and Birkin's, at the novel's end).

In its account of the birth of civilization, *Totem and Taboo* serves as the protonarrative for the founding of a new social order to supplant the decay Lawrence observes in the modern world. According to Freud's narrative, civilization began when the sons of the primal horde rose up and killed their jealous father, devoured his body, and then felt remorse and belated affection for him. From their posthumous valuation of the father was born a sense of guilt that caused them to honor his memory in the worship of a totem animal who represented him. Henceforth they would refrain from killing this animal and, by forswearing the women of the clan who had belonged to the father, they would abstain from enjoying the fruits of the murder. They would therefore mate exogamously, finding women from outside the clan. From the killing of the patriarch there thus emerged the twin taboos that form the boundaries of civilization, murder and incest; and, with them, the beginning of social organization, morality, and religion.

In symbolic terms that recall Freud's narrative, *Women in Love* provides an outline for Rupert and Gerald to kill the father (as represented by Thomas Crich)—termed in the novel "the Patriarch" (224)—by repudiating his materialism, his hypocritical Christian charity, and his false marriage based on "acceptance of the established world" (353) to forge a self-chosen community. Asserting to Gerald, "'two exceptional people make another world. You and I, we make another, separate world'" (205), Birkin suggests that they form their own community, one reminiscent of Lawrence's proposed Rananim.[4] This community would proceed from their commitment to each other, "'an impersonal union that leaves one free'" (207). Repeatedly, the novel, through Birkin, postulates a new society that begins with a bond between brothers who pledge themselves to each other and who commit themselves to a new form of marriage. While Birkin's apparent parentlessness suggests his emancipation from patriarchal domination, for Gerald there is "no escape—he was bound up with his father" (321). Although inwardly in revolt against the Name-of-the-Father, his unexpressed rebellion having been displaced in childhood onto the brother he killed, Gerald is guilt-ridden, externally compliant, taking over the mines (although subverting the father's principles in doing so), playing host for his ailing father, implacably determined "to see him through" (321). Taking his model from his parents, Gerald sees marriage as "a doom": "He was willing to condemn himself in marriage, to become like a convict condemned to the mines of the underworld . . . like a soul damned but living for ever in damnation"(353). The antidote to this "seal of his condemnation" is the new pattern for marriage that Birkin offers him: "The other way was to accept Rupert's offer of alliance, to enter into the bond of pure trust and love with the other man, and then subsequently with the woman. If he pledged himself with the man he would later be able to pledge himself with the woman: not merely in legal marriage, but in absolute, mystic marriage" (353).

Even more important than the emancipation the proposed alliance offers Gerald is the freedom it offers to Birkin himself. The idea of *blutbrüderschaft* presents Birkin with a solution to his own most pressing personal difficulty: his powerful but to him unacceptable attraction to other men. The prologue that Lawrence later deleted from the published text explicitly discusses Birkin's dilemma:

> Although he was always drawn to women, feeling more at home with a woman than with a man, yet it was for men that he felt the hot, flushing, roused attraction which a man is supposed to feel for the other sex. . . . He kept this secret even from himself. He knew what he felt, but he always kept the knowledge at bay. He never accepted the desire, and received it as part of himself. He always tried to keep it expelled from him. (Prologue 107-8)

Since "Gerald Crich was the one towards whom Birkin felt most strongly that immediate roused attraction" (Prologue 111), the *blutbrüderschaft* Birkin proposes offers him a way to resolve his ambivalent attitudes toward homosexuality by proposing a union with Gerald that is creative and life-enhancing—in fact, the fulcrum for an ideal community—while repudiating a homosexuality that is corrupt and degenerate, like that of Loerke and Leitner.

In Freud's scenario for the formation of a new society lies the meaning of the *blutbrüderschaft* Birkin proposes. The Freudian text seems to endorse, in sublimated form, homoerotic friendship and homosocial bonds. In stipulating the importance of male alliance in the formation of a new social order, *Totem and Taboo* offers support for the centrality of a male-male relationship, enacted not in directly sexual terms, but indirectly through affection, loyalty and shared endeavors. Such an alliance the modern world considers, in Ursula's words, "'a perversity'" (481).

Not only does Freud's text prove useful in positing a male-centered society that sublimates homosexual desire and contains female power: it also recalls a society in which everyday human actions are charged with religious meaning and thus provides a center of meaning for the most intense portions of the novel. Since, as Lawrence sees it, the modern world is stagnant and incapable of movement, the narrative mirrors this stasis. In place of forward progression, the narrative offers charged individual scenes that serve as pockets of value and meaning. These scenes transcend symbolism into moments of numinous revelation through the presentation of totems, animals or objects charged with spiritual import.[5] Examples of such scenes are "Totem," in which the carved figure of a "savage woman in labor" reveals the mindless sensation-seeking of Minette; "Coal-Dust," in which Gerald's cruel subjugation of a mare reveals his sadistic will to mastery; "Mino," in which Birkin's approval of a male cat's cuffing a female reveals his own desire for sexual ascendancy; and "Moony," in which the moon reflected in water reminds Birkin of Ursula's aloof autonomy, which he would like to break, just as he shatters the moon's image by his stone throwing. In these scenes, the totemic animals or objects are extensions of individual characters, serving to reveal their true natures or essential selves. Thus the totems serve to reveal what Lawrence termed the carbon of character, the unrefined, unchanging being that underlies what is commonly called personality. As Lawrence maintains, in the oft-quoted apologia for *The Rainbow* that he sent to Edward Garnett:

> You mustn't look in my novel for the old stable *ego* of the character. There is another *ego,* according to whose action the individual is unrecognizable, and passes through, as it were, allotropic states which it needs a deeper sense than any we've been used to exercise, to discover are states of the same single radically unchanged element. (Like as diamond and coal are the same pure single element of carbon. The ordinary novel would trace the history of the diamond— but I say 'Diamond, what! This is carbon' . . .). (Moore, 1:282)

Not only do the most intense scenes in the novel often focus on a totem, but they are themselves totemic, containing a ritualistic act or series of actions designed to lead the reader, as initiate, to a crucial spiritual recognition

(Freud 164-94). Thus, in "Rabbit," first Gudrun's and then Gerald's brutal subjugation of a wildly resisting pet rabbit reveals the common element or carbon in their characters that prefigures their deadly sadomasochistic sexual relationship. The religiously charged language of the chapter reveals their spiritual affinity: "There was a league between them, abhorrent to them both. They were implicated with each other in abhorrent mysteries" (242). "There was a queer, faint, obscene smile over his face. She looked at him and saw him, and knew that he was initiate as she was initiate" (243). Their "smile of obscene recognition" (243) suggests the forbidden nature of their liaison. To apply the terms of J. G. Frazer's *Totem and Exogamy,* which Lawrence read (along with *The Golden Bough*) while writing the novel (Burwell 162), Gerald and Gudrun are members of the same clan, governed by the same totem animal. Their union is therefore incestuous rather than exogamous. Dark stars bound on a collision course, they form a taboo alliance that is the opposite of the pole star equilibrium that Birkin and Ursula struggle to achieve.

Yet, if primitivism—and, in particular, the primitivist scenario of *Totem and Taboo*—provides both a rationale for the proposed action of the novel and a retrieval of the numinous in scenes of modern life, the primitive remains a problematic source of meaning for Lawrence, fraught with ambivalence.[6] As the novel proceeds, Birkin's underlying doubts about his masculinity and fear of female domination converge to undermine the reassuringly masculinist scenario for a new social order that structured the text's earlier primitivism.

In the second half of the book, the vision of the primitive originally gendered as masculine and characterized as regenerative is supplanted by a negative version of the primitive that is coded as feminine and associated with regression, loss of self, and taboo sexuality. This shift in the construction of the primitive is evident in the introduction of a second female African fetish that is much more ominous and threatening than the first fetish in Halliday's flat, over whose power and allure Birkin and Gerald had triumphed. That this second figure is more menacing and uncontainable than the first is evident in the fact that Birkin recalls her involuntarily and in isolation, and that he is unable to distance himself from her, but rather identifies her as "one of his soul's intimates" (253). Associating her "beetle face" and "protuberant buttocks" with a mindless anality and spiritual death, he projects onto her his own fear and desire: her beetle face, reminiscent of Pussum's fear of beetles, associates her with the sexual degeneracy of the prostitute, which is associated with dirt and excrement, the elements in which dung beetles live. Her protuberant buttocks serve as the stigmata of an excessive and aberrant sexuality, as identified in the Hottentot Venus and in the nineteenth-century penchant for classification, for medicalization, and for scientific information as ways of identifying, distancing, and protecting oneself from corruption by the degenerate Other (Gilman 232-38). Birkin, recalling the African statue, reflects that "[t]housands of years ago, that which was imminent in himself must have taken place in these Africans: the goodness, the holiness, the desire for creation and productive happiness must have lapsed, leaving the single impulse for knowledge in one sort, mindless progressive knowledge through the senses . . . mystic knowledge in disintegration and dissolution" (253).

This figure, onto which Birkin displaces his homosexual longing and his craving for mindless promiscuity, invites transgression but also threatens extinction. As he thinks about her, he feels frightened; and he responds to her in a variety of ways, all of them anxiety-provoking. In his identifying with her as passive sexual vessel—"She knew what he himself did not know" (345)—his masculinity is threatened. As he focuses on her "protuberant buttocks"(245), thus identifying with her implied male lover, he participates in a degenerate anality, "knowledge in dissolution and corruption" (253).

Even in attempting to distance himself from her—"How far, in their inverted culture, had these West Africans gone beyond phallic knowledge? Very, very far" (253)—his assumption of cultural superiority seems to point to an underlying sense of sexual inferiority. As Foster points out, the solitary female figure indicates the evacuation of the place of the African male so that the white subject may stand in for him, with an accompanying anxiety about inferiority to the figure he has displaced (99); much as the son in the Oedipal triangle fears the superior strength and prowess of the father he desires to supplant. In sum, Birkin's irresolvable ambivalence in this primitivist encounter, which he expresses in misogyny and racism, indicates areas of unacceptable Otherness that Birkin cannot acknowledge within himself.

For Birkin, the reappearance in his memory of the second African female fetish is a return of the repressed, precipitated by a sexual crisis in his life. This crisis has resulted from the failure of his efforts to contain the female and to sublimate his homosexual desire: specifically, from Ursula's resistance to his ascendancy over her and from Gerald's refusal of the *blutbrüderschaft* he proposed to him. As Foster points out, there is a crisis of masculinity in the primitivist encounter that is triggered by a crisis in the expression of genital sexuality that makes the subject regress to the pregenital order of the drives, especially to anal sadism and masochism (78).

Since the West, taking its cue from Freud, associates "tribal peoples with pregenital orders of the drives, especially oral and anal stages," it also correlates genital sexuality "with civilization as achievements beyond the primitive" (Foster 72). In light of this Western understanding of the hierarchy of sexuality, Birkin wishes to repudiate the allure of what he considers the regressive or taboo sexuality the statue represents to him. Torn between a desire to break down the cultural oppositions between European inhibition and primitive sensuality and an equally intense desire to strengthen his difference from the Other, Birkin runs away from this irresolvable conflict to his conventional heterosexual relationship with Ursula. In terror of succumbing to the sexual possibilities emblematically present for him in the African statue, Birkin takes refuge in monogamous marriage: "There was the other way, the remaining way. And he must run to follow it. He thought of Ursula. He must ask her to marry him. They must marry at once. . . . There was no moment to spare" (254).

After Birkin's wrestling match with Gerald in "Gladiatorial," he stages a similar retreat by turning away from Gerald, once more back to Ursula, a retreat that recalls Gerald's evasion of Birkin's initial proposal of *blutbrüderschaft* in "Man to Man." In "Marriage or Not," the ambivalence both Gerald and Rupert share about the future of their relationship receives final expression in Gerald's failure to respond to Birkin's offer of a "'perfect relationship between man and man—additional to marriage'" (352). From "Gladiatorial" on, the novel abandons much of its earlier psychological and narrative complexity for a thin and tentative resolution to Birkin's psychosexual dilemma through his exclusive relationship with Ursula, in which anal sex, so the text asserts, merely serves as a means of eradicating sexual inhibition, a variation on, not a substitute for, conventional genital heterosexuality.

Thus Lawrence, through Birkin, manages to distance and to contain the lure of the primitive and its promise of sexual transgression, but only at considerable loss. This loss is enacted literally in the sacrificial death of Gerald, who becomes the repository for the novel's unresolved conflicts and contradictions. More importantly, this loss is evidenced structurally in the novel's gradual diminution of power, as talk and exposition replace dramatic action and numinous revelation. Finally, narrative movement subsides, or peters out—rather than culminates—in the novel's indeterminate, nostalgic conclusion.

Notes

1. For an extended discussion of the problematic nature of the term "primitive," see Torgovnick 3-41. See also Rubin 74.

2. For examples of late-nineteenth-century rhetoric about the intellectual and moral inferiority, as well as sexual licentiousness, of native populations, especially in Africa, see Bolt, Brantlinger, Curtin, Gilman, and Hammond and Jablow.

3. In this scene, Birkin seems to intuit as well another meaning of this "awful pitch" of culture, that is, as awe-inspiring, although he overtly denies this interpretation. As Torgovnick points out, although Birkin insists that the fetish is "purely sensual," in her own culture "her function was probably not at all 'sensual,' was probably closer to the 'spirituality' he finds foreign to her" (162).

4. Rananim was Lawrence's name for the new society that he wanted to create. As he described his "pet scheme":

> I want to gather together about twenty souls and sail away from this world of war and squalor and found a little colony where there shall be no money but a sort of communism as far as necessaries of life go. . . . It is to be a colony built up on the real decency which is in each member of the Community—a community which is established upon the assumption of goodness in the members, instead of the assumption of [. . .] badness. (Moore, 2:259)

5. I am using the term "totem" according to Freud's definition, which, in turn, is based on Frazer's:

> What is a totem? It is as a rule an animal . . . and more rarely a plant or a natural phenomenon (such as rain or water), which stands in a peculiar relation to the whole clan. In the first place the totem is the common ancestor of the clan; at the same time it is their guardian spirit and helper, which sends them oracles and, if dangerous to others, recognizes and spares its own children. Conversely, the clansmen are under a sacred obligation (subject to automatic sanctions) not to kill or destroy their totem and to avoid eating its flesh (or deriving benefit from it in other ways). The totemic character is inherent, not in some individual animal or entity, but in all the individuals of a given class. From time to time festivals are celebrated at which the clansmen represent or imitate the motions and attributes of their totem in ceremonial dances. (Freud 5)

While Lawrence clearly interprets totems and totemic rituals to suit his own artistic purposes, at times he seems to subscribe quite literally to Freud's definition; for example, when Gudrun observes of Gerald, "His totem is the wolf," and of his mother, "His mother is an old, unbroken wolf" (9).

Relevant to the argument of my paper is the fact that Lawrence, in the course of his extensive revisions of *Women in Love,* alternately gave the title "Totem" and "Fetish" to chapter 7. Both titles appear in the variant versions of the book as currently in print.

6. Throughout, the language of *Women in Love* records Lawrence's ambivalence about the primitive: on a positive note, for example, Hermione describes Gudrun's carvings as "'perfectly beautiful—full of *primitive* passion'" (32; emphasis added); negatively, Ursula maintains of Gerald's accidental shooting of his brother, "'This playing at killing has some *primitive desire* for killing in it'" (42; emphasis added).

WORKS CITED

Bolt, Christine. *Victorian Attitudes to Race.* London: Routledge, 1971.

Brantlinger, Patrick. *Rule of Darkness: British Literature and Imperialism, 1830-1914.* Ithaca: Cornell UP, 1988.

Burwell, Rose Marie. "A Checklist of Lawrence's Reading." *A D. H. Lawrence Handbook.* Ed. Keith Sagar. New York: Barnes & Noble, 1982.

Chamberlain, Robert L. "Pussum, Minette, and the Africo-Nordic Symbol in Lawrence's *Women in Love.*" *PMLA* 78 (1963): 407-16.

Curtin, Philip D. *The Image of Africa: British Ideas and Action, 1780-1850.* 2 vols. Madison: U of Wisconsin P, 1964.

DiBattista, Maria. *"Women in Love:* D. H. Lawrence's Judgment Book." *D. H. Lawrence: A Centenary Consideration.* Ed. Peter Balbert and Phillip L. Marcus. Ithaca: Cornell UP, 1985, 67-90.

Ford, George H. "An Introductory Note to D. H. Lawrence's Prologue to *Women in Love.*" *The Texas Quarterly* 6 (1963): 92-97.

———. *Double Measure: A Study of the Novels and Stories of D. H. Lawrence.* New York: Holt, Rinehart, and Winston, 1965.

Foster, Hal. "'Primitive' Scenes." *Critical Inquiry* 20:1 (1993): 69-102.

Frazer, J. G. *Totemism and Exogamy.* 4 vols. London: Macmillan, 1910.

Freud, Sigmund. *Totem and Taboo.* Trans. James Strachey. New York: W. W. Norton, 1989.

Gilman, Sander L. "Black Bodies, White Bodies: Toward an Iconography of Female Sexuality in Late Nineteenth-Century Art, Medicine, and Literature." *"Race," Writing, and Difference.* Ed. Henry Louis Gates, Jr. Chicago: U of Chicago P, 1986, 223-61.

Hammond, Dorothy, and Alta Jablow. *The Africa That Never Was.* New York: Twayne, 1970.

Kessler, Jascha. "D. H. Lawrence's Primitivism." *Texas Studies in Literature and Language* 5:4 (Winter 1964): 467-88.

Lawrence, D. H. "Prologue to *Women in Love." The Texas Quarterly* 6 (1963): 98-111.

————. *Women in Love*. 1920. Middlesex, Eng.: Penguin, 1995.

Lodge, David. "*Tono-Bungay* and the Condition of England." *H. G. Wells: A Collection of Critical Essays*. Englewood Cliffs, N.J.: Prentice-Hall, 1976.

Moore, Harry T., ed. *The Collected Letters of D. H. Lawrence*. 2 vols. New York: Viking, 1962.

Morris, Inez R. "African Sculpture Symbols in *Women in Love*." *College Language Association Journal* 28:3 (March 1985): 263-80.

Rubin, William, ed. *"Primitivism" in 20th Century Art: Affinity of the Tribal and the Modern*. 2 vols. New York: Little, Brown, 1984.

Ruthven, K. K. "The Savage God: Conrad and Lawrence." *Critical Quarterly* 10:1-2 (Spring and Summer 1968): 39-54.

Sedgwick, Eve Kosofsky. *Between Men: English Literature and Male Homosocial Desire*. New York: Columbia UP, 1985.

Stewart, Jack F. "Primitivism in *Women in Love*." *The D. H. Lawrence Review* 13 (1980): 45-62.

Torgovnick, Marianna. *Gone Primitive: Savage Intellects, Modern Lives*. Chicago: U of Chicago P, 1990.

Widmer, Kingsley. "The Primitivistic Aesthetic: D. H. Lawrence." *The Journal of Aesthetics and Art History* 17:3 (March 1959): 344-53.

Zytaruk, George J., and James T. Boulton, eds. *The Letters of D. H. Lawrence*. 7 vols. Cambridge, Eng.: Cambridge UP, 1981.

Discovering Jane Harrison

Marianna Torgovnick

I.

I first discovered Jane Ellen Harrison on the night that the Persian Gulf War began—a fact that is more relevant than may at first appear. I had just picked up at the airport a young candidate for an assistant professorship in my department. When I parked my car and turned off National Public Radio, the United States was still at peace. But at the airport, policemen—normally absent from the scene—were everywhere. There was bustle and tension in the air. Once the candidate and I had arrived at the restaurant where we were to have dinner, we learned why: bombs were being dropped over Baghdad; terrorist reprisals were widely anticipated. It was the moment when no one really knew how short the war would be and how relatively painless for most people in the United States (I exclude, of course, veterans with chemical problems and their families). Support for the war still varied considerably, so that many people in the restaurant objected when the staff turned on television coverage by CNN. Still, whether the TV was on or not, it was not the kind of news easy to ignore.

Conversation during dinner turned quite naturally to other times of war, times the candidate and I had studied, though not lived through: the blitz in World War II, the crises of World War I. She mentioned H. D., who had been badly scarred emotionally during World War I, when H. D.'s beloved brother died at the front and her first child was stillborn. Twenty years later, H. D. wrote parts of *Trilogy* during the bombing of London, having tea with her fellow poet T. S. Eliot and sharing his sense that poetry could be a saving ritual in times of war. As we chatted about H. D., the candidate mentioned a figure she assumed I must know well: Jane Harrison, the classicist who used anthropological approaches to ritual, a strong influence on H. D. and on Virginia Woolf. *Jane Harrison, the classicist who used anthropological approaches to ritual?* I did not know her—had not even heard of her. Oh, but you should, the candidate murmured: Harrison writes about ancient Greece as the "irrational primitive." She was an important source of the idea that poetry and ritual were needed in times of war (listening to CNN, one might note, was in this case, a failed ritual)—so there was an aptness to our discussing her on this particular night. Indeed, given the subject of my own recent work, I realized that I really *should* know about Jane Harrison. That I did not previously know about her was what might be called a generational glitch.

I came through graduate school and into the profession in the mid-1970s, as Virginia Woolf was being reassessed. In chapters of my first and second books, I had written on *To the Lighthouse* and *The Waves,* which were then still in the process of being decoded. By the 1980s, many critics were studying Woolf, and the writer's reputation was booming. I had already been teaching for some six years when I began to notice references to H. D. and was inspired to turn to her poetry.

The candidate with whom I was having dinner was a newly minted Ph.D. of the nineties. Between the time when I finished graduate school and the early nineties, conceptions of Modernism and the number of women deemed worthy of serious attention had changed. At some graduate schools, such as the one this candidate was attending, the focus had clearly spread from figures like Woolf and H. D. to women who had influenced them, like Jane Harrison.

But even then, attention to Harrison—and knowledge of her work— remained quite uneven. In the early 1990s, for example, searches at leading research libraries turned up slim pickings about Jane Harrison. There were a few scattered articles, all in connection with Woolf or H. D. There was a brief mention of the "peerless" Jane Harrison in Camille Paglia's *Sexual Personae.* But there were no books about Harrison, except for a recent biography by Sarah Peacock, published in 1988. There were not even, by and large, separate encyclopedia entries under Harrison's name until the late 1980s, though she was mentioned in certain entries on Greek religion or ritual. In the same way, Harrison's work was for the most part available only in the original editions, published in the 1900s and 1910s, until Princeton University Press reprinted some of them in 1991. Although the 1970s and

1980s had been boom decades for women's studies, a time when many writers previously ignored were reprinted and reevaluated, Jane Harrison had largely been omitted from this process.

Yet in the first decades of the twentieth century, Jane Ellen Harrison was, quite simply, among the most celebrated thinkers of her day. She was the author of major books, including *Mythology* (1890), *Prolegomena to the Study of Greek Religion* (1903), *Themis* (1912), and *Ancient Art and Ritual* (1913). At Cambridge University (where she taught at Newnham College), she debated and collaborated with the likes of Sir James Frazer, Gilbert Murray, and Francis Cornford. Among writers, she influenced H. D. and Woolf, as I have said, and also T. S. Eliot, D. H. Lawrence, and many others. Toward the end of her life (she died in 1928) she was asked to write a short autobiography that was initially serialized in magazines aimed at general audiences, *The Nation* and *The Atheneum,* one sign of how her name, if not exactly a household word, was still widely recognized and known.

How did Harrison move from the worshipful attention that once surrounded her to almost complete neglect by the 1970s? Why is that neglect beginning to end and likely to end completely? This essay represents work in progress. It is my attempt to discover more about the intriguing Jane Ellen Harrison. It may include old news for some who have already discovered Jane Harrison or the few who never forgot her. But it will, I suspect, still be news, as it was for me at the dinner I have described.

II.

Jane Ellen Harrison was born in Yorkshire, in 1850; her mother died a month later. She was reared at first by her doting father and a beloved aunt. When Jane was about five, her aunt married; Harrison's father hired a governess for his children. Perhaps the inevitable happened. Jane's father married the governess and began a second, large family that diverted his attention and drained many of the family's resources.

Biographer Sarah Peacock sees these events as pivotal in Harrison's life.[1] She describes Harrison as a woman convinced that marriage and family life are ultimately incomplete forms of collectivity and hence destructive forces, much less healthy than friendship and intellectual companionship. She sees Harrison as nostalgic for earlier forms of social life, most notably among the Greeks. She also sees Harrison as marked by a lifelong compulsion to re-create her sense of deprivation as a child, neglecting the bonds of love, then feeling wounded when they are broken.

Luckily, the terms of her mother's will protected Harrison in the event of her father's remarriage by giving her direct access to an inheritance.

Harrison used her independence to study first at Cheltenham Ladies College, the first "public" school in England for young ladies, and then at Newnham College, the second college for women at Cambridge University, which opened in 1872. Unlike Girton, the first women's college at Cambridge, Newnham offered women courses of studies similar to those available for men. Harrison was one of its first students. Although she did not earn a "first" (highest honors) in classics, she clearly became a highly distinguished alumna.

Harrison spent some twenty years living in London, studying archaeology, lecturing at the British Museum, and writing important books on Greek vases and other topics. Then, having failed to win an appointment at the University of London, she returned to Cambridge in 1898 to teach as a research fellow and lecturer at Newnham. The return inaugurated the highwater period of Harrison's career when she, along with Gilbert Murray and Francis Cornford, two fellow classicists, studied the past in order to discover a more emotional and vivid reality than modern life. They combined anthropological approaches with the scholarly analysis of texts. Harrison, for example, often used archaeological fragments such as vases and pottery (subjects of books published during the London years) to develop her arguments. She was in many ways the keystone figure in the famous and influential movement called the Cambridge Ritualists.

Yet there was a canker in Harrison's personal life that ultimately helped end her career as a classicist. In 1922, she decided to leave teaching and move away from Cambridge. Partly she was feeling the aftermath of World War I, when the university was mostly shut down and the Ritualists lost ground and steam. Partly she was reacting to the death of close friends outside the Ritualist circle. Partly she was pursuing a new and passionate interest in Russian which could be freely spoken among emigrés living in the French capital. But she was also experiencing the fallout from disappointment in love.

Several times Harrison had formed what look to be affectional or love relationships with men; each time the match failed to come off. Once the prospective fiancé died suddenly; twice, he married someone else. In each case, the extent of Harrison's emotional engagement is unclear; indeed, it often looks as though she chose friendship over intimacy. Still, her sense of rejection and disappointment at the end of each relationship was strong and vivid. The apotheosis of this pattern came in Harrison's relationship to Francis Cornford.

Cornford, some twenty-five years Harrison's junior, was in many ways her intellectual alter ego. They met in the late 1890s, when Harrison was in her late forties. The two were fast friends and intellectual comrades. They talked incessantly about ideas and issues. In a very real sense, they provided mutual intellectual mentoring of a kind unavailable to Harrison in her early years. Like many intense mentoring relationships, theirs had an edge of excitement almost erotic. Oftentimes the woman in such relationships ends up being relatively silenced; perhaps because Harrison was so much older, this was not the case with Cornford.

The pair traveled together many times, especially in Greece. As far as one can tell, the relationship was always entirely platonic. Then, in 1907, Harrison introduced Francis to Frances Darwin, the daughter of a treasured friend. Frances, it seemed, had always resented and rebelled against her mother's friendship with Harrison, whom she perceived to be a rival for her mother's love. Harrison thought that Francis and Frances would like each other. Although she was an avid reader of Greek tragedy, she was devastated when liking turned to love.

Francis and Frances became engaged in October of 1908; they married in 1909. It was a marriage of mixed blessings. The match produced four children and was apparently fairly happy. Yet, in 1917, Frances had a nervous breakdown and there were intermittent breakdowns in later years. For Harrison, the engagement and marriage were the end of the world. She became ill repeatedly, descending into a quasi-invalid state. She acted like a woman scorned. She found it increasingly impossible to live and work in Cambridge, playing the maiden aunt to Cornford and his children. Her bitterness led to her decision to travel and live abroad after 1922. One of her prize students from Newnham, Hope Mirrlees, was her constant companion. For many years, Mirrlees had engaged in a rivalry with Jessie Stewart, another of Harrison's favorite students, for Harrison's attention. She remained the guardian of Harrison's legacy, always (like Stewart) planning, though never writing, a biography of her friend and mentor.

The story of Harrison and her frustrated love for Francis Cornford is among the saddest and messiest I know. It ranks with other stories from Georgian England that are also sad and messy: Dora Carrington and Lytton Strachey, Virginia and Leonard Woolf, T. S. and Vivienne Eliot, D. H. and Frieda Lawrence. Harrison's unhappiness is of a piece with the vexed dynamic of male-female relations at a time of expanding possibilities for both men and women. During this era, lovers more and more felt free to cross boundaries of age, nationality, gender, and social class once sacrosanct in England. Yet the new possibilities were not yet matched (if they ever would be) by full comfort with different kinds of roles and relationships. As a result, the era is littered with human wreckage: Violet Trefusis and Vita

Sackville-West, pulled apart by their distraught husbands; Virginia Woolf, engaged in wistful flirtation with Vita and ill at ease both with Leonard's Jewishness and with his sexuality; Mark Gertler plunged into despair by his futile love for Dora Carrington and Dora Carrington led to suicide by Lytton Strachey's death; the Lawrences, staying together in often destructive, lacerating ways; the Eliots and Fitzgeralds separating under the cover of the wives' "insanity." The list could go on and on. Harrison might well have looked to her own life when describing the dangerous effects of passion on groups and friendships. But she also would not have had to look very far in her circle of acquaintance to discover other instances where passion burned but love hurt.

Yet in summarizing Harrison's life story, many more questions than conclusions come to mind. Is it possible, for example, that so analytic a thinker as Harrison could have remained unaware of the peculiar and self-lacerating patterns in her life? More pragmatically, how could Harrison have loved Francis Cornford so very deeply without making a move of any kind to show it until it was, clearly, too late? Indeed how could she have put the attractive and much younger Frances directly in his path unless (as Peacock speculates) Harrison unconsciously wanted to break off her own intimacy with Francis? What of the companionship of Hope Mirrlees? Was there an erotic dimension in this friendship too, as unacknowledged, and perhaps unrecognized, as that in the friendship with Cornford? Might she have found comfort in the love of women to match the unease she felt in love with men? Did she perhaps actually find it?

In the 1990s we feel entitled to ask and answer questions like these. But people like Harrison saw the matter quite differently. Whatever Harrison knew or recorded of her emotional life, she took care to destroy the records. In 1922, before leaving Cambridge, she burned most of her personal papers. The archives that remain are entirely partial and often quite impersonal. There are things about Jane Harrison that will never be discovered.

III.

But there is still, I would claim, much to be gained by discovering Jane Harrison. I say that with regard to both her life and to her work. But here a certain clarification is needed. Harrison's only biographer to date, Sarah Peacock, sees the connections between Harrison's life and work as strong and fairly transparent. By beginning with Harrison's biography, I may similarly seem to be suggesting that the work is less important than, or just a function of, the life. But that is not at all my intention. All intellectual work grows from life history and personal temperament, visiting and revisiting a writer's preoccupations and obsessions. Harrison is no exception. Yet there are dangers in reading Harrison's work as fully determined by her personal history. With the exception of a few essays, Harrison's work was focused very tightly on ancient Greece, with only occasional glances at modern life. Yet Peacock's biography of Harrison tends to treat her views of Greece as veiled attacks on contemporary England and on institutions like the bourgeois family. What is more, it tends to reduce the validity of Harrison's research and writing by making her ideas the function of personal neuroses.

So I would like, at least provisionally, to treat the work and life separately, making a case for them as two separate but quite fascinating concerns. I see several advantages to this approach with regard to Harrison. First it will avoid the tendency to see the work as solely determined by the life, and so mostly out of the writer's control. (This tendency is far too frequent within biographies and pervades even literary criticism of female writers. Think, for example, of how often critics assume that Charlotte Brontë identifies herself with Jane Eyre; think also of how Woolf's fiction and Plath's poetry tend to be read as premonitions of suicide.) Second, and very important, it will allow us to see that the work grew quite organically over time, with no rupture visible before and after Cornford. Instead, Harrison's work developed from text to text, with the pattern of her ideas resembling expanding ripples in a pond. Often, a discovery that is mentioned toward the end of one work becomes the motivation and center of the next: Harrison's fertile mind retrieved "stones" from one work and tossed them into the next, with ever-expanding ripples and consequences. I want to summarize Harrison's major work, with an eye to major ideas that retain a special resonance for people today.

In 1890, Harrison published *Mythology,* still among the most accessible of her works. In this book she presents a history of how the goddesses came to be part of the Greek pantheon and initiates an interest in women that became, in various ways, a central element in her theories. Harrison's claim in *Mythology* is that the goddesses divide up among them powers once located, among the indigenous peoples of Greece, in a single Great Mother Goddess. The figures we know—Athena, Aphrodite, Hera, and so on—are associated with a limited set of attributes: Aphrodite, for example, is the goddess of love; Artemis the virgin goddess of the hunt. None is in herself a unified whole. Harrison coined the memorable phrase "departmental goddesses" to describe the fragmented figures who survive in the pantheon.

In *Mythology* and her later work *Prolegomena* (1903), Harrison set out to prove a view that, even after it was accepted by experts, would lie dormant in most sectors of Western culture until the 1980s. She believed that Greek religion, as recorded in *The Odyssey* and later texts, extended back into the shadows of prehistory and included more "primitive" forms of religion. These Ur-religions were based on ritual, not written myth or theology. In prehistory, Harrison claimed, matriliny prevailed and life assumed a certain plenitude as a result. Recent interpretations of archaeological evidence back Harrison up, though they remain disputed.

But here it becomes necessary to make a specific point about definitions. Harrison cautioned her reader against confusing *matriliny* (descent of names and social status, such as priesthood, through the female line) with *matriarchy* (complete female dominance or rule). She did not conclude that Goddess worship was accompanied by full political matriarchy, even though she was inspired by the nineteenth-century German theologian Johann Bachofen, who had famously posited the existence of prehistoric matriarchies. Critics now disagree on whether Harrison herself always maintained the distinction between matriliny and matriarchy. But there is no question that she understood it and urged it on her readers.

In *Mythology,* Harrison also broached what would become her subject after 1900: Dionysus and allied figures. In one fascinating section, she described the multiple myths that surround Dionysus. Originally, Dionysus was the son or consort of the Great Mother and firmly associated with Her power. By Euripides' day, Dionysus was usually imagined as the son of Zeus and his energies were contained within Bacchic cults fully countenanced by Greek religion. But Euripides' *The Bacchae* takes place, quite deliberately, before the final containment of Bacchic impulses had taken place. Harrison saw Dionysus as a liminal figure presiding over the transition from Goddess worship to patriarchy and the male-dominated pantheon.

In 1903, Harrison published her first indisputably major work, *Prolegomena to the Study of Greek Religion.* Using largely anthropological evidence, such as pottery shards, *Prolegomena* advanced a new theory about Greek culture and mystical or irrational experience. Dionysus, who worked through women, said Harrison, represented a "return to nature" and the valid need for ecstasy in the Greek imagination. Although it built on Nietzsche, Harrison's overall view—and the detailed proofs it presented—were nonetheless transformative.

Since the Renaissance, and with renewed intensity in the Romantic period, the Greeks had been imagined as the children of reason and light and had been studied mostly through written texts. Harrison believed that this literary bias had truncated Greek culture by ignoring the long centuries before Homer, which left a record too—but an unwritten one, in archaeological artifacts. The first half of *Prolegomena* discusses evidence of ritual in ancient Greece based on the unwritten evidence. Its purpose was to emphasize "the primacy of act over word, of rite over myth" in understanding the Greeks (Ackerman xviii).[2] In effect, *Prolegomena* collaborated with other texts to overturn images of the Greeks dominant since the Romantic period.

In Harrison's work, the Greeks participate fully in irrational acts, and often dangerous rituals, which contrasted with other aspects of their culture. Harrison does not ultimately endorse as a "higher form" what Nietzsche called the Apollonian over the Dionysian. Instead, her book balances traditional respect for Greek rationality with a questioning and critique of its limitations. In fact, *Prolegomena* validates the Dionysian return to the emotions, and celebrates the emergence of chthonic, mystical cults in Greece. "The Greeks of the sixth century B.C.," Harrison wrote, "may well have been a little weary of their anthropomorphic Olympians, tired of their own magnificent reflection in the mirror of mythology, whether this image was distorted or halo-crowned." The figure of Dionysus offered "a 'return to nature'" (444). Although she felt reservations about animal sacrifice and other violent acts associated with Dionysus, Harrison valued positively women's association both with Dionysus and with nature.

Prolegomena introduced Harrison's interest in mystic Orphism. This would become the stone producing ripples in her next major work, *Themis*. For Harrison, the figure of Orpheus opened a way to resolve her ambivalence about both the effete elegance of the pantheon and the violent vigor of Dionysus. Harrison believed that Orpheus and Dionysus represent, in many ways, a "spiritual antagonism" (455): Orpheus is human, musical (harmonious), and gentle, while Dionysus is divine, mad, and wine-crazed. Yet Orphic asceticism had, for Harrison, a crucial similarity to Dionysian excess: it too sought to break through the hollow forms of life to essence and intensity. "The religion of Orpheus," Harrison said, "is the worship of the real mysteries of life, of potencies, rather than personal gods." In other words, it is "the worship of life itself in its supreme mysteries of ecstasy and love" (657). I find these views extremely suggestive not only when applied to the Greeks, but also with regard to later Western traditions. They help explain, for example, the role of martyrdom and mortification of the flesh within Christian and Jewish traditions of religious mysticism. These are "excessive" modes that shadow and accompany more tranquil spiritual methods of transcendence, such as meditation (Torgovnick, *Quest).*

Themis (1912) revisited the question of the origins of religion using anthropological approaches—but it was more radical than *Prolegomena.* By pursuing the implications of Dionysian and Orphic rites, the book sought not just the origins of Greek religion but the origin of the religious sense in general. Harrison set out to prove Emile Durkheim's principle that (in Harrison's words), "religious representation arises from *collective* action and emotion" (*Themis* xi; emphasis added). Ultimately, the book conceived of "collectivity" quite broadly. In fact, *Themis* displays "an almost mystical appreciation of the interdependence of things" (Peacock 195).

In one of the loveliest passages in *Themis,* Harrison regrets the passing of totemism and the human imagination of deities in plant or animal form. Such imaginings, she says, may have been "superstitions," but they were "full of beautiful courtesies" (449-50). The lost sense of unity between human, animal, and plant life was usually seen by intellectuals of Harrison's time as an evolutionary gain, part of the progress from group to individual, primitive to civilized. Indeed, comparisons between human prehistory and indigenous cultures in Africa and elsewhere were common. Harrison did not exactly deny the evolutionist view: she thought like an evolutionist, though she did not applaud all evolutions. But she also saw the rupture between humans and other forms of being as producing "a sense of chill and loneliness" (450).

The linchpin of Harrison's theory in *Themis* is the figure of Themis herself. In Harrison's words, Themis "is herd instinct, custom, conventions slowly crystallized into Law and abstract right." She is similar to social conscience, but, Harrison says, with a "warmth and emotional lift" characteristic of religion more than "the chill levels of ethics." In fact, she is "the stuff of which religious representation is made" although, by her very nature, she could not become a personified deity (485). In effect, Themis is collective religious feeling, before it becomes hardened and localized in the figure of a God.

Harrison compared religious feeling, as symbolized by Themis and similar figures, such as Dike, to Buddhism and the Chinese Tao. She points out that "Buddhism knows no God" (488). Harrison sums up her conclusions in a short monograph called *Epilogemena to the Study of Greek Religion* this way: "the idea of god is a byproduct arising out of rites and sanctities"; theology is "the science of the images of human desire, impulse, aspiration" (6, 34). In addition, although "[t]he Praying Wheels of the Lamas and of Buddhism generally have long been the butt of missionaries and ignorant Anglo-Indians," Harrison writes, "they enshrine a beautiful and deeply religious thought" (*Themis* 526). That thought is the unity of good fortune and bad, Olympus and Hades, Life and Death, Human and Nature, Earth and Cosmos in a magical glow that is recognized and not denied by what Harrison called "the social conscience."

Although published in 1913, at the end of Harrison's most creative period, *Ancient Art and Ritual* (the last book I shall discuss) remains in many ways the best overall introduction to Ritualist theory. In it, Harrison contrasts ritual and art, using theater as her primary example of artistic activity. She celebrates the immediacy of ritual, which she defines as action able to involve all its participants in a greater whole. Ritual is the Ur collective experience, a threshold to ecstasy. Harrison admires, but clearly feels a certain distance from, theater and other artistic expressions. For Harrison, the great dramatic achievements of Greek culture reflect the emergence of an individualized consciousness. But they simultaneously mark a loss of energy and intensity and a certain kind of collective feeling for the whole.

Harrison's work is indisputably important. Indeed I now think it is in indispensable dialog with the most important debates of her time. Harrison's work refined, for example, the ideas of Bachofen; it extended, but also challenged and revised, Nietzchean paradigms. It dialogued in interesting ways with Engels's critique of the family under capitalism. It advanced topics associated also with Emile Durkheim, most especially his preoccupation with ritual and the religious sense. It took up issues of prehistory that also arrested Freud from the teens through the twenties. Most of all, Harrison's work addressed issues involving gender and power— and it did so in a female voice. Nietzsche, Engels, Durkheim, and Freud have all become indispensable names in cultural history. During the teens and twenties, Harrison's name floated alongside theirs as a name to be reckoned with. Yet today, as I have said, it is necessary to rediscover Jane Harrison. To do so leads to a greater understanding not just of the early modern age, but also of our own.

IV.

Harrison's work—for, in this final section, I will begin there—opens windows onto meanings attributed to ritual in the first part of the twentieth century. More important, it reveals some of the *need,* even *hunger* for ritual that arose then and, I would argue, has never since been fully satisfied.

In Harrison's theories, ritual marks the difference between participation and representation. To perform ritual is to be placed fully within an action, participating with a group. In a sense, it is to be beyond the divide between mind and body, action and analysis, deeds and words. It is "authentic" experience, direct and unmediated—in contrast to dramatic performance, in which actors are aware of mimesis and of feigning, and in which the audience occupies a mediated role at one remove from the action.

Harrison's extremely resonant idea of ritual appealed to many in the opening decades of the twentieth century, and it still does, though her name has been largely forgotten. Versions of this idea of ritual can be found in writers and thinkers probably unknown to Harrison—as she was likely to have been to them—such as the Hasidic scholar and philosopher Martin Buber who wrote in Eastern Europe.[3] Others who read Harrison, such as D. H. Lawrence, praised her ideas about art and ritual in his letters but dismissed her in gender-biased terms as "school marmy."[4] He paraphrased Harrison's definitions of ritual quite closely. Indeed, in Lawrence's essays on Mexican and American Southwest Indians ("Indians and Entertainment" and others) the description of Indian ritual as having only participants, no spectators, is so close as to verge on plagiarism, since Harrison's name remains unmentioned.

The appeal of Harrison's ideas on ritual can be traced, often quite directly, to the anxieties created by modernity and the perceived loss of organic communities. These anxieties were intensified by World War I. Civilization appeared then, to many, to have irretrievably broken down. The Germans, once seen as occupying the apogee of cultural life, had become the barbaric "Huns." In a very real way, such images pointed to an unsettling of what was then the European world order. Germans, British, and other colonial powers were to be on top: white lords, ruling the world and nursing along "savages" in the long voyage toward civilization. But now savagery had erupted at home in Europe. Comparisons between the state of the Continent and earlier or "primitive" life were frequently made—for example, by Sigmund Freud.[5] Harrison herself freely made such comparisons, especially in very late works like *Epilogomena to the Study of Greek Religion* (published in 1921) and *Alpha and Omega* (a book of collected essays). Ways of understanding the eruption of the irrational—and ways to contain and channel it—were much on people's minds.

Harrison's work on ritual—most of it published between 1903 and 1913—both anticipated and, later, clarified many activities and emotions that surrounded World War I. Indeed, Harrison's work helps explain, to give just one more example, T. S. Eliot's assertion, in *The Waste Land,* of the efficacy of poetry to stand against ruin; it also explains in part Eliot's use of "exotic" religions in effecting the climax of that poem. Eliot is almost certain to have read Harrison's work, given his interest in ritual and membership in Bloomsbury. Yet he makes no mention of her work in, for example, the notes to *The Waste Land.* Evidence suggests that Eliot knew Harrison's work but never felt the need to acknowledge it, although primitive ritual remained one of his strong preoccupations.[6]

The appeal of Harrison's ideas on ritual also, I believe, helps explain the renewed interest in her work today. Many aspects of Western culture—from the New Age to pervasive self-help groups to phenomena like the Promise Keepers and Million Man March—can be illuminated, though of course not subsumed, by Harrison's theories. Now, as in the past, the desire for community, spirituality, and the wholeness of the group leads to ritual. Sometimes contemporary people try to reenact rituals from other cultures (Indian or African drumming or dance, for example); sometimes, people today strive to invent new rituals of their own. Much as in the second and third decades of this century, we today feel the need of ritual and want to access once again its power. That is why—as I said at the beginning of this essay—there is a certain aptness in the fact that I learned about Harrison on the brink of war, at a time of perceived cultural crisis that tried out new forms of "ritual," like watching CNN.

Harrison's work holds still other revelations, and these about her primary topic, ancient Greece. Since at least 1945, for example, Western culture has by and large returned to Romantic images of Greece—images that Harrison mistakenly believed had been dispelled forever. In fact, Harrison declined to reprint *Prolegomena* in 1907 in a second edition. She was convinced that knowledge had moved on with regard to ancient Greece and that the case for prehistory and the persistence of the irrational been irrefutably made. Yet it once again became an axiom of thought that Greece is the first stop in the great train of Western civilization. Greece is the cradle of literature, of art, of culture, of rationality—or so we have been taught to think, reflexively. Of course this idea was already being refurbished in Harrison's day; T. S. Eliot, in essays like "Tradition and the Individual Talent," would become one of its vivid spokesman; in *Being and Time,* Heidegger asserts that Greek and German are the only possible languages for philosophy. But Harrison's work is proof that, in the opening decades of the twentieth century, Greece represented many other things as well.

In *Mythology,* for example, Greece is a cauldron of cultural conflicts. It is, above all, a meeting ground between indigenous groups and colonizing cultures from the North. It is a model, almost, of how invasions occur and of how "native" and invasive groups can and often must merge over time. In this case, it was necessary for patriarchal invaders to live alongside and with indigenous matrilineal beliefs. According to Harrison, the accommodation took place, over many centuries, by intermarriage and the symbolic merger of female and patriarchal gods in the Greek pantheon.

In *Prolegomena* and *Themis,* Harrison continued to explore how, in part as a legacy of this cultural conflict, images of gender continued to have real and perceptible consequences within religions. "Female" ecstasy needed to channel itself through masculine figures such as Dionysus and Orpheus. But, according to Harrison, the pressure of old matrilineal beliefs continued to be exerted within mystical religions and women remained a sign of ecstatic spiritual traditions.

What is more, and very important, for Harrison Greece was *not* the cradle of Western civilization in any narrow or exclusive way. In Harrison's work, especially in the later work, Greece is shown to be a site of irrationality as well as of rational conduct: the traditional view stressed the rational only. In addition, Harrison's work did not insist on the singular status of Greece. She believed that the processes that took place in Greece took place in other cultures as well; her late work deals with the origins of religion, not just of Greek religion. In fact, in the teens and twenties, other sites were also commonly thought of as the origins of "Western" culture, along with Greece. Egypt, for example, counted, too—as it did for Lawrence and H. D., among many others. In fact, the ideas so splendidly documented by Martin Bernal in *Black Athena* concerning the role of Egypt in the rise of Western civilization would have been less startling in the 1920s than they were in the 1980s, when Bernal's work appeared.

Harrison's work, then, is highly relevant to the nineties. One additional point of relevance should be mentioned as well: the history she outlines of Mother worship, displaced by the patriarchal pantheon. Since the mid-1970s, there has been a growing revival of interest in the Goddess (or Great Mother) and speculation about what prehistory was like. Harrison provides a full and coherent historical account of how the Goddess was supplanted in ancient Greece, one that offers full sympathy for the Mother and for her survival in Orphic cults. Indeed, Harrison's idea of "departmental goddesses" has been used in best-selling recent books like Jean Shinoda-Boden's *Goddesses in Everywoman* and Marilyn Woolger's *The Goddess Within.* It is a commonplace of Jungian therapies that many archetypes of femininity exist in the culture and in the collective unconscious: one task necessary to achieve psychological wholeness is the balancing of the archetypes and retrieving any that have been unduly neglected in the development of individual personalities. I do not know what Harrison would have made of the current assumption that "everywoman" can and should have the plenitude of the Great Goddess: I suspect she might have dismissed the idea as a utopian dream even as she felt strongly attracted to it. But one thing is clear: Harrison's ideas are in step with our times, as they were distinctly not in step with the antifeminist assumptions of the decades from about 1940 through the feminist revival of the late 1960s.

Still, in the end, I want to say more about the relevance of Harrison's life and career—and not just her published work and ideas—to those of us alive and doing intellectual work today. Here is Harrison, a vibrant thinker, a woman who confidently worked and debated with the most famous male thinkers of her day. What does it say that their names have been remembered and hers was so long forgotten? One thing it says, I believe, is that the networks of citation—and hence of influence and fame—are often biased by gender. Catherine Lutz has concretely shown such bias within her field, anthropology: men are much more likely to discuss male scholars in their own texts, and to cite them in footnotes, than they are to discuss or cite women scholars. In fact, citations of men by men dominate at every level. Anecdotal evidence suggests similar patterns in many fields, continuing even today, when so much scholarship is by women. As one of the first published female intellectuals, Harrison was, without doubt, an early casualty of this trend. She was one of only a smattering of female professors at Cambridge, all of them housed, as a matter of course, within the women's colleges. But I do not mean to cast her as a weak and vapid "victim," someone who could not hold her own against the forces arrayed against her. That would be very far from the truth of her life and the impact of her career. Instead, I am referring to the after-history of that career, eclipsed and effaced for many decades. In a very real sense, Harrison's renewed fame depended on the "discovery" of women writers like Woolf and H. D. who used her work and admitted its influence. That is one reason why any revival of Jane Harrison's work was likely to depend on the prior revival of theirs.

Then there are more delicate matters, such as love, marriage, and work. Harrison clearly perceived these states as potentially antagonistic and acted consistently, if not necessarily wisely, to fend off men in order to protect her identity. At the same time, she apparently *needed* men for her work, collaborating with them frequently while she collaborated with women only rarely. Indeed, Sarah Peacock notes that Harrison seems to have valued women as friends and students; but she also seems to have respected more the judgments of men about her work. It would be pretty to think that all tensions between love, marriage, and work have vanished in the 1990s, when family and career certainly go more freely together than they did in the early 1900s. It would be lovely to say that gender issues have become irrelevant at the workplace and in the academy. But anyone who is utterly sanguine about the peaceful coexistence of love, marriage, and work is probably both very lucky and not in contact with the reality of very many people's lives.

In a similar way—and this really is a delicate matter—Harrison's life suggests certain paradigms about who may love whom in our culture. It is very hard to imagine many powerful men—not to mention male teachers and scholars—who would fall deeply in love with much younger colleagues but hold back declarations of love, as Harrison did with Francis Cornford. In fact, college communities are filled with marriages between male teachers and former students who became (or, in some cases, might have become) colleagues: the situation scarcely causes comment. But the marriage of a female teacher and a former student happens rarely and, when it does, it continues to cause a certain frisson. Unlike a man, Harrison was unlikely to succeed when wooing a younger colleague. She may have been wise, at least initially, in deciding not to try. But her ambivalence was surely a matter of gender coding and acceptable gender patterns. It reflects a certain impoverishment of imagination in our culture. In fact, it is perhaps not too strong to say that had Harrison been male and Cornford female, she would have become not a devastated person, but a reinvigorated one: one of the legion of gray-haired new daddies who populate almost any college town.

Harrison's vexed relationship with her own college town, Cambridge, has a similar gender coding. Harrison came to Cambridge to teach rather late, after a twenty-year career in London. Cambridge is a beautiful place to visit. But it is a hard place, I would imagine, to live for anyone who feels at all like an outsider. Many of the thirty-odd colleges at Cambridge back up to the river, with splendid Gothic buildings, magnificent grounds and gardens, punts gliding serenely along as tourists gape and ogle. When I visited there, I walked and walked, gaped and ogled, and then settled down to business, searching out Newnham College. Had I sought Girton, I would have had to go several miles: the first woman's college was, quite deliberately, isolated from central Cambridge. Newnham is just across the river, but it is distinctly on the "other side of the tracks." Its buildings are in a red brick, heavily chimneyed style that says "nineteenth century," not Gothic; industrial nouveau riche, not aristocratic. Its gardens and grounds are handsome, but not breathtakingly so, like King's College's, or Trinity's, St. John's, or even relatively Spartan Clare's. Anyone teaching at Newnham, however famous, would have taken a back seat socially to men teaching at the most prestigious colleges. Anyone who became the subject of gossip, as Harrison surely did with regard to Francis Cornford, would have had to tolerate being picked over in conversation. That is simply the way things were. That is likely to be the way things are.

Yet the discomforts Harrison felt as a female academic cannot be dismissed as a British pattern or even as a pattern from the past. When we look into women's careers in the academy (and we rather rarely do) there is often something askew or something odd. Perhaps the noted woman is overshadowed by a husband, like Q. D. Leavis; perhaps she is frustrated and rejected at various points in her career, like Ruth Benedict. Perhaps she is mysterious and largely unsung despite her obvious brilliance, like Dorothy Van Ghent. Perhaps she has been at rather public odds with her home institution, like Carolyn Heilbrun, or lacked a proper academic appointment at all, like Margaret Mead (who was never a tenured professor at Columbia).

The sample of academic women in the past has been small, to be sure. Too small, perhaps, to explore the problem, though the small size of the female professoriate is in itself part of the problem. Today the sample is much larger. But women still occupy a disproportionately small share of tenured full professor positions, as statistics in all fields demonstrate, some (the natural sciences, engineering) quite egregiously. So I would claim an evocative power in the pattern of Jane Harrison's life and career that I felt just walking through the streets of Cambridge. I felt it there. She must have felt it every day—year in, year out.

NOTES

1. I take most of the biographical information from Sarah Peacock, *Jane Ellen Harrison: The Mask and the Self;* I have also relied on information given by Robert Ackerman in his "Introduction," *Prolegomena.* Also helpful is *The Cambridge Ritualists Reconsidered,* which includes several essays on Harrison.

2. This view is associated also with William Robertson Smith and Sir James Frazer.

3. Neither Buber nor his biographers mention Harrison or the Cambridge Ritualists in print. I found only one suggestive reference to Gilbert Murray, in a postscript to a letter. Although the letter is written in German, Buber quotes from Murray in English: "God is the helping of man by man" (2:119-20).

4. There are three references to Harrison in Lawrence's letters, in the fall of 1913. He says that *Ancient Art and Ritual* "helps one immensely" and adds, "You have no idea how much I got out of [it]" (2:114, 119).

5. See, for example, not just noted works like *Totem and Taboo* (1913) and *Civilization and Its Discontents* (1930) but also "Thoughts for the Times on War and Death" (1915), reprinted in *On Creativity and the Unconscious* (206-35).

6. In *The Savage and the City in the Work of T. S. Eliot,* Crawford lists Harrison as a source for Eliot's 1913 Harvard seminar paper, "Essay on the Interpretation of Primitive Ritual." He reviewed books by other Cambridge Ritualists and corresponded with Harrison in 1923 as a potential contributor to

The Criterion. Eliot does cite Sir James Frazer and Jessie Weston in the notes to *The Waste Land.*

WORKS CITED

Ackerman, Robert. Introduction. *Prolegomena to the Study of Greek Religion.* By Jane Ellen Harrison. Princeton: Princeton UP, 1991, xiii-xxx.

Bernal, Martin. *Black Athena: The Afrocentric Roots of Classical Civilization.* New Brunswick: Rutgers UP, 1987.

Buber, Martin. *Briefwechel aus sieben Jahrzeiten.* Band 2. Heidelberg: Verlag, Lambert, Schneider, 1973.

Calder, William M., III. *The Cambridge Ritualists Reconsidered.* Atlanta: Scholars Press, 1991.

Crawford, Robert. *The Savage and the City in the Work of T. S. Eliot.* Oxford: Oxford UP, 1990.

Freud, Sigmund. *Civilization and Its Discontents.* 1930. Ed. James Strachey. New York: Norton, 1962.

———. "Thoughts for the Times on War and Death." *On Creativity and the Unconscious.* Ed. Benjamin Nelson. New York: Harper, 1958, 206-35.

———. *Totem and Taboo.* 1913. New York: Norton, 1989.

Harrison, Jane Ellen. *Alpha and Omega.* London: Sidgwick and Jackson, 1915.

———. *Ancient Art and Ritual.* 1913. New York: Greenwood Press, 1969.

———. *Epilegomena to the Study of Greek Religion.* 1921. New York: New York University Books, 1962.

———. *Mythology.* 1890. London: Harrap, 1924.

———. *Prolegomena to the Study of Greek Religion.* 1903. Princeton: Princeton UP, 1991.

———. *Themis.* 1912. Cleveland: World Publishing, 1962.

Lawrence, D. H. *The Letters of D. H. Lawrence.* Vol. 2. Ed. George J. Zytaruk and James T. Boulton. Cambridge, Eng.: Cambridge UP, 1981.

Peacock, Sarah. *Jane Ellen Harrison: The Mask and the Self.* New Haven: Yale UP, 1988.

Torgovnick, Marianna. *Primitive Passions: Men, Women, and the Quest for Ecstasy.* New York: Knopf, forthcoming 1997.

"The Bloomsbury Fraction" Versus War and Empire

Patrick Brantlinger

Early in "The Bloomsbury Fraction" (1980), Raymond Williams writes:

> Nothing more easily contradicts the received image of Bloomsbury as withdrawn and languid aesthetes than the remarkable record of political and organizational involvement, between the wars, by Leonard Woolf, by Keynes, but also by others, including Virginia Woolf, who had a branch of the Women's Cooperative Guild meeting regularly in her home. The public record of Keynes is well enough known. That of Leonard Woolf, in his prolonged work for the League of Nations, for the Cooperative movement, and for the Labour Party, especially on anti-imperialist questions, is especially honourable. (155)

Williams follows up this positive assessment, however, with a quite different conclusion, according to which the ultimate but elitist political value of Bloomsbury was a cultured, bourgeois individualism with little comprehension of real-world politics (165). The Bloomsbury artists and intellectuals were "against cant, superstition, hypocrisy, pretension and public show"; their primary value, however, "was the unobstructed free expression of the civilized individual"; they carried "the classical values of bourgeois enlightenment" and "liberal thought" (165).

Like numerous other male critics, including some connected to Bloomsbury, such as Quentin Bell, Williams has little to say about Virginia Woolf's feminism. He also quotes Bloomsbury against Bloomsbury, as when he cites Leonard Woolf's autobiography: "we had no common theory," according to Woolf; everything was "purely individual" and idiosyncratic; there was no connection between Roger Fry's art criticism, John Maynard Keynes's economics, and his wife's *Orlando*. Besides failing to deal with feminism or to give adequate recognition to the ties of several Bloomsburyites to Fabian Socialism and the Labour Party, Williams does not distinguish between the value of a cultivated individualism as an ideal or a utopian goal—one that he himself shared—and an exclusive, class-bound social conservatism. Because of their liberal individualism and elitism, Williams believes, the Bloomsburyites were unable to construct systematic social theories about the various social ills they loftily disliked and sometimes "honourably" opposed. But several members of Bloomsbury supported versions of democratic socialism close to Williams's, while perhaps going further than he did in the directions of pacifism, anti-imperialism, internationalism, and feminism.[1]

I will first examine Bloomsbury's responses to war, especially World War I; I will then turn to the related topic of their responses to imperialism; in the concluding section, I will examine Virginia Woolf's synthesis of these responses in her feminist critique of patriarchy, war, and empire in *Three Guineas*. Anti-feminist attitudes toward her political essays, coupled with her centrality to literary-critical accounts of Bloomsbury, have underwritten the view, shared by Williams, that both she and Bloomsbury peered down their upper-class noses at politics and at the everyday struggles of ordinary people. But Virginia, like her husband Leonard, considered herself a socialist (*Letters* 2:595). And most of Leonard's career as also a quite prolific writer involved impassioned advocacy of radical, if idealistic, forms of pacifism, internationalism, anti-imperialism, and socialism.

WAR

"The war is a nightmare," wrote Virginia Woolf in 1916 (*Letters* 2:100). The liberal humanism and elitism that E. M. Forster, John Maynard Keynes, Leonard Woolf, Bertrand Russell, and others imbibed at Cambridge, partly from G. E. Moore, came in for a shock on August 3, 1914. Through relentless self-questioning, most of this group were led to versions of pacifism, socialism, and anti-imperialism more or less antithetical to their original liberal views and attitudes. Virginia Woolf's critique of war and empire also emerged in direct response to World War I; she quite early connected war and empire to patriarchy.

Partly because of her mental illness, and perhaps also because she viewed politics in general as "all phantasies . . . only mudcoloured moonshine" (*Letters* 2:582), Woolf took no activist role in antiwar efforts. But as early as *The Voyage Out* (1915), she was clearly unhappy with the imperialist mentality of the Richard Dalloways of the world: "A vision of English

history, King following King, Prime Minister Prime Minister, and Law Law
had come over him while his wife spoke. He ran his mind along the line of
conservative policy, which went steadily from Lord Salisbury to Alfred,
and gradually enclosed, as though it were a lasso that opened and caught
things, enormous chunks of the habitable globe" (*Voyage* 51). Woolf is
here critical of what might be called the cowboy mentality underlying
jingoism and territorial aggrandizement by Britain (among other Western nation-states). On January 23, 1916, Woolf wrote to Margaret
Llewellyn Davies: "I become steadily more feminist, owing to the Times,
which I read at breakfast and wonder how this preposterous masculine
fiction [of the war] keeps going a day longer—without some vigorous
young woman pulling us together and marching us through it" (*Letters*
2:76). While this statement leaves unclear whether the "vigorous young
woman" is to be a righteous warrior like Joan of Arc, leading the British
(and French, of course) to victory over the Germans, "masculine fiction"
suggests that the ultimate warfare must be, and perhaps already was being,
waged by women against the male ideology that combined sexism with
patriotism and militarism in a deadly brew.

I will return to Woolf's "feminist pacificism" (Ouditt 175), especially
in *Three Guineas*. The primary response to World War I of Bertrand Russell,
Lytton Strachey, Clive Bell, and some of the other male members of
Bloomsbury was also pacifism, albeit unconnected to feminism. *Three Guineas* itself, of course, takes the form of a letter from the author to a male
friend who has invited her to write on behalf of his all-male pacifist organization. Woolf may partly be recalling the organizations formed in 1915 and
after to oppose conscription, such as the Union for Democratic Control,
which Leonard, Bertrand Russell, the Stracheys, and other Bloomsburyites
joined. Leonard was unwilling to call himself a pacifist, and perhaps
would have followed his brothers into battle if it had not been for
Virginia's mental illness; when conscription began he was not drafted
on medical grounds (*Beginning* 176-78). But other male members of
Bloomsbury—Clive Bell, Duncan Grant, Bertrand Russell, the Strachey
brothers—claimed conscientious objection. Russell famously spent six
months in prison in 1916 for his pacifist activities. If it hadn't been for
his frail health, Lytton Strachey might have followed Russell to prison.
The war affected Lytton, as it did all of Bloomsbury, as "a personal tragedy" (Holroyd 574), and not least when the prospect of his own conscription loomed. Yet, when confronted with the possibility of doing clerical
work in England as alternative service, Lytton declared: "I'm willing to go
to prison rather than do that [safe] work" (quoted in Holroyd 624).

For a while, Russell found his closest Bloomsbury ally in Lytton Strachey, for whom political activism of any sort was painfully distasteful. But like his brother James, Lytton chose pacificism, and at his tribunal hearing on March 7, 1916, stated:

> I have a conscientious objection to assisting, by any deliberate action of mine, in carrying on the war. This objection is not based on religious belief, but upon moral considerations. . . . [M]y feeling is directed not simply against the present war: I am convinced that the whole system by which it is sought to settle international disputes by force is profoundly evil; and that . . . I should be doing wrong to take part in it. (Quoted in Holroyd 626)

Although Lytton was excused from military service on medical grounds (his request for exemption as a CO was denied), there is no reason to doubt either his sincerity or his courage.

Keynes was less sure how to respond than Russell or the Stracheys, or perhaps just more willing to trim his sails to the winds of war. Because of his position with the Treasury, he escaped having to make a decision about conscription. By not resigning from government, he greatly disappointed his Bloomsbury friends (Moggeridge 254-61; Holroyd 620). But Keynes nevertheless used his influence to try to protect Russell, the Stracheys, and other COs. Perhaps also because he saw history largely in economic instead of political terms, Keynes did not respond to the war by revising his early liberalism in the radical directions taken by Russell, the Woolfs, and some of the other members of Bloomsbury.[2]

Both during and after World War I, it was easy for prowar writers like H. G. Wells to attack pacifists, including Russell and the Stracheys, as unpatriotic, even treasonous. Here is another reason why Bloomsbury has been condemned as limp-wristed and retrograde by presumably red-blooded, progressive patriots such as the Leavises.[3] It is true that Russell, for example, could afford to be a pacifist; even when imprisoned in 1916, he was, through the intervention of Arthur Balfour, well treated (Russell 29-34). But the fact that wealthy COs were protected while others were not does not explain how and why Bloomsbury's pacifism and internationalism arose. No doubt their international sympathies derived from liberal cosmopolitanism rather than socialist internationalism as exemplified by the First and Second Marxist Internationals. With the outbreak of the war, many liberals wondered how Britain and Germany, especially given the British monarchy's long-standing familial connections to German royalty, could have become enemies. After all, hadn't Queen Victoria and Prince Albert been joined in holy matrimony not too long ago? The most common answer was that all of the belligerents, despite or perhaps even because of their high level of civilization, had reverted to barbarism.

During the war, Russell, Forster, the Woolfs, the Stracheys, and many other previously good liberals reformulated their liberalism in directions that were more powerfully and consistently critical of war and imperialism—and of civilization, which after all had produced or at any rate not prevented war—than some supposedly more radical brands of politics and social theory, such as Fabian Socialism. Though there were strong connections between Fabian Socialism and several members of Bloomsbury, including Russell and Leonard Woolf, the official position of the Fabians was in favor of Britain's entry into the war and also in favor of the British Empire as the best form of internationalism the world had yet experienced (Wilson 60, 80-81).

Keynes's most important early work, *Economic Consequences of the Peace* (1919), was a scathing critique of British and Allied policy toward defeated Germany—a critique in basic agreement with Russell and Leonard Woolf, both of whom argued passionately for the establishment of new forms of "international government" that would at least reduce the chance of future wars. Their voices, along with many others' during and after the war, led to the formation of the League of Nations. Woolf's most influential work, his 1916 *International Government,* which he wrote for the Fabian Society, has been called "the book which became the blueprint for the League of Nations" (Gottlieb 242). It is at least, "in its own right . . . a landmark in the study of international affairs" (Wilson 67; see also Woolf, *Beginning* 186-89).[4]

By the end of the war, in contrast to Keynes, both Russell and Leonard Woolf had connected advocacy of "international government" to their versions of socialism and Labour politics. "War is only the final flower of the capitalist system," Russell wrote in 1918 (120). Competition among individuals for scarce resources was magnified on the global level as strife among nations. Only a social system based on cooperation and the common ownership of resources could bring about lasting peace. Russell believed that in the British context, the best hope for the future lay with the Labour Party. As a Labour candidate in 1922, Russell told the voters of Chelsea: "I see no hope of improvement from parties which advocate a continuation of the muddled vindictiveness which has brought Europe to the brink of ruin. For the world at large, for our own country, and for every man, woman and child in our country, the victory of Labour is essential" (Russell 241).

Leonard Woolf arrived at his own version of socialism, his collaboration on various projects with the Fabians, and his adherence to the Independent

Labour Party partly by way of the Women's Cooperative Guild and the inspiration of its leader, Margaret Llewellyn Davies (Wilson 50-54). For the Fabian journal *New Statesman,* Woolf wrote a number of articles on the cooperative movement (Wilson 58), projects that drew him further into Fabianism and Labour politics. His *Co-operation and the Future of Industry* (1919) expresses his "vision of a socialist society based on consumers' control" (*Beginning* 106). Like Russell, Woolf also came to see the alternatives both domestically and internationally as capitalist, imperialist rapacity and war versus "industrial democracy" (the title of Sidney and Beatrice Webb's influential book) and "international government."

Assessing Woolf's impact on the formation of the League of Nations, Duncan Wilson writes: "The historian may regretfully say that the human race has not benefited much from the machinery of the League of Nations . . . or of the United Nations. . . . The less sceptical may reflect that these experiments in international machinery have still been worth making. . . . And Leonard Woolf did as much as any man to lay the foundation for their work" (Wilson 91). In his later writings, Woolf continued to try to explain World War I and war in general. The two-volume *After the Deluge* (1931, 1939) and its sequel, *Principia Politica* (1953), combine Woolf's theory of "economic imperialism" with an attempt to fathom the psychology of human aggression. This combination—apparent economic rationality on the one hand and deep individual and social irrationality on the other—partly echoes the work of Woolf's acquaintance J. A. Hobson in *The Psychology of Jingoism* (1901) and *Imperialism: A Study* (1902), while adding a psychoanalytic dimension that mirrors *Three Guineas* and looks forward to Alix Strachey's *The Unconscious Motives of War* (1957).

Perhaps partly because of the failure of the League of Nations to stem the tide of dictatorship and barbarism that led to World War II, the ideas and work of Bertrand Russell and Leonard Woolf have been overlooked or underestimated by later radicals as just more ineffective, liberal idealism. But the later radicals (including Williams) have too often themselves lacked positive ideas about how national rivalries and war might be overcome. Russell and Woolf's advocacy of "international government" was at least based on a clear-sighted, radical analysis of the causes of war that pointed both to irrational elements of "communal psychology" and to capitalism and imperialism.

EMPIRE

Keynes's early work for the India Office, Leonard Woolf's seven years (1904-11) as a district administrator in Ceylon, and E. M. Forster's travels to India and employment, in 1921, as private secretary to the Maharajah of Dewas suggest that Bloomsbury had ties to the British Empire that might have led them to view it through approvingly Kiplingesque lenses. But this is hardly the case. Keynes's attitudes toward the empire and imperialism are difficult to fathom. For both Woolf and Forster, however, service in India and their assessment of imperial rivalries among the European powers as a major cause of World War I led them to versions of anti-imperialism directly related to their internationalism.

Even before the war, Forster was critical of at least jingoistic versions of imperialism. Near the conclusion of *Howards End* (1910), an automobile passes Leonard Bast while he is walking through the countryside. The driver, the narrator says, was a "type whom Nature favours—the Imperial":

> Healthy, ever in motion, it hopes to inherit the earth. It breeds as quickly as the yeoman, and as soundly strong is the temptation to acclaim it as a super-yeoman, who carries his country's virtue overseas. But the imperialist is not what he thinks or seems. He is a destroyer. He prepares the way for cosmopolitanism, and though his ambitions may be fulfilled, the earth that he inherits will be grey. (323)

Earlier in the novel, Ernst Schlegel equates "Pan-Germanism" with British imperialism, adding: "'It is the vice of a vulgar mind to be thrilled by bigness, to think that a thousand square miles are a thousand times more wonderful than one square mile, and that a million square miles are almost the same as heaven'" (29). Forster undoubtedly also saw British imperialism as little different from the German variety, and believed that both arose partly from a jingoism that dismissed the ideals of international cooperation, friendship, and cultural interchange as unpatriotic.

Forster's *A Passage to India* (1924) may not be the definitive anti-imperialist novel of the modern era, but it is nevertheless a stark contrast to, say, Kipling's *Kim*.[5] As Edward Said suggests, Forster does just the opposite of Kipling. Whereas the Ethnographic Survey in *Kim* will, through espionage, science, and proper policing, map and master all of India despite its vastness and colorful multiplicity, the experience of all of the European characters in *Passage* is ultimately one of failure—of coming up against the limits of knowledge and of the imperialist attempt of any society to map and master others. "Almost by virtue of its liberal, humane espousal of Fielding's views and attitudes, *A Passage to India* is at a loss, partly because Forster's commitment to the novel form exposes him to difficulties in India he cannot deal with" (Said 201).

The omniscient narration of *Kim* confidently explains all mysteries of diverse customs and creeds, including the minds and hearts of Indians as

well as Europeans. The omniscient narration of *Passage* is much less confident, and ultimately not omniscient when confronted with the larger mysteries of its own story—what actually happened in the Marabar Caves, what
do Muslims and Hindus finally want, what can any mere mortal (perhaps
especially an Englishman or -woman) ever come to know about "India's
massive incomprehensibility" (Said 202) except that it is massive and incomprehensible? Like the Edwardian realism that Virginia Woolf rejected, *Kim* remains within the framework of Victorian empiricism as well as imperialism,
according to which everything can eventually be known and mastered. But in
Passage, the "imperial archive" turns Gothic, or proves to be haunted by
the excess of all that remains unknowable, and therefore by the knowledge
of the ultimate failure of the imperialist project, even when that project is
carried on by such liberal, humane agents as Fielding and Mrs. Moore.[6]

Informing all aspects of *Passage,* the failure of the imperialist enterprise in India implies the triumph of Indian nationalism. Forster does not
portray Aziz's and Godbole's nationalism as already clearly triumphing.
But he understands that independence is inevitable—that the days of the
Raj are numbered. How to quit India on positive terms, rather than with the
fear and violence exhibited by General Dyer in the Amritsar Massacre of
1919? In *Passage,* Forster portrays some of "the unlovely chaos that lies
between obedience and freedom—and that seems, alas! the immediate future of India" (*Abinger* 311). But perhaps politics always involves balancing acts between obedience and freedom. At least this is one theme in
Forster's politics and that of the other Bloomsbury intellectuals. G. K. Das
notes that Forster's "outlook belonged primarily with the outgoing liberalism of the pre-war generation" (xi). But such liberalism was often anti-
imperialist in sentiment if not always in deed—compatible with Forster's
"deep sympathy with India's democratic aspirations . . . as expressed in the
revolutionary ideas of Gandhi's Non-cooperation movement" (Das xviii).

Das sums up Forster's liberalism, contrasting it to the muddled orthodoxy of the Liberal party in Britain, in terms of the ideal of a "democratic
Empire." This oxymoron was at once "a sincere, personal ideal," that of a
"liberal individualist," and an insistence that the political destinies of both
Britain and India depended upon the quality of the personal relationships
"between individual Indians and Englishmen, and between their two communities." Forster "knew that if Indian nationalism was turning wholly anti-
British after the First World War, it was because the Government of India,
under an imperialist system, whether Tory or Liberal, had failed to create
the conditions in which Indians and Englishmen could live together in an
atmosphere of social equality and friendship" (Das 43). After independence

in 1947 and Gandhi's assassination the following year, Forster wrote that Gandhi was "likely . . . the greatest [individual] of our century" (quoted in Das 116). But Forster never made common cause with Indian nationalism, and his own personal ties were to Indian aristocrats of the backward, highly conservative princely states who themselves dreaded independence and saw Gandhi only as the destroyer of their wealth and power.[7]

At once admiring of Indian aristocratic tradition, pomp, and civility and sympathetic to Gandhi and Indian nationalism, Forster developed an idealistic liberalism that was also an antipolitical politics or an aestheticized anarchism of the sort often charged against Bloomsbury. But he believed that politics as usual resulted in fanaticism and war and was destructive of the personal relationships that he most valued. In "What I Believe" (1938), Forster bitterly declared that "faith" both religious and secular was what destroyed humanity. "Democracy is not a beloved Republic, and never will be. But it is less hateful than other contemporary forms of government," in part because it respected the individual (66-67). Beyond this, what mattered most—the main article of Forster's own antipolitical faith—was "personal relationships" (65). Forster added that "I believe in aristocracy," though only from a democratic, liberal perspective: "Not an aristocracy of power, based upon rank and influence, but an aristocracy of the sensitive, the considerate and the plucky. Its members are to be found in all nations and classes . . . and there is a secret understanding between them when they meet. They represent the true human tradition, the one permanent victory of our queer race over cruelty and chaos" (70). Forster's description of this sensitive, democratic aristocracy suggests the Bloomsbury circle, and perhaps also Virginia Woolf's Society of Outsiders in *Three Guineas,* also expressive of an aestheticized anarchism in which personal relationships take precedence over politics, laws, and institutions, including armies and empires.

Apart from Virginia's *Three Guineas,* Leonard Woolf's *Empire and Commerce in Africa* (1920), *Economic Imperialism* (1920), and *Imperialism and Civilization* (1928) are the most sustained anti-imperialist analyses produced by Bloomsbury. These build upon Hobson's *Imperialism* by demonstrating the causal connections among capitalism and industrialization, the search for new markets, rivalries among the Western nation-states, and the impact of unofficial adventurers in such places as Abyssinia and Uganda. Hobson's focus was mainly on South Africa and the causes of the Boer War. In *Empire and Commerce in Africa,* Woolf's focus is on the more general "scramble for Africa" between the 1880s and 1914; his conclusion in all three books is that "the struggle among the Great Powers for the control of African territory had a most disastrous effect upon European international relations" and was a main cause of World War I (*Economic Imperialism* 62-63). This conclusion seems obvious today, but was perhaps less apparent in the 1920s.

More remarkably, especially in *Imperialism and Civilization,* Woolf explores the response of imperialized peoples around the globe and predicts the demise of the European empires as a result of independence movements and of future catastrophic warfare among the European nation-states. Resistance to Western rule, Woolf makes clear, was apparent from the start in the Far East: both China and Japan had to be "opened up" to Western capitalism via military means (the Opium Wars of the 1840s; Commander Perry's gunboat diplomacy in Japan in 1853), and both remained resistant to direct imperial encroachment. In India, the 1857-58 mutiny marked the beginning of the end of the British Raj. From the early 1900s, Woolf remarks, the subcontinent has entered "a period of complete revolt" which by the 1920s had clearly demonstrated "the ultimate impossibility of [continued] imperialism in India" (*Imperialism* 70-76).

Hobson and Woolf both understand "economic imperialism" to mean the pursuit of new markets and profits abroad on the part of individuals and private commercial enterprises at the expense of the imperializing nation-state. "The objective wealth of the State, as distinguished from that of individual subjects or citizens of the State, has certainly not been increased by the possession of Empire" (Woolf, *Empire* 318). Again like Hobson, Woolf sees "jingoism" as a form of ideology that both justifies and mystifies economic exploitation at home and abroad. Especially in *The Psychology of Jingoism,* Hobson had analyzed the workings of that ideology from the perspective of Gustave Le Bon's "crowd psychology." Woolf does not spend much time on ideology; nevertheless, he writes that "economic imperialism" arises from "the beliefs and desires . . . of individual men and women" who think that they will profit from imperial expansion, or that such expansion will enhance the "power and prestige" of their nation-state (*Empire* 316-17).

Woolf's fuller exploration of the "communal psychology" underlying war and empire would come in *After the Deluge* and *Principia Politica.* With their explicitly psychoanalytic orientation, these later works approximate Virginia Woolf's antiwar novels and essays, including *Three Guineas.* But before turning to that ultimate critique of patriarchy, war, and empire, it may be worth recalling one more example of Bloomsbury's general anti-imperialism: Lytton Strachey's portrait of General Gordon, the essay that concludes *Eminent Victorians* (1918). Strachey illustrates that imperialist's heroism but also his religious fanaticism, his insubordination, his craziness, his alcoholism. Gordon's "martyrdom" at Khartoum, Strachey suggests, is the irrational stuff that empires, including Britain's, are made of. Strachey gives the story an ironically happy ending, equivalent to the "healthy" destructiveness of "the Imperial" type in *Howards End.* The final sentence of *Eminent Victorians* reads: "At any rate, it had all ended very happily—in a glorious slaughter of 20,000 Arabs, a vast addition to the British Empire, and a step in the Peerage for Sir Evelyn Baring" (Strachey 192).

THREE GUINEAS

In "The Bloomsbury Fraction," Williams mentions "sexual . . . discrimination," but he fails to say that Virginia Woolf elaborated a feminist theory that exposed and condemned the ages-old connections among patriarchy, war, and empire.[8] In *Jacob's Room* (1922), *Mrs. Dalloway* (1925), and *To the Lighthouse* (1927), Woolf's "technique may be oblique"—her famously subjective impressionism—but "the effect is inflammatory. . . . [Woolf manages] to initiate an investigation of the ideologies that structure our ways of seeing and to allow the shock of the war to *remain* a shock, rather than permitting its assimilation into the codes of sentimentality" (Ouditt 188). In all three novels and in *Three Guineas,* Woolf, despite her reservations about Freud's theories, conducts her "investigation of the ideologies" that produce war, empire, and fascism within the general framework of psychoanalysis. In *Three Guineas,* by "both writing and departing from Freud's position . . . Woolf inscribes the question of war in a dialogue conducted with psychoanalysis across and about the sexual division" (Abel 103-4).

In *To the Lighthouse,* the seemingly gratuitous deaths that punctuate the "Time Passes" section, including Andrew Ramsay's death in battle in France, are of a piece with the violent Oedipal emotions that James feels at the start of the novel: "had there been an axe handy, or a poker, any weapon that would have gashed a hole in his father's breast and killed him, there and then, James would have seized it" (4). Both the deaths and the emotions are also of a piece with Mr. Ramsay's feelings of inadequacy and insatiable craving for sympathy. Mr. Ramsay's militaristic fantasies as he marches around the garden spouting lines from "Charge of the Light Brigade" ("'Stormed at with shot and shell. . . . Someone had blundered'" [17, 18]) foreshadow the bracketed news of Andrew's death: "[A shell exploded. Twenty or thirty young men were blown up in France, among them Andrew Ramsay, whose death, mercifully, was instantaneous]" (133). The "continuity" of British imperial history, so admired by Richard Dalloway, was of course a continuity of war, leading through the Crimean to the Boer War and on to the catastrophe of World War I. Woolf implies that Mr. Ramsay's patriarchal inadequacies are the ultimate cause of the death of his son in France. The phallic imagery of *To the Lighthouse* (including the lighthouse, of course) involves a critique of phallocentrism without the name, as into the "fountain and spray of life, the fatal sterility of the male plunged itself, like a beak of brass, barren and bare" (37). And if the "beak of brass" metaphor does not make the link to war explicit, "the arid scimitar of the male, which smote mercilessly, again and again, demanding sympathy" (38), more clearly connects the two.

But it isn't just Mr. Ramsay's masculinist lack that causes both psychological and political damage to others, spreading war and death. The patriarchal system cannot sustain itself without the cooperation of "the angel in the house," Mrs. Ramsay, who "expects chivalry and valour and, in return, offers men psychological security, unquestioningly revering their authority in government, whether national or domestic" (Ouditt 202). If Woolf saw anything positive arising from the appalling death and destruction of World War I, it lay in alternatives to patriarchy and the Victorian and Edwardian confinement of women (bourgeois women, at least) to the domestic sphere. The war "altered civilisation's focus, it smashed some prohibitive traditions; it offered the means to destroy the angel in the house" (Ouditt 22).

Nevertheless, as Woolf would more explicitly analyze in *Three Guineas,* nationalist, imperialist rivalries and the disasters of war would indeed form the continuity of British history into the foreseeable future unless somehow the heritage and consequences of patriarchy could be subverted more completely than they had been during World War I. To think of anything positive coming from war was problematic, to say the least. Moreover, to understand war as an ideological construct—that is, as a "preposterous masculine fiction" masquerading male insecurities, "barrenness," and "sterility"—meant that the story had to be changed, renarrated or completely scrapped in favor of a new telling. Woolf's Modernist efforts to unhinge Victorian and Edwardian realism and create an alternative form of the novel should be understood as attempts to rewrite "the dominant [patriarchal] Symbolic Order" in light of her "feminist pacifism" (Ouditt 175).

What is it, Woolf asks in *Three Guineas,* that separates women's sphere from men's—supposedly the private from the public, or the inward and intimate from the political? Is this separation natural, logical, fair, sane? And is the divisive power that causes it related to—perhaps identical to— the power that drives men and nations to war? For the author has been asked by a male friend to support a society for the prevention of war. But why should she or any woman do so, she replies, if in general women have been deprived of political influence by men, and if in general war is the result of a male "instinct" to competition, domination, and bloodshed? "For though many instincts are held more or less in common by both sexes, to fight has always been the man's habit, not the woman's. Law and practice have developed that difference, whether innate or accidental. Scarcely a human being in the course of history has fallen to a woman's rifle; the vast majority of birds and beasts have been killed by you, not us" (6).

"Law and practice," buttressed by the strange sentiment known as "patriotism," have erected a vast system of power and institutions—church and state, the schools and universities, the nation and its colonies—from the running of which women are virtually excluded. This vast apparatus of wealth and power, buttressed by professions and disciplines from which women are generally excluded, constitutes the great war machine of Britain (or France, or Germany, et cetera). It may be understandable that the war machine should elicit the state-worship known as patriotism from the men whose own power and prestige are derived from it, but women, Woolf thinks, do not have similar motives for patriotism. Women have passions and interests, but they do not have these other motives—at least not until the men they love, or try to love, go to war. Rather than becoming a patriot, a reasonable woman will instead join the ever-expanding Society of Outsiders and will, as an outsider, not automatically wax patriotic when asked to do so by a man.

Woolf suggests that the alienation of the Society of Outsiders is parallel to that of peoples and cultures dominated by Britain through its empire—"the Indians or the Irish, say" (108). Having treated woman "as a slave" throughout history, "our country" has no claim on her loyalty: "as a woman, I have no country. As a woman I want no country. As a woman my country is the whole world" (109). Therefore the member of the Society of Outsiders, Woolf says, "will bind herself to take no share in patriotic demonstrations; to assent to no form of national self-praise; to make no part of any claque or audience that encourages war; to absent herself from military displays, tournaments, tattoos, prize-givings and all such ceremonies as encourage the desire to impose 'our' civilization or 'our' dominion upon other people" (109).

If "patriotic demonstrations" and the rest are public activities leading up to war, Woolf leaves no doubt that the initial motives for war are planted in private, in childhood, in the inwardness and intimacy of family life. On the issue of admitting women to the priesthood of the Church of England, Woolf cites a Freudian theologian, Professor Grensted of Oxford, who points out that whatever the rational merits of the case, it raises a "strong emotion" that is governed by an "infantile fixation"—a "non-rational sex taboo" (126). Woolf extrapolates from Grensted the suggestion that this same "infantile fixation" is the "egg" or "germ" from which other "strong feelings" of exclusion grow—indeed, from which the entire system of patriarchy grows: "Society it seems was a father, and afflicted with the infantile fixation too" (135).

Although Woolf doesn't use the word, fetishism describes many of the symptoms of this generalized "infantile fixation," and above all the male rituals of exclusion and domination that lead to war. In an early passage listing the centers of power "crowded together" in London—"St. Paul's, the Bank of England . . . the Law Courts . . . Westminster Abbey and . . . Parliament" (18)—Woolf enumerates the ornaments that its male denizens wear: "every button, rosette and stripe seems to have some symbolical meaning" (19). Woolf adds that the

> wearing pieces of metal, or ribbon, coloured hoods or gowns, is a barbarity which deserves the ridicule which we bestow upon the rites of savages. . . . Even stranger, however, than the symbolic splendour of your clothes are the ceremonies that take place when you wear them. Here you kneel; there you bow; here you advance in procession behind a man carrying a silver poker; here you mount a carved chair; here you appear to do homage to a piece of painted wood. (20)

In his accounts of the "communal psychology" that produced wars and empires, Leonard also describes the modern ideologies of patriotism, jingoism, and fascism as versions of fetishism: "Men have always worshipped images, sometimes of cats, sometimes of gods, sometimes of men, and now of States. They made strange sacrifices to their cats in Egypt and to their gods in Israel; and they make strange sacrifices to-day upon the altar of the State" (*Empire* 318). As in Marx's analysis of commodity fetishism and Freud's of sexual fetishism, at the very heart of Britain's supposedly civilized institutions of national and imperial power reside savage or infantile beliefs and practices no different in kind from primitive idolatries, including those that involve human sacrifice, as in war. This fetishistic behavior is, moreover, indistinguishable from the equally barbaric deployment of political symbols by the dictatorships in Germany and Italy, a connection that Leonard would reiterate in his anti-fascist tracts, *Quack, Quack!* (1935) and *Barbarians at the Gate* (1939).[9]

In insisting that no aspect of the Society of Outsiders be bound by rules, rituals, and symbolic displays, and also that it involve no hierarchies of power or distinction, Virginia Woolf writes:

Here . . . the example of the Fascist States is at hand to instruct us—
for if we have no example of what we wish to be, we have, what is
perhaps equally valuable, a daily and illuminating example of what
we do not wish to be. With the example then, that they give us of the
power of medals, symbols, orders and even, it would seem, of decorated ink-pots to hypnotize the human mind it must be our aim not
to submit ourselves to such hypnotism. (114)

Fetishistic rituals involving objects like "decorated ink-pots" or "painted
pieces of wood," flags or medals, are of course instances of patriotism—
that is, of the general fetishization of the nation-state. Rooted in an "infantile fixation" at least on the part of the male sex, patriotism is the product of
neurotic, compensatory, dominative behaviors first within families and then
beyond them, in the world at large, in the phenomena associated with the
growth of nation-states, the acquisition of empires, and war.

Woolf's quasi-utopian Society of Outsiders will take no part in the
state-building, war-mongering phenomena of ages-old politics. I say "quasi-
utopian," not because her society was fictive or didn't really exist but
because to be fully utopian would involve imagining the reconstitution
of society on the basis of different, positive premises and values. Because Woolf refuses to imagine the reconstitution of society, her Society
of Outsiders must necessarily remain inside—complicitous with—the
given, flawed, patriarchal society that it opposes. But direct opposition
is not what Woolf advocates; she calls instead for a seemingly apolitical
"indifference." The objection that the Society of Outsiders isn't utopian
is beside the point also because its membership in a sense consists of all
women throughout history—that is, of all women under patriarchy. Woolf
remorselessly, ironically refuses to be political in the standard, common
sense of the term, partly because politics refuses to include women, and
partly because politics means empire and war. Why redesign society,
when society does not provide women with any tools for redesigning it?
This seemingly indifferent, apolitical stance is calculated, through irony,
to be highly troublesome to Woolf's male lawyer friend, correspondent,
and political animal—perhaps a Bloomsbury friend, perhaps even her
husband—and just as troublesome to somewhat solemn male critics like
Raymond Williams.

The Bloomsbury artists and intellectuals felt much guilt over their
own inability, as would-be leaders of "civilization," to stem the "tide of
barbarism" that swept over Europe in 1914, again in the Spanish Civil
War, and then even more catastrophically in World War II. Their own
confessions of naiveté and failure, of ineffectiveness at and distaste for
politics, have helped to diminish the record of their actual political and

social theories, struggles, and achievements. If the record is difficult to sum up, that is also because the range of their views and their activities, over entire careers and lifetimes, was enormous. Leonard Woolf alone evolved, especially under the impact of World War I, from being a loyal liberal imperialist during his time in Ceylon into democratic socialism and an anti-imperialist advocacy of world government. From 1914 forward, he did not hesitate to identify both capitalism and its offspring, imperialism, as the main causes of war and modern "barbarism." And in *Three Guineas,* Virginia Woolf authored one of the most radical anti-war, anti-imperialist, and feminist essays ever written. These alone are accomplishments that greatly exceed the narrow, bourgeois liberalism and elitism that Williams for one attributed to the Woolfs, to Forster, and to the rest of "the Bloomsbury fraction."

NOTES

1. For Williams and feminism, see Jenny Bourne Taylor; for Williams and imperialism, see Edward Said (14, 41) and also Gauri Viswanathan.

2. See especially Keynes's 1925-26 essays "Am I a Liberal?" and "Liberalism and Labour," in *Essays in Persuasion.*

3. F. R. Leavis was even capable of blaming Bloomsbury, via Keynes, for helping to start World War II (Holroyd, "Bloomsbury" 50-51), while Q. D. Leavis "savaged" *Three Guineas* as "Nazi dialectic without Nazi conviction" (quoted in Alexander 180). See also Noel Annan in Marcus 23-38.

4. Laura Moss Gottlieb goes even further when she describes *International Government* as "the book which became the blueprint for the League of Nations" (Gottlieb 242).

5. Leonard Woolf's *The Village in the Jungle* (1913) offers a contrast both to *Kim* and to *A Passage to India.* It is neither explicitly pro- nor anti-imperialist, largely because its focus is so completely on its Sinhalese characters. That is, it is so completely ethnographic that the British presence seems irrelevant. The British judges who pass sentence on Babun and Silindu are not unsympathetic, but they are uncomprehending—unable to render justice in the first place, and therefore inadvertent causes of further injustice and tragedy. For Woolf's attitude toward imperialism prior to World War I, see *Growing* and also *Beginning Again* 100.

6. For the concept of the "imperial archive," see Thomas Richards.

7. The personal experience of India that Forster was able to incorporate into *Passage* came mainly from his 1921 service as private secretary to the Maharajah of Dewas Senior, Sir Tukoji Rao Puar III, an experience celebrated in *The Hill of Devi.*

8. It is now evident that not just the unsympathetic Leavises but many of the more sympathetic male critics and biographers who have written about her have downplayed her quite radical political ideas; most of these male-authored commentaries conclude that she was either innocent about or didn't care about political issues. Even Leonard Woolf claimed that she was "the least political animal that has lived since Aristotle invented the description" (quoted in Gottlieb 242), though this is surely partly ironic. Most such commentaries, including Quentin Bell's biography, also downplay the significance of Leonard Woolf's political ideas and activities as influences on Virginia and as significant contributions to modern pacifism and internationalism. But that the Woolfs shared fundamental political attitudes and values is manifest, though the extent to which Leonard shared his wife's feminism is unclear.

9. While perpetuating the view that Virginia was thoroughly apolitical, Peter Alexander says that Leonard "profoundly disagreed" with the views she expressed in *Three Guineas,* even though she was there expressing Leonard's views about the analogy between "the psychological ascendancy of Hitler and Mussolini" and "the blind fetish-worship of savage tribes" (Alexander 177). The correct judgment is surely Selma Meyerowitz's; she sees *Three Guineas* "as a companion piece to Leonard's *Quack, Quack!,* as both analyze the communal psychology of barbarism and link it to fascism and war" (Meyerowitz 18).

Works Cited

Abel, Elizabeth. *Virginia Woolf and the Fictions of Psychoanalysis.* Chicago: Chicago UP, 1989.

Alexander, Peter. *Leonard and Virginia Woolf: A Literary Partnership.* Hemmel Hempstead: Harvester Wheatsheaf, 1992.

Annan, Noel. "Bloomsbury and the Leavises." *Virginia Woolf and Bloomsbury: A Centenary Celebration.* Ed. Jane Marcus. Bloomington: Indiana UP, 1987, 23-38.

Bell, Quentin. *Virginia Woolf: A Biography.* New York: Harcourt Brace Jovanovich, 1972.

Das, G. K. *E. M. Forster's India.* Totowa, N.J.: Rowman and Littlefield, 1977.

Forster, E. M. *Abinger Harvest.* New York: Harcourt Brace, 1936.

———. *The Hill of Devi and Other Indian Writings.* Ed. Elizabeth Heine. London: Arnold, 1983.

———. *Howards End.* 1910. New York: Vintage, n.d.

———. *A Passage to India.* 1924. Harmondsworth: Penguin, 1961.

———. *Two Cheers for Democracy.* 1951. Ed. Oliver Stallybrass. London: Arnold, 1972.

Gottlieb, Laura Moss. "The War between the Woolfs." *Virginia Woolf and Bloomsbury: A Centenary Celebration.* Ed. Jane Marcus. Bloomington: Indiana UP, 1987, 242-52.

Holroyd, Michael. "Bloomsbury and the Fabians." *Virginia Woolf and Bloomsbury: A Centenary Celebration.* Ed. Jane Marcus. Bloomington: Indiana UP, 1987, 39-51.

————. *Lytton Strachey: A Biography.* New York: Holt, Rinehart, and Winston, 1971.

Keynes, John Maynard. *Essays in Persuasion. Collected Writings.* Vol. 9. London: Macmillan, 1972.

Meyerowitz, Selma. *Leonard Woolf.* Boston: Twayne, 1982.

Moggeridge, D. E. *Maynard Keynes: An Economist's Biography.* London: Routledge, 1992.

Ouditt, Sharon. *Fighting Forces, Writing Women: Identity and Ideology in the First World War.* London: Routledge, 1994.

Richards, Thomas. *The Imperial Archive: Knowledge and the Fantasy of Empire.* London: Verso, 1993.

Russell, Bertrand. *Autobiography.* Vol. 2. Boston: Little, Brown, 1968.

Said, Edward. *Culture and Imperialism.* New York: Knopf, 1993.

Strachey, Lytton. *Eminent Victorians: The Illustrated Edition.* London: Bloomsbury, 1988.

Taylor, Jenny Bourne. "Raymond Williams: Gender and Generation." *British Feminist Thought: A Reader.* Ed. Terry Lovell. London: Blackwell, 1990, 296-308.

Vellacott, Jo. *Bertrand Russell and the Pacifists in the First World War.* New York: St. Martin's, 1981.

Viswanathan, Gauri. "Raymond Williams and British Colonialism: The Limits of Metropolitan Theory." *Views Beyond the Border Country: Raymond Williams and Cultural Politics.* Ed. Dennis Dworkin and Leslie Roman. New York: Routledge, 1993, 217-30.

Williams, Raymond. "The Bloomsbury Fraction." *Problems in Materialism and Culture.* London: Verso Books, 1980, 148-69.

Wilson, Duncan. *Leonard Woolf: A Political Biography.* New York: St. Martin's, 1978.

Woolf, Leonard. *After the Deluge: A Study of Communal Psychology.* 2 vols. London: Hogarth, 1931, 1939.

————. *Beginning Again: An Autobiography of the Years 1911 to 1918.* London: Hogarth, 1964.

————. *Economic Imperialism.* 1920. New York: Howard Fertig, 1970.

―――. *Empire and Commerce in Africa: A Study in Economic Imperialism.* 1920. New York: Howard Fertig, 1968.

―――. *Growing: An Autobiography of the Years 1904-1911.* London: Hogarth, 1961.

―――. *Imperialism and Civilization.* New York: Harcourt Brace, 1928.

―――. *Principia Politica: A Study of Communal Psychology.* London: Hogarth, 1953.

―――. *The Village in the Jungle.* 1913. Oxford: Oxford UP, 1981.

Woolf, Virginia. *The Question of Things Happening: The Letters of Virginia Woolf.* Vol. 2. Ed. Nigel Nicolson. London: Hogarth, 1976.

―――. *Three Guineas.* 1938. New York: Harcourt Brace Jovanovich, n.d.

―――. *To the Lighthouse.* 1927. New York: Harcourt Brace Jovanovich, 1989.

―――. *The Voyage Out.* 1920. New York: Harcourt Brace Jovanovich, n.d.

Part Four

Looking and Looking Again: Two Views of Two Writers

Forster, the Environmentalist

Wilfred H. Stone

I.

In 1950 the Santa Clara Valley of California was perhaps the richest fruit-growing area in the world. In the springtime, the redolence of fruit blossoms was intoxicating, and a sea of color stretched fourteen miles from Palo Alto to San Jose at the foot of San Francisco Bay. You could drive for miles through lanes of shade. Today that valley is Silicon Valley—paved over—and San Jose, once a sleepy agricultural city of 50,000, has metamorphosed into the second largest metropolis in the state. The fruit trees, save for a few ceremonial survivors, are gone. That transition is commonly called "progress." It has brought jobs, monetary wealth, a real estate boom; it has also brought air, water, soil, and noise pollution—and congestion so heavy that traffic densities and casualties are reported daily on the air, as if the area were a war zone.

Any inhabitant of the developed world since World War II could tell a similar story of "then and now." Radical change has been the rhythm of modern life and the argument still rages as to whether that change has been for good or for ill. Few would question that modern medicine, electric lights, central heating, refrigeration, and zippers are improvements; few would want to return to the outdoor privy or the foot-powered dentist's drill; and most seem to be voting—at least with their pocketbooks—for computers. Nevertheless, ever since the industrial revolution (and even before), subversive voices have been heard questioning whether this "progress" has been worth it; and in the last few decades these malcontents—led by so-called environmentalists—have begun to question whether the machinery of progress is compatible with human survival itself.

But this question is not new. "Environmentalism" is a new word, but the worry it organizes has been alive in the West ever since the introduction of machinery—especially in the consciences of writers and poets. Forster, in *Howards End,* wrote a chapter of that worry for the Edwardian period. Appearing in 1910, that novel in its rhythms captures brilliantly the movements of an age of radical change, an age in which an aggressive capitalism was making an impact on everything—cities, culture, taste, morals, classes, but especially on "nature," or what would now be called the environment or the ecosystem. Of this age, Orwell wrote, "There never was, I suppose, in the history of the world a time when the sheer vulgar fatness of wealth, without any kind of aristocratic elegance to redeem it, was so obtrusive as in those years before 1914" (357). Forster acknowledges the poor in the character of Leonard Bast, but the novel never leaves the middle class, and its main people are rich—and the uses of riches is one of its central concerns. But rivaling that concern, and inseparable from it, is the sense that the age doesn't know where it is going, that it is speculating with a priceless inheritance and flirting with catastrophe. In 1908, two years before the novel appeared, Forster saw the new machines as bringing not progress but pestilence:

> It's coming quickly, and if I live to be old I shall see the sky as pestilential as the roads. It really *is* a new civilisation. I have been born at the end of the age of peace and can't expect to feel anything but despair. Science, instead of freeing man . . . is enslaving him to machines. Nationality will go, but the brotherhood of man will not come. . . . God what a prospect! The little houses that I am used to will be swept away, the fields will reek of petrol, and the airships will shatter the stars.[1]

This is a lament, as well, for the death, or dying, of the Liberal dream of progress—for the idea that "civilisation" was on a steady trajectory of moral, as well as material, improvement. But neither is that lament, in its emotional content, anything new. The underground sense that the present is somehow a falling-off from a greener, happier past is probably as old as the Western imagination; and the notion that an agricultural golden age once actually existed has been a persistent dream (Williams 35-45). Eden, wherever it is, is in the past—unless in some future perfect—and this elegiac sense is still probably lurking in those romantic arguments pairing nature against industry, poetry against trade. As Raymond Williams says: "We have heard this sad song for many centuries now: a seductive song, turning protest into retrospect, until we die of time" (83).

Forster is in that company, but he had plenty of precursors. Blake, George Eliot, Meredith—to name but three from the last century--all saw the machine in the garden and shuddered; and Hardy in *The Woodlanders*—like Forster in *The Abinger Pageant* (1934) and *England's Pleasant Land* (1940)—wept for the trees, lamenting, as Mary Jacobus says, "a lost mythology as well as the rape of the woods by rootless predators from the modern world" (116). The word "smog" didn't appear in the language until 1905,[2] but its reality had been passionately noted well before. Dickens in *Our Mutual Friend* (1865), after conducting us from the unpolluted upstream Thames down into London (where the river becomes a sewer), takes us into a smog-bound heart of darkness, a city whose atmosphere is "a gigantic catarrh": "Even in the surrounding country it was a foggy day, but there the fog was grey, whereas in London it was, at about the boundary line, dark yellow, and a little within it brown, and then browner, and then browner, until at the heart of the City . . . Saint Mary Axe—it was rusty black" (438). And Ruskin, notably in *Fors Clavigera* (1871-74) and its strange offspring, *The Storm-Cloud of the Nineteenth Century* (1884), raged against the "sulphurous chimney-pot vomit" and the "foul chemical exhalations" (34:38) that were poisoning air and water; and saw in the heavens of 1871 and 1884 what he came to call a dark and dirty "plague-cloud," with its "plague-wind," that seemed to him an omen of the age's disease, its soul-and-body pollution: "It looks partly as if it were made of poisonous smoke; very possibly it may be: there are at least two hundred furnace chimneys in a square of two miles on every side of me. But mere smoke would not blow to and fro in that wild way. It looks more to me as if it were made of dead men's souls" (34:33).[3]

Forster, a "fag-end" Victorian, picks up the elegiac refrain and adds his own witness. If Ruskin can remember a youth when "the beauty and blessing of nature, all summer long" fitted his spirit like a long embrace, he lived to feel that "harmony" broken—and "broken the world round" (34:78). Forster, less apocalyptic than Ruskin and less melodramatic than Dickens (to name but two differences), registered the same sense of loss, not only in *Howards End* but in the real world that followed it, and as late as 1960: "I am glad to have known our countryside before its roads were too dangerous to walk on and its rivers too dirty to bathe in, before its butterflies and wild flowers were decimated by arsenical spray, before Shakespeare's Avon frothed with detergents and the fish floated belly-up in the Cam" ("Aspect" 1230).

He is "glad" to have known an England before those changes: he counts his blessings and frames his ironic protest in personal, and largely aesthetic, terms—in the seeming expectation that the mere expression of his sensibility, with no raising of the voice, might make a difference. Ian Watt has called such faith an expression of the "Canute syndrome," the delusion, common to liberals, that mere words might hold the waves back.[4] While it is indeed delusion to suppose that recalling the smell of fruit blossoms will unpave Silicon Valley, there is nevertheless a certain "redress"—to borrow Seamus Heaney's meaning (15-16)[5]—in making a poetic statement of a proper course, just as stenciled bird shapes on a glass window can "change the direction of the real birds' flight" (15). Words do not work of themselves, and a lot of cries are cries in the wilderness, but without them the slippery slope is a lonely and uncelebrated place. Forster honored Ruskin even in his "weakening whining" mood (*Commonplace* 167) and though a lot of Forster's protest was laced with self-pity and class interest, it was nevertheless an acutely sensitive register of the connections between personal and public loss.

"Only connect . . . ," the epigraph of *Howards End,* is, as Alistair M. Duckworth wisely observes, "an optative, not an imperative," a wish that the radical disconnections of that Edwardian world could be joined, and a pointer—indicated by the ellipsis—that the novel's project is open-ended and not one proposing solutions to the problems it raises (8). The point is well taken, but it would be wrong to suppose that Forster is neutral, or even-handed, in the way he treats his characters and themes. In surveying his world between 1918 and 1939, he wrote: "there is a huge economic movement which has been taking the whole world . . . from agriculture towards industrialism . . . personally I hate it" (*Two Cheers* 281); and in many ways *Howards End,* especially in its depiction of the male Wilcoxes, is a register of that hate—though occasionally Forster tucks in some modifying passages of fairmindedness. But "Only connect . . . " is not only an optative, it is a declarative (without the form), a formula for survival, another way of saying, after Auden, that "we must love one another or die" (*Two Cheers* 275). Forster, along with Lawrence, is the last great English novelist to attempt to get a whole society in his scope; and part of their common vision was a sense that aesthetic values—industrial ugliness itself—could be a clue to what was wrong. "The real tragedy of England," writes Lawrence, "is the tragedy of ugliness. The country is so lovely: the man-made England is so vile" (137). Forster agrees, but he does not agree easily, for he saw that beauty (which depends on space⁶) may be only another word for special privilege.

At the end of World War II, the Ministry of Town and Country Planning "commandeeded" some 160 acres of land around "Rooksnest," Forster's childhood home in Hertfordshire (and the original of Howards End)—land he thought "the loveliest in England"—to build a "satellite town" for 60,000 people. It was like a doom: the local farmers were dislodged, "the ancient and delicate scenery" obliterated. In facing this issue, Forster's sense of social justice was put to a severe test:

> "Well," says the voice of planning and progress, "why this senti-mentality? People must have houses." They must, and I think of working-class friends in north London who have to bring up four children in two rooms, and many are even worse off than that. But I cannot equate the problem. It is a collision of loyalties. I cannot free myself from the conviction that something irreplaceable has been destroyed, and that a little piece of England has died as surely as if a bomb had hit it. I wonder what compensation there is in the world of the spirit for the destruction of the life here, the life of tradition. (*Two Cheers* 70)⁷

He cannot "equate" the problem, but he admits it, and in so doing he gives expression to a conflict that is raging worldwide today: the conflict between trees and jobs, farmland and housing, rivers and mills, wildlife and oil, to name but a few formulaic simplifications. That these often come down to conflicts between the haves and the have-nots goes without saying, but they are not neat conflicts, with the bad guys on one side and nature on the other. To be unable to "equate" the problem is no disgrace—and cannot be reduced merely to an issue of class privilege, though that is involved. It is a case beyond individual morality and calls for political solutions—however crude they may be. It is a case in which "connection"—the need to see the problem "clearly" as well as "whole"—is required. This formula for connection is put to a fictional test in *Howards End.*

That novel was, among other things, a confrontation with what C. F. G. Masterman had called, in 1909, the "Condition of England" question.⁸ In his book of that title and his earlier *In Peril of Change* (1905), Masterman had painted a devastating picture of London as nature's antithesis, the heart of a spirit-dead society, "a civilisation becoming ever more divorced from Nature and the ancient sanities" (*Peril* xii). The close of *Howards End* is, on the surface, a pastoral idyll, in which the two loving sisters, Margaret and Helen, are shown exulting over Helen's new baby and a bumper crop of hay and the house they have finally made their own. It is a scene of Virgilian beauty and contentment. But as they gaze out southward across the meadow—across "eight or nine meadows"—something spoils the view. "All the same," says Helen, "London's creeping," noting in the distance an ominous "red rust"—the same that Dickens, seeing it up close, knew was really black. "'You see that in Surrey and even in Hampshire now,' she continued. 'I can see it from the Purbeck Downs. And London is only part of something else, I'm afraid. Life's going to be melted down, all over the world'" (339). This pattern runs throughout the novel—antipastoral invading pastoral—and, as Barbara Rosecrance observes, a "vision of cosmic evil" works against any final unity in the novel: "the rhetoric affirms connection, but the undercurrent describes collapse" (146, 116). Howards End, that semirural citadel of sensitivity and privilege, is under siege by forces against which its strength is no more than that of a flower.[9] Margaret's hope that the century-old "craze for motion" will be followed "by a civilization that won't be a movement because it will rest on the earth" (339) seems, by the testimony of her own narrative, wishful thinking; and when she says, "I feel that our house is the future as well as the past" (339)—a house symbolizing "England"—one weeps for the confusions of liberalism.

Nevertheless, Forster's picture of the creeping evil is powerful and prophetic: "The city seemed Satanic, the narrower streets oppressing like the galleries of a mine. No harm was done by the fog to trade, for it lay high, and the lighted windows of the shops were thronged with customers. It was rather a darkening of the spirit which fell back upon itself, to find a more grievous darkness within" (84).[10] The fog, now actually smog, is symbolic. Mrs. Wilcox, who presently ascends the lift of her flat at Wickham Place, is described as "going up heavenwards, like a specimen in a bottle"—"And into what a heaven—a vault as of hell, sooty black, from which soots descended" (85). Heaven and hell, even to the agnostic Forster, are still usable images, but there is never any doubt that he is speaking of man-made realities, or that the other name for those soots, as Dickens also saw (149-50), was money.[11] *Pecunia non olet*[12] does not apply in *Howards End,* for the rich in their "throbbing stinking" motorcars (23), "oozing grease on the gravel" (317) cannot, any more than the poor, escape the omnipresent "odours from the abyss" (117). "If there is a villain to be found in *Howards End,*" writes Merritt Ellen Cole, "it is no single human being but rather the motorcar" (232)[13]—the machine that sent clouds of dust over the village, which "percolated through the open windows," "whitened the roses and gooseberries of the wayside gardens," and in due course "entered the lungs of the villagers" (18). (Charles Wilcox confronted this minor ecological disaster by invoking progress: "I wonder when they'll learn wisdom and tar the roads" [18-19].) All classes—as in Carlyle's democracy of typhus[14]—are part of the same organism and breathe the same polluted air: "the earth is explicable—from her we came, and we must return to her. But who can explain Westminster Bridge Road or Liverpool Street in the morning—the city inhaling; or the same thoroughfares in the evening—the city exhaling her exhausted air?" (108). The city, though man-made, is a living mystery—becoming a "muddle" in 1937[15]—but it is always a presence greater than the sum of its parts, a force independent of human agency and moving to its own sinister rhythms. In a passage like the following, the remorseless *pace,* as well as quality, of change is brilliantly registered, bringing to mind Helen's goblins "walking quietly over the universe from end to end" spreading "panic and emptiness" (34) and, needless to say, pollution:

> This famous building had arisen, that was doomed. Today Whitehall had been transformed: it would be the turn of Regent Street tomorrow. And month by month the roads smelt more strongly of petrol, and were more difficult to cross, and human beings heard each other speak with greater difficulty, breathed less of the air, and saw less of the sky. Nature withdrew: the leaves were falling by mid-summer; the sun shone through dirt with an admired obscurity.[16]

"Month by month!"—not year by year or decade by decade, but *month by month!* The hydrocarbons are coming, bringing noise as well as chemical pollution. (And global warming is on its way.) The same phrasing reappears two pages later as Forster adds the "architecture of hurry" and the "language of hurry" to the swift-moving stream: "Month by month things were stepping livelier, but to what goal? The population still rose, but what was the quality of men born?" (109) The phrasing echoes that of Ruskin as he spoke of the "fragments" that still exist from an organic past: "month by month darkness gains upon the day" (34:78).

II.

But it is not just the speed of these changes, it is also their *size* that worries Forster; and the conflict of bigness versus littleness is one of the critical issues of value negotiated in the novel—and outside it.[17] Forster is prescient in seeing that the quality, as well as quantity, of things changes with their scale; and in trying to connect Henry Wilcox and Margaret in marriage, he effects a collision—and an argument—between the "big machinery" and the "little." The Schlegels, however much they live off the bounty of the great world, fear and dislike it and refuse to pretend it is good. The dialectic of the novel, as I have argued elsewhere (*Cave* 236), can be subsumed in a statement of Alfred North Whitehead's: "Sensitiveness without impulse spells decadence; impulse without sensitiveness spells brutality" (287); and there is no doubt that Henry, with his energetic commitments to big business, big money, big empire, big city, belongs in the latter court. This bigness is another word for brutality—to nature as to people—and is inseparable from the "red rust."[18] Margaret after her marriage—even in the courtship stage—senses that "the big machinery, as opposed to the little, had been set in motion" (166). The big machinery cannot handle emotion or the personal; it cannot say "I." Margaret, by insisting on it, throws a wrench in the works; and Forster is brilliant in showing how the big machinery that Henry runs, his financial empire, has also mechanized his soul. Margaret, though embarrassed by Henry's cold lovemaking and his inept reaching "for possessions that money cannot buy" (165), plays along at first and tries to "connect" with bigness. She argues:

> "If Wilcoxes hadn't worked and died in England for thousands of years, you and I couldn't sit here without having our throats cut. There would be no trains, no ships to carry us literary people about in, no fields even. Just savagery. No—perhaps not even that. Without their spirit, life might never have moved out of protoplasm." (175)

Helen's reply—with, I think, Forster's backing—is "'Rubbish!'" And this riposte is immediately followed by one of the most passionate descriptive passages in the novel, one celebrating a natural and unspoiled England that evokes a vision of "the whole island at once, lying"—after the words of John of Gaunt in *Richard II*—"as a jewel in a silver sea":

> There was a long silence, during which the tide returned into Poole Harbour. "One would lose something," murmured Helen, apparently to herself. The water crept over the mud-flats towards the gorse and the blackened heather. Branksea Island lost its immense foreshores, and became a sombre episode of trees. Frome was forced inwards towards Dorchester, Stour against Wimborne, Avon towards Salisbury, and over the immense displacement the sun presided, leading it to triumph ere he sank to rest. England was alive, throbbing through all her estuaries, crying for joy through the mouths of all her gulls, and the north wind, with contrary motion, blew stronger against her rising seas. (175-76)

Here, plain—despite the objections of F. R. Leavis and I. A. Richards[19]— is Forster's patriotism and religion. This is the kind of bigness that moves him—the great natural sweeps that convey an idea of "space" on the way to infinity, something that human beings have left alone. "The moment nature is 'reserved' her spirit has departed for me," he writes; "she is an open-air annex of the school, and only the semi-educated will be deceived by her" (*Two Cheers* 369). And if the "semi-educated" are also the poor? There is snobbery here, but Forster's religion cannot exist without the sanctuary of unpeopled or secret places, like the "dell" of *The Longest Journey* (19-20) or those pastoral fields that have been treated gently, like the ancient agricultural land around Abinger, where he lived from 1917 until 1945.[20] That there is something antisocial in craving empty space in a crowded world, Forster, as we have seen, recognizes. To love space is to wish people elsewhere—and if there is nowhere else to go? Forster cannot "equate" the problem, but it is the same problem that every "no growth" movement faces today and is inseparable from the environmental problem of a world filling up with people. His testimony, for all its bias, is worth listening to. "The sort of poetry I seek," he writes, "resides in objects Man *can't* touch—like England's grass network of lanes a hundred years ago, but to-day he can destroy them. The sea is more intractable, but it too passes under human sway" (*Two Cheers* 369). He finds consolation in nature's "unmating things"—in those objects "with which we are not naturally in contact, such as the rocks and the sea" ("Notes" 767); and in 1960 he wrote, "There is no forest or fell to escape to today, no cave in which to curl up, no deserted valley for those who wish neither to reform nor corrupt society but to be left alone" (Gardner 477). These are late-life statements, but Forster makes the point again and again: "For some of us who are non-Christian, there still remains the comfort of the non-human, the relief, when we look up at the stars, of realizing that they are uninhabitable" (*Two Cheers* 276). These may seem strange preferences for a humanist, but they are ambiguities at the heart of Forster's religion, his need for something inviolate, even at the expense of social justice, in a world being overrun. There is a nihilistic strain in Forster, and he is sympathetically drawn even to nature's violent side—to the "sense of something vaguely sinister, which would do harm if it could . . . of something which rises upon its elbow when no one is present and looks down the converging paths" (*Two Cheers* 368).[21]

In a talk I had with Forster in 1965, he told me that he had lost the "reverential" view of nature he had held as a youth and had expressed in *The Longest Journey,* that one could no longer look to the hills for help when one knew they might be bulldozed for housing tracts tomorrow. This impermanence he associated with his own impermanence, but he most lamented the loss to the earth: "The death of our countryside [which will *never* be renewed] upsets me more than the death of a man or a generation of men which [can] be replaced in much the same form" (*Commonplace* 244). Like Wordsworth, he came to learn that nature *could* betray the heart that loved her but, even worse, man could betray nature. Once the open spaces are turned into real estate, they lose their sacredness, for—as E. F. Schumacher has acutely said—"there can be nothing sacred in something that has a price" (43). Estuaries and mud flats may once have seemed safe from the developers and bulldozers, but today we know that is not so, and even back in 1910, Henry Wilcox was showing the way. To him the reaches of the Thames held no "mysteries": "He had helped to shorten its long tidal trough by taking shares in the lock at Teddington, and if he and other capitalists thought good, some day it could be shortened again" (131).[22]

Henry Wilcox would cite such projects as evidence that "the tendency of civilization has on the whole been upward," but Helen sees just the opposite: "You grab the dollars. God does the rest" (192)—words that, no doubt unwittingly, call up Adam Smith's notion of the God-like "invisible hand" of the market. Henry, missing the point, was disgusted to hear the girl "talk about God in that neurotic modern way" (192). He, after all, had the backing of such authorities as Nassau Senior, who said in 1825 that "the pursuit of wealth . . . is, to the mass of mankind, the great source of moral improvement" (quoted in Schumacher 39).

Thus do the energies of the "big money" eat up the land and block the view. The "phantom of bigness" that haunts Margaret in London, the manmade bigness that wipes out the "sense of space" and ends in "one dirtiness" (204), drives her to the country in search of peace and sanity, as one escaping claustrophobia:

> Penned in by the desolate weather, she recaptured the sense of space which the motor had tried to rob from her. She remembered again that ten square miles are not ten times as wonderful as one square mile, that a thousand square miles are not practically the same as heaven. The phantom of bigness, which London encourages, was laid for ever when she paced from the hall at Howards End to its kitchen and heard the rains run this way and that where the watershed of the roof divided them. (201)

The motor had "tried" to rob her—thus does Forster personalize the threat of the machine, while at the same time holding out a hope that the Schlegels and their culture might, after all, prevail. But the "undercurrent" of the book suggests that this is a wild hope, that only in fantasy will the meek inherit the earth. Nevertheless, Forster again and again proclaims this wild hope, whistling to keep up his courage ("the strong are so stupid" [*Two Cheers* 80]), and delivers fictional comeuppance to the big ones, the public school redbloods who had bullied him at school and went out to rule the empire and bully the natives.[23]

The phrasing of the above passage echoes an earlier one in which the Schlegel father rebukes his visiting German relatives for their unimaginative love of bigness and power and money. Their presence is an ominous foreshadowing of World War I, in which the "big machinery" got its first great show of strength in the century. "'Do you imply that we Germans are stupid, Uncle Ernst?'" "'To my mind,'" he replies (and he is a transplanted German himself), "'you use the intellect, but you no longer care about it. That I call stupidity'" (29). He delivers a passionate speech in which he laments that gone are the philosophers and poets and musicians of the "'little courts'" of the last century, of Esterhaz and Weimar, along with the creative impulse that made them—all sacrificed on the altar of big empire and big money and the dangerous notion that the only things of value are things one can *use*—money first of all, imagination not at all. Over their protest, Uncle Ernst rubs it in:

> "No—your pan-Germanism is no more imaginative than is our Imperialism over here. It is the vice of a vulgar mind to be thrilled by bigness, to think that a thousand square miles are a thousand times more wonderful than one square mile, and that a million square miles are almost the same as heaven. That is not imagination. No, it kills it." (29-30)

Had Forster lived long enough to read E. F. Schumacher's *Small is Beautiful* (1973), he would have known some wonderful support for these, and other, views. Schumacher, like the father Schlegel, was a transplanted German who found a spiritual, and economic, haven in his adopted country. He served for twenty years as economic advisor to Britain's National Coal Board, and had a Bloomsbury friend in John Maynard Keynes, some of whose ideas are sharply invoked in the book.[24] Schumacher argues not only that smaller is better but that slower is better as well; and he indicts an economic system—moved by "greed and envy"(29)—that is wasting its natural resources, its real "wealth," at a prodigal, criminal, and utterly stupid rate, thus spending its "capital" as though it were income, a process no sane businessman would ever approve (19). A slow awakening to this self-destructive course has brought the terms "pollution, environment, ecology" into sudden prominence (16), but the system is still in radical denial. War, he argues, is the natural product of such a system, for it is obvious that the exploitation "at an ever-increasing rate" of the world's limited supply of nonrenewable fuels "is an act of violence against nature which must almost inevitably lead to violence between men" (57). In one passage he practically takes the words out of Father Schlegel's mouth:

I was brought up on the theory that in order to be prosperous a country had to be big—the bigger the better. This . . . seemed quite plausible. Look at what Churchill called the 'pumpernickel principalities'
of Germany before Bismark; and then look at the Bismarkian Reich.
. . . [But] if we make a list of the most prosperous countries in the
world, we find that most of them are very small. (59-60)

The First World War—the war that "spoilt everything," in Forster's phrase—
was the perfect expression of that hostility to organic life implicit in the
industrial juggernaut; and its energy, Schumacher argues, has intensified
down the century. "Today," he writes, "we suffer from an almost universal
idolatry of giantism"(62); and thanks to that, combined with the "sin of
greed," we have been "delivered . . . over into the power of the machine"
(34). Again and again the generalizations of *Small is Beautiful* make a perfect gloss on the central themes of *Howards End:* "Ever bigger machines,
entailing ever bigger concentrations of economic power and exerting ever
greater violence against the environment, do not represent progress: they
are a denial of wisdom" (31).

We cannot go far into Schumacher's argument, but an important part
of it is his recommendation for an "intermediate technology," for simple
machines within the means of poor nations that they could adapt to local
needs and conditions and thus, among other things, free themselves from
their crushing indebtedness to the West. The general direction of that
argument—though of course not its details—coincides at every turn with
what we might call the "economics" of *Howards End:* a favoring of smallness and simplicity against bigness and complication, and a sensitivity
to the balance of nature. "The economics of giantism and automation,"
writes Schumacher, "is a left-over of nineteenth-century conditions and
nineteenth-century thinking and it is totally incapable of solving any of
the real problems of today" (70). Indeed, that economics is itself the
problem, and he inveighs against the "large-scale mechanisation and
heavy chemicalisation" that has turned agriculture into big business,
making it "impossible to keep man in touch with living nature," and that
therefore supports "all the most dangerous modern tendencies of violence, alienation, and environmental destruction" (107).[25] Schumacher
would doubtless have seen a benign version of that alienation in the
vacationing Wilcoxes who could not even go swimming "without their
appliances" (210)—could not even use the country as a playground without mechanizing it. "The amount of real leisure a society enjoys," writes
Schumacher, "tends to be in inverse proportion to the amount of labour-
saving machinery it employs" (140); and the Wilcoxes make work even

out of their play. But not so Tom's father at novel's end, who, using intermediate hay-cutting technology, passes "again and again amid whirring
blades and sweet odours of grass, encompassing with narrowing circles
the sacred centre of the field" (335)—as the sisters, in counterpoint,
discuss their chances for happiness. That is a picture, if not of paradise,
at least of survival.

"The doctrine of *laissez-faire* will not work in the material world,"
writes Forster; ". . . On the other hand, the doctrine of *laissez-faire* is the
only one that seems to work in the realm of the spirit" (*Two Cheers* 68).
Schumacher would agree, for his "Buddhist economics," with its respect
for "simplicity and non-violence" (54), "water and trees" (56), is the spiritual antithesis of the Wilcoxian world of "telegrams and anger"—which is
only another way of saying "greed and envy." He quotes Bertrand de Jouvenal
to the point, a point that could summarize the novel's main theme: "As the
world is ruled from towns where men are cut off from any form of life other
than human, the feeling of belonging to an ecosystem is not revived" (56).

But if the city's bigness is "Satanic," it is a puny threat to the ecosystem compared with that of the atomic bomb and atomic wastes. Here is
giantism in the most ogreish form it has assumed in this century and Forster,
needless to say, opposed it. It is not certain that he actually joined the first
march to Aldermaston in the spring of 1958 (he was, after all, nearly eighty),
but he certainly supported the ban-the-bomb protest.[26] And again Schumacher spoke for a posthumous Forster in voicing outrage at a society permitting the accumulation of atomic toxins—in sites that nobody knows how
to make "safe"—and in calling it "an ethical, spiritual, and metaphysical
monstrosity" (137).

III.

But in spite of his love of nature and his sensitivity to its violation by the
industrial machine, Forster is no "environmentalist" in the modern sense.
(Indeed, the word itself is only about three decades old.) Though the "red
rust" was a social and political problem, his lament for a despoiled nature is
essentially the voicing of a personal fear and grief—the heartbreak and outrage of one who sees his private estate invaded by the barbarians—and only
incidentally a moral argument for the health and welfare of the planet. Rachael
Carson's *The Sea Around Us* (1951) or *Silent Spring* (1962) was not, I suspect, his kind of reading[27] and his readings in Eddington and Hoyle return
him quickly from the universe back into himself—to feelings of carpe diem
and personal helplessness: "nothing matters for humans but the immediate—

error starting when we deduce from it what is likely to happen next" (*Commonplace* 246).

Such feelings grew stronger with age. In a 1959 entry in his *Commonplace Book,* Forster wrote: "I sometimes pretend to myself that I am public-spirited. I am not. I am a hedonist who wants pleasant sensations. On the other hand I am not the usual type of hedonist, for I want sensations *to be had*—if not by myself, then by someone else. The show shouldn't end with my death, which becomes a minor boo-hoo" (211). And a year earlier he had written—while expressing disaffection for the characters of *Howards End* and their "non-sexual embraces"—that "Perhaps . . . I am more hedonistic than I was, and resent not being caused pleasure personally" (*Commonplace* 204). He is, to be sure, a hedonist with a conscience—if that can be allowed to one so reluctant to enter the public arena[28]—but the impulse to "eat, drink, and be merry" is strong (though Forster would doubtless prefer other words) and acted as a powerful deterrent to any impulse to engage in political action. His distaste for the modern world is largely aesthetic, a distaste for what was spoiling the view, and he was depressed largely "because the human race seems advancing to disaster via vulgarity" (*Commonplace* 206). To escape into the "non-human"—in the event that consciousness would survive after death—seemed to him attractive, "an adventure worth attempting after roads full of cars, skies full of aeroplanes, and the very heart of night throbbing with little noises that man has made" (*Commonplace* 41). An environmentalist has defined "conservation" as "humanity caring for the future" (McPhee 74), but by that measure Forster is found wanting. He can entertain nostalgia for the past and take pleasure in the present, but he expresses little hope for, or interest in, the future. When P. J. M. Scott asked him, "Do you think the human race will survive?" Forster replied (after determining that Scott would answer yes): "I can't see it myself" (197). Forster is no doomsayer (though hedonism and pessimism are easy bedfellows), but his optimism is hardly vigorous and seems to be limited to the bounds of his own life span. He says he "cannot agree with Sophocles that it were better never to have been born" (*Two Cheers* 81), but it is not a very energetic denial.

Nevertheless, just once in his fiction, Forster did confront the future—and found it decidedly unattractive. That was in his remarkable short story "The Machine Stops" (1909). This anti-Wellsian dystopia shows the "big machinery"—the biggest in all his fiction—grinding to a halt and bringing all mankind down with it. It is science fiction, but it is also a cautionary tale in which the consequences of man's alienation from nature are seriously projected. In the story, civilization has retreated underground; people everywhere in the world are living in a honeycomb of little air-conditioned hexagonal rooms, like the cells of bees, connected by what might today be called "interactive media," a kind of wired TV and telephone. But the whole establishment is the "machine," not just its parts. This is not the machine *in* the garden, for apparently gardens no longer exist (the source of food in the story is a puzzle). But the point is that the *machine* has taken over, and the people can no longer conceive of existence without it or outside it. The central conflict is between Kuno and his mother, Vashti, who is a devotee of the establishment, lectures on it (*The Book of the Machine* is her bible), and follows its gospel religiously: she loathes wasting time, bodily contact, and everything that fails to give her "ideas." Kuno rebels against this mother and the institution she represents: he honors and exercises the body, seeks direct experience, and attempts to escape through one of the "vomitories" to the upper earth—that strange, forbidden place where freedom and fresh air and an unspoiled nature still exist, "as it was in Wessex, when Aelfrid overthrew the Danes" (*Stories* 146).[29] He is dragged back by the "mending apparatus," castrated, and threatened with "homelessness" for his heresy (for being "unmechanical"). But he wins, or is proved right, after all, for the machine collapses from its own decadence. Over the years, part after part had broken down and no one living any longer understood its total workings: "Humanity, in its desire for comfort, had overreached itself. It had exploited the riches of nature too far" (138). The light dimmed, the air became foul, and one day "the entire communication-system broke down, all over the world, and the world, as they understood it, ended" (*Stories* 142). Men had disastrously become the victims of their own technology.

Schumacher uttered the same warning, and saw the "ideas of the fathers" of the nineteenth century as "visited on the third and fourth generations" in the second half of the twentieth: "To their originators, these ideas were simply the result of their intellectual processes. In the third and fourth generations, they have become the very tools and instruments through which the world is being experienced and interpreted" (83). And the Forster scholar John Colmer is, I think, quite on target in seeing the relevance of the story to conditions in our day:

> Most original . . . is Forster's insight into the possibility that man will become so uncritically dependent on the machine that he will not notice its gradual deterioration: he will accept the jarring sounds as part of the harmony, the foul air and diminished light as natural. The relevance of this to modern-day world pollution and the breakdown in basic social services is obvious. (39)

Evidence for that "relevance" is all around us, most strikingly perhaps in the parallels between the world of "The Machine Stops" and that of "cyberspace"—of computers, e-mail, and, in particular, the world of the Internet, which should include not only its aficionados but also those "unmechanical" heretics who, like Kuno, have difficulty accepting virtual space as the real thing. The World Wide Web, for example (an application of the Internet), offers to Web surfers many of the same blessings that Vashti cherished. One can possess a "home" on the Internet where, without leaving one's comfortable chair, one can gossip, exchange information, sell products, hear music, get ideas, even have virtual sex with others one need never meet in the flesh—and perhaps even taste the terror of "virtual rape"[30] (though such libidinous dangers were not in the scope of the Victorian Vashti). As Sherry Turkle says (approvingly), "Interactive and reactive, the computer offers the illusion of companionship without the demands of friendship" (Lehmann-Haupt 30), an idea Forster would find reprehensible. One can, of course, get creative "ideas" via this medium—even ideas about how to green the environment—but it is not the same, as Clifford Stoll points out, as planting a garden. "An on-line home," writes John Seabrook, "is a little hole you drill in a wall of your real home to let the world in." This is your own "hive"—as an Internet homesteader actually called it (66)—but Stoll, to name but one dissenter, finds this "home" weird and confining and ultimately dehumanizing. His book, *Silicon Snake Oil* (a kind of *Kuno's Handbook)*, sees the fellowship of the Internet as an "impoverished" community, where people do not touch, "[a]nd no birds sing." It is a "metaphorical" community, but "[h]ow sad—to dwell in a metaphor without living the experience" (43). And, like all machines, this one tends to break down. Stoll, though an expert with computers, says he spends "almost as much time figuring out what's wrong with my computer as I do actually using it" (30). And what about the day when the know-how is lost, the energy gives out, and the cyberspace dwellers—out of boredom or exasperation or poverty—just stop being interested and, like Kuno, leave the virtual world for real space, real nature, real people, and perhaps even for some real love?

To the machine-dwellers, such a question is blasphemy, a form of the "unmechanical" heresy. But it is a heresy that Forster encouraged throughout his life. When machines are in the saddle and ride mankind—to torture Emerson's metaphor—Forster had no doubt of their malignancy, and he saw the danger clearly. In a 1943 entry in the *Commonplace Book*—on the day Mussolini was deposed—Forster had some long thoughts about the machine age and its downward slide. He was convinced that "there will be no betterment in my lifetime—or that betterment like worsement is something too deep to be observed at any particular moment":

> What I do see and this morning hear is machinery used for evil. And machinery will be used increasingly. That is the knockout first intercepted by Ruskin [and others] now . . . by punies like . . . myself. I cannot rid myself of the theory that one day men will stop making & using machines, and revert with a tired sigh to the woods. (*Commonplace* 156)

But in the next sentence he calls the bluff of this "theory" and asks "who will start the stopping?" Certainly not the "Managerial Class" and certainly not people like himself, spiritual Luddites, who "fake the remoter future . . . to help [themselves] bear the present." The vision of a machineless world is, Forster recognizes, an impotent fantasy, but he nevertheless clings to that vision as something better than any ideal of "progress." It may be silly to plead (as Forster parodies himself doing): "I say chaps—don't let us develop machinery any more—let's be less organised," but it is a plea on the same level of earnestness as that of Gerard Manley Hopkins, in the lines with which Forster closes the entry:

> What would the world be, once bereft
> Of wet and wildness? Let them be left
> O let them be left, wildness and wet:
> Long live the weeds and the wilderness yet. (156)[31]

Wildness and wet! The words suggest rainforests and mangrove swamps, whereas Forster's forests were tame copses and beloved trees so domesticated that they could be itemized and named. To imagine Forster in a real wilderness, making like a Thoreau or a John Muir with blanket and backpack, is more than a little funny. Nevertheless, wildness and wet were real needs for him, however much they shared their reality with the fantasy of such a "wildwood" as the one closing *Maurice*—a place of imaginative escape and sexual bliss rather than any actual place. But he cherished the real thing as well, however little he mixed himself up with it, and in the Epilogue of *England's Pleasant Land,* his environmental pageant play, he challenged his hearers, if they would save the countryside, to do so "through good laws rightly applied, through Parliament, through the nation as a whole" (79). That's easier said than done, and perhaps Forster was just passing the buck, but his behest would have the blessing of the Audubons, the Izaac Walton League, the Nature Conservancy, and all those people and organizations fighting to have some part of nature left alone and some bit of the wilderness left intact. But he also deserves the blessing of the "new environmentalists" who have appeared since his death—especially since Earth Day in 1970—and who have concentrated less on the view and more on the technology and chemistry and politics of industry's assault on the natural environment, on such things as air pollution, water pollution, noise pollution, waste disposal, pesticide poisoning, and radiation.

Forster, were he alive, would perhaps be a bit overwhelmed by all this and opt still to "revert with a tired sigh to the woods." But he gave a damn and he left a moving witness to how much he cared. "Wildness and wet" is more than a romantic's indulgence. It is the very definition of life for space station earth if it wishes to survive.

NOTES

1. Quoted from Forster's notebook journal entry for January 27, 1908 (Duckworth 131).

2. A Dr. H. A. des Voeux in July 1905 was apparently the first to use the term. See *Oxford English Dictionary*, 2nd. ed., 1989, 798.

3. For the validity of Ruskin's observations, see Rosenberg 212-14 and Sherburne 174-76. Forster often cites Ruskin. See *Commonplace* 167.

4. These wise words were uttered at a Stanford NEH Summer Seminar in July 1980 and have never, I think, gone into print.

5. See also Vendler's splendid review "A Nobel for the North."

6. Note "the sense of space, which is the basis of all earthly beauty" (*Howards* 204).

7. For an account of the later effort to preserve this "Forster Country"—a successful effort—see *Commonplace* 349-50.

8. At least three of Masterman's books are relevant here: *The Heart of the Empire* (1901), containing essays by Masterman and others, *In Peril of Change* (1905), and *The Condition of England* (1909). Masterman had reviewed the first three of Forster's novels most favorably and had written one of the first signed reviews of *Where Angels Fear to Tread* (1905), an important event since it encouraged Forster to write at a time of acute self-doubt. They shared similar views about the empire, the poor, and the economic system, and held a similar humanist "religion," in which the dualisms of orthodoxy are secularized to a dichotomy between the "seen" and the "unseen." See *Peril* xii.

9. The Forsters took pains not to let "farming" spoil the view. They leased the meadow on the condition that no "obnoxious animals" were allowed to be there, and fenced it off from the garden with wire, so that they could see through. See "Rooksnest," *Howards End* (Abinger Edition) 347.

10. Consider J. Hillis Miller's comment: "though it is impossible to tell whether man has excluded God by building his great cities, or whether the cities have

been built because God has disappeared, in any case the two go together" (209).

11. I have written elsewhere on the money issues in Forster's work. See "Forster on Love and Money" 107-21 and "Forster on Profit and Loss" 69-78.

12. "Money doesn't stink" is a phrase erroneously attributed to Vespasian. See my essay "Forster on Love and Money" 118.

13. But at least once it would seem to be a clown, when "their motor is regarding them placidly from its garage across the lawn" (185).

14. In *Past and Present,* Carlyle cites a case showing typhus as the great leveler, doing its work with no respect for social rank. See "Gospel of Mammonism" 359-60. Benjamin R. Barber updates the observation by saying: "When it comes to acid rain or oil spills or depleted fisheries or tainted groundwater or fluoro-carbon propellants or radiation leaks or toxic wastes or sexually transmitted diseases, national frontiers are simply irrelevant" (12).

15. See "London is a Muddle" (*Two Cheers* 361-65). Here he finds "bits" of London to love and does not "loathe" it as he did when young. Those "bits"— Lower Thames Street and Magnus Martyr—are the same that T. S. Eliot celebrated in *The Waste Land.* The "yellow smoke that rubs its muzzle on the window panes" from *Prufrock* is not mentioned.

16. Whitehall House appeared in 1904 and housed the Office of Woods and Forests. Nash's "splendid creation" of Regent Street was in this period being destroyed to make way for commercial development. See Oliver Stallybrass's note to *Howards End* (Abinger) 359. The "admired obscurity" may refer to paintings by Turner and/or Whistler.

17. In a letter to Noel Annan dated February 21, 1963, Forster wrote: "I have a growing—perhaps *in*growing—respect for smallness, and you are increasingly attracted by largeness" (*Letters* 2:285).

18. London is, of course, a cleaner city today than it was in 1910. Since the "killer fogs" of the 1970s—in which some 4,000 people died—oil and electricity have generally replaced coal as a heating fuel. Worldwide, of course, smog and pollution (along with population) have increased exponentially.

19. See Gardner for an account of their objections—which strike me as ill taken (32, 38). Richards didn't like the "mysterious nervous shiver" of the passage, but I like it, and don't even mind the pathetic fallacies.

20. In 1926 Forster bought a piece of woodland near West Hackhurst, his Abinger home, and wrote a delightful essay about it. It was called "Piney Copse." See "My Wood" (*Abinger* 33-36).

21. See also *Commonplace* 271.

22. Oliver Stallybrass notes that the lock at Teddington dates from 1811 (*Howards,* Abinger 129n).

23. "The bully and his victim never quite forget their first relations" (*Journey* 41). Actually, Forster, being a day boy at Tonbridge, was not badly bullied; but the fiction shows this to be a relative matter.

24. But he disagrees when Keynes says that the time is not yet ripe for a "return to some of the most sure and certain principles of religion and traditional virtue—that avarice is a vice, that the exaction of usury is a misdemeanour, and the love of money is detestable." The time *is* ripe, Schumacher claims (28).

25. Schumacher emphasizes that to treat agriculture as "just another industry" is to fail to note the *essential* difference between industry and agriculture, "a difference as great as that between life and death." We could survive without the former, but not the latter (103-4). Schumacher would delight over R. L. Duffus's "late-setting hen who had just laid the world's finest egg in spite of not understanding the poultry business" (13).

26. These marches (more like pilgrimages), organized by the Committee for Nuclear Disarmament, have occurred every Easter since 1958. See also *Cave* 360.

27. This is a guess, since I don't have access to a checklist of Forster's library. But note how Helen changes the subject when Leonard starts to talk about E. V. Lucas's *Open Road* (118).

28. He was at times, however, active in causes. He was briefly president of the National Council for Civil Liberties, active in the PEN Club, and a defender of D. H. Lawrence and others in censorship trials.

29. The idealization of Alfred's kingdom as a "Dream of ancient time" goes back a long way. See Williams 79.

30. See Lehmann-Haupt, "The Self in Cyberspace" B4.

31. The verse is the final quatrain of "Inversnaid" (1881). Forster has taken some liberties with the punctuation. See Philip Gardner's long footnote to this passage (*Commonplace* 328).

WORKS CITED

Barber, Benjamin R. *Jihad vs. McWorld.* New York: Random House, 1995.

Carlyle, Thomas. "The Gospel of Mammonism," *Past and Present. The Works of Thomas* Carlyle. Vol. 6. New York: Collier, 1987.

Cole, Merritt Ellen. "In Search of a Mythic View: The Early Fiction of E. M. Forster." Ph.D. dissertation, 1988. Case Western Reserve University. DEV88-19870.

Colmer, John. *E. M. Forster: The Personal Voice.* London: Routledge and Kegan Paul, 1975.

Dickens, Charles. *Our Mutual Friend.* 1865. N. Y.: Modern Library, 1960.

Duckworth, Alistair M. *Howards End: E. M. Forster's House of Fiction.* New York: Twayne, 1992.

Duffus, R. L. *Nostalgia, U.S.A.* New York: Norton, 1963.

Forster, E. M. *Abinger Harvest.* 1936. London: Arnold, 1953.

———. "Aspect of a Novel." *The Bookseller.* 10 Sept. 1960: 1230.

———. *Collected Short Stories.* 1947. Harmondsworth: Penguin, 1954.

———. *Commonplace Book.* Ed. Philip Gardner. 1978. Stanford: Stanford UP, 1987.

———. *England's Pleasant Land.* London: Hogarth, 1940.

———. *Howards End.* 1910. New York: Vintage, 1959.

———. *The Longest Journey.* 1907. New York: Vintage, 1962.

———. "Notes on the Way." *Time and Tide* 15 (1934): 767.

———. "Rooksnest." *Howards End.* Abinger Edition. Ed. Oliver Stallybrass. London: Arnold, 1975.

———. *Selected Letters of E. M. Forster.* Vol. 1, 1879-1920. Eds. Mary Lago and P. N. Furbank. Cambridge, Mass.: Harvard UP, 1983.

———. *Selected Letters of E. M. Forster.* Vol. 2, 1921-1970. Eds. Mary Lago and P. N. Furbank. Cambridge, Mass.: Harvard UP, 1985.

———. *Two Cheers for Democracy.* London: Arnold, 1951.

Gardner, Phillip, ed. *E. M. Forster: The Critical Heritage.* London: Routledge, 1973.

Heaney, Seamus. *The Redress of Poetry.* New York: Farrar, Straus and Giroux, 1995.

Jacobus, Mary. "Tree and Machine: *The Woodlanders.*" Ed. Dale Kramer. *Critical Approaches to the Fiction of Thomas Hardy.* London: Macmillan, 1979, 116-34.

Lawrence, D. H. *Phoenix. The Posthumous Papers of D. H. Lawrence.* Ed. Edward D. McDonald. 1936. New York: Viking, 1968.

Lehmann-Haupt, Christopher. "The Self in Cyberspace." Review of *Life on the Screen,* by Sherry Turkle. *New York Times.* 7 December 1995, B4.

Masterman, C. F. G. *In Peril of Change.* New York: Huebsch, 1905.

McPhee, John. *Encounters with the Archdruid.* Farrar, Straus and Giroux, 1971.

Miller, J. Hillis. "The Theme of the Disappearance of God in Victorian Poetry." *Victorian Studies* 6 (1963): 207-27.

Orwell, George. "Such, Such Were the Joys." *Selected Essays.* Vol. 4. London: Secker and Warburg, 1968, 330-69.

Rosecrance, Barbara. *Forster's Narrative Vision*. Ithaca: Cornell UP, 1982.

Rosenberg, John D. *The Darkening Glass: A Portrait of Ruskin's Genius*. New York: Columbia UP, 1961.

Ruskin, John. *The Works of John Ruskin*. Ed. E. T. Cook and Alexander Wedderburn. 39 vols. London: George Allen, 1908.

Schumacher, E. F. *Small is Beautiful: Economics as if People Mattered*. New York: Harper and Row, 1973.

Scott, P. J. M. *E. M. Forster: Our Permanent Contemporary*. London: Vision, 1984.

Seabrook, John. "Home on the Net." *New Yorker*. 16 Oct. 1995, 66-76.

Sherburne, James Clark. *John Ruskin or the Ambiguities of Abundance. A Study in Social and Economic Criticism*. Cambridge, Mass.: Harvard UP, 1972.

Stoll, Clifford. *Silicon Snake Oil: Second Thoughts on the Information Highway*. New York: Doubleday, 1995.

Stone, Wilfred H. *The Cave and the Mountain: A Study of E. M. Forster*. Stanford: Stanford UP, 1966.

————. "Forster on Love and Money." *Aspects of E. M. Forster*. Ed. Oliver Stallybrass. New York: Harcourt, 1969, 107-21.

————. "Forster on Profit and Loss." *E. M. Forster: A Human Exploration*. Eds. G.K. Das and John Beers. London: Macmillan, 1979, 69-78.

Vendler, Helen. "A Nobel for the North." *New Yorker* 23 Oct. 1995, 87.

Williams, Raymond. *The Country and the City*. New York: Oxford UP, 1973.

Forster's Italian Comedies: Que[e]rying Heterosexuality Abroad

Margaret Goscilo

If in *Maurice* (1913-14) Clive Durham's sojourn in Greece marks his retreat from the hero's embrace into classical sublimation, in E. M. Forster's two Italian comedies, *Where Angels Fear to Tread* (1905) and *A Room with a View* (1908), a Mediterranean stay has the opposite effect on frigidly conventional, or inhibited, Britons. Of course, in these earlier novels, the central—indeed, the only avowed—romances are heterosexual. Therefore the "new order of experience" that John Sayre Martin regards as a corollary of travel in Forster's fiction (5) here involves ethnicity and class rather than sexual preference. Yet at the same time, in both cases Forster codes foreignness, and particularly Italianness, to include the tabooed "Otherness" of homosexuality, displacing onto nationality some of the themes that he tackles directly in *Maurice*. So both texts are "queer" in accord with Alexander Doty's use of that word to describe "the nonstraight work, positions, pleasures and readings of people who either don't share the same 'sexual orientation' as that articulated in the texts they are producing or responding to . . . or who don't define themselves as lesbian, gay, bisexual (or straight, for that matter)" (xviii). In their screen adaptations of *Where Angels Fear to Tread* (1991) and *A Room with a View* (1985), respective directors Charles

Sturridge and James Ivory preserve Forster's implicitly homoeroticized Italy, neither proleptically outing the author on the basis of his more explicit *Maurice* (unpublished until 1971) nor minimizing the queerness in/of the original narratives. In Doty's terms, such adaptation might seem problematic in perpetuating the notion of *sub*textuality and therefore, by extension, *sub*sexuality (104); yet these period pieces' representations of displaced male love actually serve the author well, by reflecting his cultural positioning as a young, closeted Edwardian author cognizant of the recent Labouchère Amendment's criminalization of "gross indecency" between men (1885)[1] but less aware of his own sexual identity.

As Paul Fussell observes in *Abroad,* it was particularly between the wars that Italy came to represent sun, life, and vitality to the English. The Mediterranean country's more specific identification with homoerotic desire, however, had appealed to and influenced European writers—including Winckelmann, Byron, Pater, Cocteau, and Mann—since the 1750s (Aldrich x-xi). Thus by setting his protagonists' quickening of body and soul in an Italian landscape as early as 1901, the year he first visited the country with his mother, Forster followed not only an autobiographical imperative but also "a clear itinerary in European gay history" (Aldrich 4) that would later merge with post–Great War iconography. Even in the earliest versions of his "Lucy novel"—later *A Room with a View*—drafted during his extended Italian sojourn with his mother, Forster already constructed the locale as a site of fulfillment: the land that, in P. N. Furbank's words, had "warmed Forster and given him a vision" found its way into his notes as "the beautiful country where they say 'yes,'" "'where things happen'" (96). Despite Forster's later deletion of this line, his Italy emerges as just such a charmed place for his protagonists in both *A Room with a View* and in the similar novel he completed before it, *Where Angels Fear to Tread.* And although homosexuality is never overtly among the "things [that] happen," Forster nonetheless tacitly affirms it alongside his conventional couples' involvements. Here too, then, as in *The Longest Journey,* Forster practices what Scott Nelson calls a "narrative inversion"—that is, a "duplicitous [inscription of] homosexuality as the subtext . . . of the Edwardian 'master narrative' of heterosexual, homosocial (and necessarily misogynist) desire" (311). Yet whereas *The Longest Journey* shares the openly gay *Maurice*'s English setting, these two traditional romances gain much of their "homotextuality" (Nelson 311) from the unabashedly androcentric Italian culture that serves for their backdrop.

Appositely enough for screen adaptation, the novelist's construction of a homoerotic rather than merely homosocial Italy owes something to three of the four discourses that Albert LaValley has distinguished as main-stays of films with covert gay appeal: aestheticism, camp, rebellion, and the evocation of the natural man (29-34, 70). Such tacitly homoerotic discourses, LaValley maintains, were "born with the emergence of gay identity in the late-nineteenth century, the same period that gave birth to film" (30). This was also, uncoincidentally, the period of Oscar Wilde's trial, a spectacularly public warning against revealing homosexuality alongside, or instead of, aestheticism and rebellion; pronounced only eight years before Forster took up his career as a writer, Wilde's 1895 sentencing to hard labor reaffirmed the wisdom of reliance on indirection and encoding for homosexual concerns in art (as well as in life). Certainly both the aestheticism—"the earliest important gay discourse" (LaValley 29)—and the rebellion that figure so prominently, even complicitously, in the growth of Forster's protagonists abroad spill over into connoted homoeroticism. Furthermore, the Tuscan setting proves most apt for what LaValley considers the gay discourse that prevailed over aestheticism and camp in the 1980s: that of the natural man (34).

In *Where Angels Fear to Tread,* the discourses of aesthetics, rebellion, and the natural man converge in the figure of Gino Carella, the young peasant from Monteriano with whom three Britons—the hero, Philip Herriton; his sister-in-law, Lilia; and their friend Caroline Abbot—all become enamored as the embodiment of Italian beauty, intensity, and spontaneity. These discourses fuse, moreover, with another pattern suggestive of homoeroticism: the remarkable correspondence between Philip's Italian experiences and those of his female counterparts. For in this first novel, as in his later, more explicit short story, "The Obelisk" (1939), where a woman's fling with one sailor echoes her husband's similar liberation with another, Forster indirectly explores attraction between men by "emphasiz[ing] the equivalence of heterosexual and homosexual expression" (Summers 283). Hence for all three—Lilia, Caroline, and Philip—Gino Carella becomes a forbidden object of desire; too Mediterranean and lower class in general, he is also too young for Lilia, too earthy for Caroline and—most subtextually—too same-sexed for Philip. While Harriet, Philip's rigid sister, remains impervious to Gino's (and all other) Italian "enchantment" (96), the others rebel against their insularity and class snobbery to attain varying degrees of intimacy with this natural man, after whom Forster initially named the narrative his "Gino novel."

Like the book, the film begins with Philip's vicarious pleasure in Lilia's trip to Italy, which he has recommended to her for a "transfiguration" through artistic and natural beauty. Philip himself gradually becomes transfigured, in Lilia's wake, through his two visits to Monteriano: stuffily censorious toward Lilia when he first arrives to rescue her from a mercenary seducer, he modulates on his second stay into the openness that Lilia and Caroline have experienced before him—not least through his attraction to the same Italian youth desired openly by the first woman and secretly by the second. Although the screenplay cuts much of the summarizing narrative and the dialogue that establish just what Italy means to Philip, the film's musical score by Rachel Portman nicely captures Forster's initial opposition between the two countries in question. Regularly paced, even constrained, during Lilia's railroad departure, the music swells expansively into longer, lusher phrases with the first cut to equally lush vistas of the Italian countryside, filmed with Leonardoesque sfumato. A piano enters with a new theme in a voice separate from the rest of the orchestra, suggesting the parallel individuation through beauty and passion lying ahead for all three British travelers.

Whereas the novel from the outset emphatically distinguishes Philip from his fellow Sawstonians through his aestheticism—including his appreciation of a field of violets and of Gino's striking face—the film minimally singles out his love of art, most notably in a medium close-up of him sitting in front of a bust in his mother's drawing room. Overall, until his second trip, the aesthetic pull to the Mediterranean becomes generalized through long shots of the numinous Tuscan countryside awaiting the women and through Lilia's later joy over having her "lovely, lovely boy." Once the Britons return for the baby, however, the cinematic Philip's concern with beauty becomes central, as he prods his sister about the landscape in words from the novel—"Don't you see any beauty in it at all?"—and insists that they spend their first evening at a performance of Donizetti's *Lucia di Lammermoor.* That Philip might prove as susceptible as his female predecessors to Gino's Italian charisma becomes additionally clear from Sturridge's mise-en-scène: the director frames the second drive between railroad station and Monteriano in exactly the same way, except for seating Philip, divested of glasses and his stuffy interviewer's notepad, where Caroline sat earlier, while Harriet takes her brother's former—stiff and judgmental—position in the carriage.

Besides indicating his artistic interests, Philip's eagerness to attend the local performance of precisely an opera also enables Forster to dovetail "the affective male bonding and utopian visions of male camaraderie" characteristic of the natural-man discourse (LaValley 34) with the aesthetics of an art consistently associated with gay sensibilities or identity. First aesthetics and nature fuse in the Monteriano audience's passionate, unruly, and spontaneous appreciation of friends and of the singers, while Forster's narratorial comments stress the virtual symbiosis of Italy's natural and cultural vitality:

"The audience accompanied [the chorus] with tappings and drummings, swaying in the melody like corn in the wind" (119); "as she sang the theatre murmured like a hive of happy bees." At this point, Philip feels that "he had been in this place always. It was his home" (120). Then, Gino and his comrades appear in a box far above Philip, in all the vigorous exuberance of youth and pleasure, welcoming him with "kind, cheerful voices . . . laughter that was never vapid, and the light caress of an arm across his back" (123). So magical is the moment that Philip's ascent into their company vies briefly with Lucia's drama on stage—a drama that, besides being one Forster himself saw in Florence with "an enraptured and very noisy audience" (Furbank, 1:104), fits neatly into the narrative as an Italian adaptation of a tale by the Anglo-Saxon Sir Walter Scott.

In Sturridge's version, spellbound expressions and body language aptly convey the crowd's vitality and Philip's growing enchantment, especially in contrast to his sister's repressiveness. Moreover, non-diegetic music replaces the opera score to emphasize the dramatic off-stage moment, and it reaches an expansive crescendo—recapitulating the opening credits' shift from England to Italy—as Philip and Gino embrace.

But even before Gino appears here, the way Forster—and after him, Sturridge—constructs the operatic scene as a crisis in Philip's emotional life accords with the weight that Wayne Koestenbaum attaches to opera as a gay venue: "You can date the moment you began to speak as a gay person, with a gay heart, from the moment you began, truly, to listen" (Queen's 42). Likewise, the congruence between Philip's subsequent lament to Caroline, "'I don't die—I don't fall in love'" (151) and the moral lesson that Koestenbaum finds inherent in opera testifies to the consistency of this art's discursive function in gay texts: "Opera has the power to warn you that you have wasted your life. You haven't acted on your desires. You've suffered a stunted, vicarious existence. You've silenced your passions" (Queen's 44).

Interestingly, Sturridge omits Forster's continuation of this vocal symbolism in an intervening scene with Caroline, when she comes upon Gino in his own home, "singing fearlessly from his expanded lungs, like a professional. Herein he differed from Englishmen, who always have a little feeling against music, and sing only from the throat, apologetically. . . . [Caroline's own] throat was dry when he turned away" (127). For this upward displacement of sexual liberation and appeal, Sturridge substitutes a more visual version of "the natural man as gay icon" (LaValley 34) by displaying Gino's nude torso. At the same time, however, the motif of swelling chords and organs colluding with body taboos still finds its way into the film. For the diva who sings Lucia di Lammermoor, only mentioned in the novel as a "hot lady" on the train from Florence before she appears onstage in Monteriano (120), becomes in Sturridge's adaptation the anonymous fat woman at Monteriano station whose Italian extroversion (and girth?) repel the fastidious Harriet. Such a transposition would make sense to Koestenbaum, who notes: "Singers are supposedly fat. The body must be huge. . . . There are cultural and emotional affinities between large women and gay men; both are entrusted with understanding the body as shame and as difference, the body all mouth . . . the body a clue that a mistake has been made" (*Queen's* 101).

Of course, the diva is already crucial in Forster's original text as part of another, recurrent homoerotic dynamic: a woman's mediation of desire between men. It is, after all, this coloratura who brings together the two youths by throwing out to the audience a bouquet—with love note—tossed to her from a box. When Philip catches both and seeks to return them to the prima donna's "innamorato," he

> deserted his ladies and plunged towards the box. A young man was flung stomach down over the balustrade. Philip handed him up the bouquet and the note. Then his own hands were seized affection-ately. It all seemed quite natural. . . .
> "No! no!" cried the young man. "You don't escape me now."
> For Philip was trying feebly to disengage his hands. (122)

The exhilaration on both sides suggests that, thanks to the singer's presence, the bouquet has reached its proper destination—complete with overtones of Romeo's balcony scene. In fact, the diva's liaison function here is the cen-tral instance of a repeated pattern of female mediation between Philip and Gino, true to the displacement of same-sex desire prevalent—as Sedgwick first noted—in homosocial yet homophobic culture (3, 16). Just as at the opera the diva serves to reunite the youths, so earlier Lilia introduces them and later Caroline reconciles them after the death of the baby. For that mat-ter, on a grander scale, Italy itself seems the femininized source of such camaraderie, striking Philip as a land that "really purifies and ennobles all who visit *her. She* is the school as well as the playground of the world" (8; emphasis added).

While Lilia's pivotal role between Philip and Gino is clear enough from the story's structure, Sturridge concretizes his source's homoerotic nuances through his framing. In Lilia's introduction of Gino to her dis-approving brother-in-law, Forster merely mentions an awkward hand-shake and "murmurs of approval from the stairs" (29). Sturridge, however, frames the scene with Lilia standing between and slightly be-hind the two youths as they shake hands, and a voice simultaneously calling out, "Siete proprio la bella copia [You are truly a lovely couple]!" Immediately thereafter, it is Gino's abashed face that we see over Philip's shoulder, Lilia relegated briefly offscreen. By improvising such a "queer moment," such a seeming misalignment between the compliment "obviously" intended for Gino and Lilia and the two figures most coupled by the mise-en-scène, Sturridge follows Forster's lead in conflating Italian expression with intimations of sexual Otherness.

Caroline's intercession is, however, the most weighted, since she not only encourages Philip's relationship with Gino throughout (as she encouraged Lilia's) but also binds them lastingly through an ad hoc sacrament. At her instructions, the grief-stricken Gino moves from beating Philip to sharing the dead baby's milk with him in a gesture of loving forgiveness. While her comfort of Gino has more erotic undercurrents in the novel than in the film—despite Philip's insistence on seeing her as *untouchably* transcendent—in both cases she is a conduit for considerable intimacy between the two men. First, she encourages Gino to transfer his tenderness from the dead baby to Philip. Then, although she seals their bond with the milk inspiration, she herself does not imbibe any of the fluid they share, in what suggests itself as a variation on both blood brotherhood and seminal exchange. She is, instead, a wise spiritual mother who has subdued two fighting brothers, even a priestess, whose triangulated function becomes all the more emphatic when the film shows her taking the youths seated on either side of her by the hand. Granted, both Gino and Philip respect her as a superior woman, and in the novel Gino even endorses her as a worthy fiancée for Philip, but this shared admiration serves rather to cement the male closeness than to make her anyone's heterosexual partner. In her humble service to the relationship between "brothers" who plan a reunion while she means never to see Italy or Gino again, Caroline echoes the function of the second wife whom Gino courts only for his son's sake.

Caroline's surrogacy and recessiveness in the milk scene seem all the more pronounced in the context of that other coding, found at both the erotic and the homophobic ends of "the homosocial continuum" (Sedgwick 1-2), on which Forster relies here: men in the physicality of struggle. Gino and Philip's brutal fight minutes before Caroline's civilizing advent is a high point of passionate release in the book—in some ways, the only climax of all the unrealized or unacknowledged feelings between Gino and his two English friends. From first to last, Forster's language in describing the encounter is sexually connotative. Philip confesses his part in the baby's death with the words, "'You are to do what

you like with me, Gino. Your son is dead, Gino'" (172). Once Gino obeys
by grasping Philip's broken arm, "the Englishman" calls him a "'brute'"
(168) and strikes him down, only to "raise him up, and [prop] his body
against his own. He passed his arm around him. Again he was filled
with pity and tenderness. He awaited the revival without fear, sure that
both of them were safe at last" (169). In light of the narrative's connotations
for opera and singing, it is significant that pain to his throat and windpipe in
particular makes Philip lose consciousness. When he comes to, he resists
Gino's effort to help him gently because his "body had suffered too much
from Gino. It could not bear to be touched by him" (172).

The fight is all the more suggestive because it is embedded in a frame
of reference that suggests Italian fusion of sex and violence, or the substitution of the one intensity for the other. Philip himself first voices this primal
duality when he tells his mother about Caroline's interference, "'The man
who wrote [this letter] will marry her, or murder her, or do for her somehow'" (92). He seems to speak from his wisdom of Gino's earlier "assault"
on him, in which the bridegroom pushed Philip onto a bed (and in the film,
playfully yet painfully slapped him on the leg). Shortly afterward, Harriet
picks up the connection when she refers to Gino as "'a man [who's] murdered
a woman [Lilia]'" and then crossly tells Philip, "'If you don't look out he'll
murder you'" (98). The motif recurs when Philip reminds Caroline that "'Italians are essentially dramatic; they look on death and love as spectacles'" (110).

In addition to keeping most of this dialogue in the screenplay, Sturridge
uses a few niceties of mise-en-scène to accentuate the sexual undercurrents
in Gino's assault on Philip. Earlier in the film, an erotic scene of Lilia and
Gino on their bed seems unnecessary for reaffirming their attraction but
instrumental in echoing Gino's pseudo-aggressive push of Philip onto the
bed. This playful contact obviously prefigures the serious encounter at the
end, in which Sturridge positions Philip in the frame exactly where Lilia
stood in her quarrel with Gino about her rights within their marriage.

While playing up ambiguous bodily contact between Gino and Philip,
the adaptation opens up even more queer space in the narrative by minimizing the original insistence on Philip's romantic involvement with Caroline.
In the interests of the "master narrative's" orientation, Forster himself prepares for a heterosexual resolution by suggesting that Philip and Caroline's
mutual appreciation of Gino can draw them together into couplehood. But
long before Caroline's last-minute avowal of her love for Gino thwarts
Philip's hopes, such a resolution seems contrived. For the narrator's repeated
documentation of Philip's attraction to her lacks conviction, despite out-
right declarations like "it was an increasing pleasure to him to be near her,

and her charm was at its strongest today" (148) or "By this time he loved her very much" (176). Part of the credibility problem is Philip's continuing idealization of Caroline as a "goddess" (172), a muse or teacher rather than a flesh-and-blood woman. As Summers observes, Philip's perception of her as the Virgin Mary with child and donor—in her intimate moment of bathing the baby with Gino—is "cruelly appropriate" (42) given his "weak intellectual response" to her (48), certainly feeble compared to the intensity of his attraction to Gino.

In Sturridge's version, cinematic inaccessibility to Philip's consciousness erases both the growing love for Caroline and his image of her as a Madonna—in other words, both his explicitly heterosexual desire and its lukewarm, reverential nature. Granted, the screenplay also loses some of the novel's most homoerotically suggestive lines this way, including Philip's early assessment of Gino—"And Philip had seen that face before in Italy a hundred times—seen it and loved it, for it was not merely beautiful" (31), and his later realization that he is "bound by ties of almost alarming intimacy" to Gino and has "not a secret corner left" (174-75). But crucially, the film assigns Philip no lingering glances nor new speeches as substitute testimonials to his incipient heterosexual interest, even as it maintains or intensifies signs of his attachment to Gino. The most we get, in fact, is his exclamation to Caroline, in the novel's exact words, "'You are wonderful!'" (151)—a minimal concession, after all, given that her reciprocal remark, "'You are so splendid, Mr. Herriton, that I can't bear to see you wasted'" (151), proves entirely disinterested by narrative's end.

Moreover, Sturridge's insertion of a scene where Gino plays *pallone,* only mentioned in the novel, and of another where Philip becomes assimilated into Gino's band of rollicking, embracing cohorts as they walk home after the opera, stresses the ease and frequency of male physical contact; by contrast, his female counterpart, Caroline, is enough the Edwardian lady to faint at the palpability of Gino's presence across the bedroom threshold (in the film, he is bare-chested) and to gain greatest proximity to him in bathing his baby! Similarly, after the reconciliation, it is Gino rather than Caroline who nurses the wounded Philip, intensifying their intimacy.

Consequently, Philip becomes a far more ambiguous lover on the screen than in the novel, his desire channeled only most tenuously into a normative pattern. By the time Caroline prepares to tell him the truth in their final scene together, Forster has put a heterosexual imprimatur—however contrived—onto Philip's inclinations; on screen, by contrast, it is far easier to assume that when Philip begs her to be the first to voice her passion, his own avowal relates not to her but to Gino. Only his chivalrous gesture of throwing his coat over her shoulders—and perhaps the implication that he'll wait for her to "get over" Gino—invokes the possibilities of heterosexual resolution. In the absence of blatant disappointment and withdrawal in Philip's demeanor to relay visually such lines as "He smiled bitterly at the thought of them together" (182), his echo, "I love him too!" cannot help resonating with gay implications.

By the end of the novel's narrative, the male bonding to the exclusion of women that Forster initially deplores as a patriarchal liability of Monteriano's Latin culture assumes a slightly different face because of its homoerotic resonance. While Forster's parallel of the three Britons' travels suggests that the broader, warmer horizons of the Mediterranean beckon the sexes alike, his structure gradually reveals the limits enforced by cultural gender asymmetry (especially in Italy but also in England). Obviously the narrator sympathizes with Lilia's disillusionment soon after her marriage: "Italy is such a delightful place to live in, if you happen to be a man. . . . [There] the brotherhood of man is a reality. But is accomplished at the expense of sisterhood of women" (47). Albeit missing from the film, this passage is condensed and transposed into Lilia's screen rebuke to Gino: "If you wanted an obedient Italian wife just to stay at home and eat with you and sleep with you, you should have married one." But whereas at the outset both versions of the fiction align homo- and heterosexual liberation with women's rights, soon narrative tensions remind us that, certainly, "profound and intuitable as the bonds between feminism and anti-homophobia often are . . . the two forces are not the same" (Sedgwick 20). For although Mediterranean wives—whether native or foreign—need enfranchisement despite glorious Italian expansiveness, the story concerns itself most with freeing the passive Philip from his mother's matriarchal grip—precisely through the bonding with Gino.[2] Whereas Lilia's gender subsumes both her class and national privileges under her wifehood, Philip is able to shake off his Englishness for assimilation into Gino's life. Thus toward the end of the narrative, Philip joins Gino at the Caffè Garibaldi—explicitly the symbol of the body in the novel (146), and an emphatically all-male setting intruded upon by harridan Harriet in the film—where their laughing depreciation of how "the ladies" have run the affair takes on the accents of misogyny, whether homophobic or homoerotic. Yet this gendered disloyalty to class and nation seems to be at the heart of what Forster mentioned as the "object of the book," namely, "the improvement of Philip" (Beauman 163).

Indeed, the myth of the homoerotic Mediterranean looms large enough in Forster's design to overshadow the issue of female fulfillment, even to make the backgrounding of women seem as much a function of his authorial strategies as of Southern machismo: Lilia lives just long enough to endow Gino with the male heir of paramount patriarchal importance to him; Caroline self-sacrificingly reconciles the youths; Harriet disintegrates to make room for the more benign sister, Caroline, and the true brother, Gino; and "Philippo"—as the celluloid Gino calls him before their fight—intends to return eventually to "paint Siena red for a day or two with some of the new wife's money. It was one of the arguments for marrying her" (175)! Only several years later, however, in his counterpart Italian novel, *A Room with a View,* Forster interweaves feminist and homoerotic agendas more smoothly by redistributing the gender and nationality of the figures seeking or offering Mediterranean erotic-spiritual salvation. And onscreen, the homoeroticism, although muted, is by no means lost.

In *A Room with a View,* Italy's continuing role as midwife of selfhood is simultaneously more pervasive and more attenuated. The permeation comes from a veritable chorus of characters who join the narrator in extolling Mediterranean *savoir vivre,* which includes "the eternal league of Italy with youth" (61) and Florence's proffering of the "most priceless of all possessions—her own soul" to Lucy Honeychurch, the young heroine (128). Lucy herself considers Florence "a magic city where people thought and did the most extraordinary things . . . Was there . . . in her . . . the power, perhaps, to evoke passions, good and bad, and bring them speedily to a fulfillment?" (65). Both of Lucy's suitors, George Emerson and Cecil Vyse, find themselves drawn to Italy—though in radically different ways—with George assigning the same miraculous power to the country when he suggests that Italy is just another word for "'Fate'" (148). Minor characters as varied as Mr. Beebe, Mr. Emerson, and Miss Lavish also unite in appreciating the beauties and possibilities of their host country, the last characterizing Lucy onscreen as "the young English girl transfigured [Philip's word] by Italy." And again aesthetics, nature, and rebellion conspire to bring the three protagonists into intimacy. This time, though, the figures in the romantic triangle are all Britons abroad, and Forster sets only the first third and the closure of the novel in Florence, preferring to show the impact of Italian experiences on English lives back home. Without a Florentine representative among the main characters to carry the subtextual taboos, the queer coding becomes dispersed among four males: most obviously George Emerson, whose lower-class earthiness is reminiscent of Gino's; Lucy's rejected suitor, Cecil; her brother, Freddy; and the clergyman, Mr. Beebe.

Strikingly, the same triangulation as in *Where Angels Fear to Tread*— two men and a woman—here becomes a more convincing mainstream romance even as it indicates a Forster already more committed to gay expression. As Summers observes, the book may owe its popularity "to the fact that it is Forster's fullest celebration of heterosexual love. Ironically, however, the novel is actually a product of Forster's self-conscious attempt to discover a homosexual literary tradition, and it is suffused with homoeroticism and with the ideology of the late nineteenth-century homosexual emancipation movement" (101). For one thing, Forster studded the novel with references to numerous artists and writers associated with homosexuality—ranging from A. E. Housman, John Addington Symonds, and Samuel Butler to Luca Signorelli and Michelangelo (Summers 101; Fletcher 65); for another, during the book's composition, he fell under the influence of Edward Carpenter's *The Intermediate Sex* (1906), an outspoken defense of male love (Beauman 207; Summers 101). Perhaps the two types of sexual fulfillment harmonize so well in *A Room with a View* partly because Carpenter was also a feminist whose pleas "for more equal and more open relationships between the sexes" Forster found almost as congenial as his activism for homosexuality (Beauman 209). Indeed, it is Mr. Emerson, modeled on Carpenter (Summers 101), who first suggests not just the parallels between the book's male and female quests—as in *Where Angels Fear to Tread*—but also the mutuality: "'I don't require you to fall in love with my boy, but I do think you might try and understand him. . . . Let yourself go. . . . By understanding George you may learn to understand yourself. It will be good for both of you'" (31). By having Mr. Emerson, the Carpenter figure, be the one both to elicit Lucy's love for George and to preach the importance of male comradeship to his son, Forster establishes a basic congruence between the narrative's romance and its illicit-love subtext.

Then too, he allies art and nature with *both* types of love more persistently than in the previous novel—although the Carpenterian influence ultimately privileges nature as the more crucial force in saving one's body and soul. Passion and violence likewise reappear as the two poles of Italian intensity, but this time they catalyze heterosexual courtship as well as hinting at taboo impulses. Consequently, what Barbara Rosecrance calls the "pattern of schism between explicit ideals and real energies" in Forster's fiction (50) involves fewer implications of misogyny here than in *Where Angels Fear to Tread.*

It is through the nature motif that Merchant-Ivory's adaptation most fully represents the original narrative's doubling of sexual interest. Although various other hints at homoerotic impulses disappear, the film emphasizes felicitously the three outdoor scenes of physical and spiritual connection through which Forster iconographically aligns traditional romance with homoerotic bonding. The first such scene combines nature and art as Lucy stands in the Piazza Signoria bemoaning—in terms reminiscent of Philip's—the uneventfulness of her life; moments later, "bickering" between two male Italians leaves her watching blood trickle from a dying man's lips, and George Emerson snatches her up as she sways in a faint. There is absolute concurrence on the momentousness of this incident as the narrator comments, "She had complained of dullness, and lo! one man was stabbed, and another held her in his arms!" (49), Lucy herself vaguely realizes that "she, as well as the dying man, had crossed some spiritual boundary" (50), and George exclaims, "'For something tremendous has happened; I must face it without getting muddled. It isn't exactly that a man has died'" (51). As Lucy simultaneously realizes and denies their sudden intimacy, she and George assume identical positions in a mirroring that the narrator associates with "eternal comradeship" (52). The chapter ends with George throwing Lucy's bloodied photographs into the Arno, "whose roar was suggesting some unexpected melody to her ears" (53). Of course, Florence's particular association with the Renaissance makes it the ideal setting for such an epiphany and for George and Lucy's subsequent rebirth through passion.

The second communion takes place in a field in Fiesole, when George impulsively takes Lucy in his arms again, to kiss her on the cheek. His inspiration is triply Italian, in that the beautiful setting has moved him, the Florentine driver has made love to a female companion on their journey there, and Lucy has unwittingly come upon him through the same driver's intercession. In this episode, the Florentine driver, dubbed "Phaethon" by both the narrator and Mr. Beebe, appears for the first and also the last time; henceforth, however, Forster deliberately transposes his Italian spontaneity, passion, and affinity with nature—including sun imagery—onto George, who carries them home with him. The entire narrative actually elaborates on his and Lucy's British mirroring of the two lovers, Phaethon and Persephone, "ordered to disentangle" by Mr. Eager but defended by George's father because "lovers must on no account be separated" (73).

And the third such episode finds Freddy, George, and Mr. Beebe extemporaneously skinny-dipping in a Surrey pond called the "Sacred Lake," until Lucy, her mother, and Cecil interrupt them. Forster opens the scene by having Freddy and Mr. Beebe investigate George's library, which includes Byron, *A Shropshire Lad,* and *The Way of All Flesh*—all gay-inflected references. Then, Freddy's abrupt introduction to George, "'How d'ye do? Come and have a bathe,'" strikes Mr. Beebe as something that "'will only act between men,'" (145) who, he tells Mr. Emerson, are closer to the Garden of Eden than women because "'we despise the body less than women do. But not until we are comrades shall we enter the garden'" (146). It is important, of course, that the word "comrade" reappears moments before the male communion, to echo Lucy's potential for "eternal comradeship" with George. Similarly, Forster pairs these two chapters containing initiations into intimacy through their understated titles—"Fourth Chapter," "Twelfth Chapter"—so different from all the other comical headings. Then, during the fraternal baptism itself, George appears "Michelangelesque on the flooded margin" (150), in an allusion simultaneously Italian, homoerotic, and intensified from Lucy's early connection of his face to that of a figure "on the ceiling of the Sistine Chapel, carrying a burden of acorns" (29).

Essentially the bathing scene is the locus of homosexual desire in the novel, as most critics observe. The cinematic adaptation conveys precisely the three episodes' subtextual energies, while adding some extremely felicitous touches possible on film. In the Piazza Signoria, the shift from tourism to transcendence is communicated through music and editing, heavy notes adumbrating the violence that a fast montage matches to sculpted moments of discord. Besides a Perseus brandishing Medusa's head, a snarling dog, and a contorted, self-shielding body, the montage includes a groin-level shot of Perseus's sword, which harmonizes well with Forster's tendency to link sex and violence and with the frontal nudity to follow in the Sacred Lake scene. Conceivably the shot also substitutes for the palace tower in Forster's passage, "an unattainable treasure throbbing in the tranquil sky" on which Lucy gazes "wistfully"! Although the film loses the emphasis on Neptune's fountain with its "men and satyrs who idled together on its marge" (48) and thereby a crucial parallel to the male communal bathing in the Sacred Lake back home,[3] a shot of George washing his hands in a fountain cuts to an establishing shot of the Arno as background for his talk with Lucy; later, an extreme close-up of a turbulent Arno sweeping away Lucy's bloody photographs conveys the elemental attraction between the couple (here a background tower appears) and anticipates the watery medium of the male communion. Moreover, by changing Forster's sequence of events to have Lucy play Beethoven's Opus III on the piano *before* any sightseeing— perhaps incredibly for her first morning in Florence—the filmmakers showcase the narrative's link between music and the heroine's emotions. Hence, the tumultuous *non*-diegetic music accompanying the Arno close-up emphatically corresponds to her inner upheaval and confusion.

The Fiesole outing's music likewise expresses Lucy's state of being, but in even more Forsterian terms—in an aria from an Italian opera. As Lucy leaves Miss Lavish and Miss Bartlett to look for Mr. Beebe, the first notes of "Chi il Bel Sogno di Doretta," a love song from Puccini's *La Rondine,* begin on the soundtrack, swelling as the driver leads Lucy to the field where she finds George; at his appearance the music builds, reaching a crescendo as he plants a passionate kiss not on her cheek as in the novel but on her lips. That such use of the aria is not fortuitous but congruent with Forster's own emphases becomes clear from the music's overlap with a direct allusion to the previous novel, in which opera played a crucial bonding role: as Lucy leaves them to the opening strains of the aria, Miss Lavish and Miss Bartlett gossip about a female tourist who wed an Italian ten years her junior in a church in Monteriano. At the same time, the aria anticipates a scene in both book and film where Lucy, in an intertext repeated from *Where Angels Fear to Tread,* expresses her Charlotte-like self-repression through a song from Sir Walter Scott's *Bride of Lammermoor,* "'Vacant heart and hand and eye / Easy live and quiet die'" (222). It is worth noting that Lucy's other Fiesole precedent for liberated love, namely the Italian driver's dalliance with his blonde companion, receives operatic emphasis as well, by a masked close-up of the embracing couple through opera glasses, from Lucy's point of view.

Levine observes quite validly that Puccini's "meltingly beautiful song overflows with enough romantic feeling to swamp the frequently ironic tone of the novel" (73-74); but Merchant-Ivory improvise a deflatingly comic touch before the George-Lucy kiss that also provides a visual correspondence later in George's all-male communion. While the rest of the English party splits off according to gender, a solitary George climbs a tree to proclaim what his father calls "his creed" and his "eternal Yes": he yells out, "Beauty . . . *L'espoir* . . . Love . . . Joy"—and then topples to the ground as the branches give way. When months later in England the onscreen George grasps the branches of a tree overhanging the Sacred Lake, it is difficult not to connect the two scenes as his dual intimacies with nature. The film further relates the two episodes by the mise-en-scène, working its own variation on the novel's emphasis on fluidity in Fiesole. Although Levine complains that the film "unaccountably uses yellow-flowering barley, spoiling the water image" (70), in fact the narrator's descriptions of George standing "like a swimmer who prepares" and of flowers "beat[ing] against [Lucy's] dress in blue waves" (80), although crucially linked to the Surrey swim, defy exact translation to the screen.[4] And meanwhile, by substituting waist- and chest-high foliage through which the lovers move, lower bodies immersed in nature, Merchant-Ivory prefigure first the Surrey greenery enveloping the three men on their way to bathe, and then their actual immersion in the lake.[5]

Finally, the onscreen swim is a painterly version of Forster's scene that possibly even more than its original evokes comparison with Whitman's bathers in *Song of Myself,* the twenty-eight young men "'who float on their backs, their white bellies bulg[ing] to the sun . . . not ask[ing] who seizes fast to them'" (Meyers 92-93; Summers 90). Apportioning the swim at least one-and-a-half minutes of screen time to match Forster's leisurely four-page description, Merchant-Ivory create images of expansiveness within lush nature whose only equal in the film is the field kiss in Fiesole. From discreet long shots and obscured angles, the scene—an enactment of George's words to Lucy near the Piazza Signoria, "'I shall want to live, I say'" (53)—progresses to closer frontal nudity. The sunlight plays on all the bodies to excellent effect, suggesting a Mediterranean inflection, a Pagan-Arcadian ritual, and a human climate that captures the spirit of Forster's reference elsewhere in the novel to a democratic Italy "where any one who chooses may warm himself in equality, as in the sun" (127). There is also an effect of marmoreal figures come to life, especially when George spurts water into the air like a classical statue—and rather like the Italian driver in earlier close-up at Fiesole, face turned up to the sun, sensuously inhaling it along with a perfect cigar.

The episode ends even more exuberantly than the book's chapter, because the film adds considerable amusement, even conspiratorial glee, to Lucy's reaction. For although John Colmer suggests that "Lucy can hardly be expected to be as stimulated by naked men as her creator nor as amused by the antics of the three men around the sacramental pool" (51), her screen reaction fittingly underlines the novel's frequent emphasis on irrepressible youthful rebellion against familial and social conventions. Altogether, then, Merchant-Ivory successfully cinematize the scene that represents "Forster's attempt to anglicize the Pan motif and to combine social comedy and symbolic significance" (Colmer 50).

Obviously, Cecil's exclusion from this "sacramental pool" is as telling within the homoerotic subtext as in the dominant romantic triangle. By a Forsterian twist well transferred to the screen, Cecil, the self-proclaimed "Inglese Italianato" (112) who announces his engagement to Lucy with the phrase "I promessi sposi" (100)—both expressions execrably accented in the film—becomes the narrative's repository of repressed desire, both heterosexual and same-sexed. His appreciation of both Italy and Lucy, while it does him credit, has the failing of being aesthetic and snobbish rather than vital; indeed, his references to Lucy in terms of Italian art—particularly of Leonardo's *Ginevra Benci*—consistently contrast with the natural settings in which George courts her.[6] In the film, body language, costuming, and intonation all add to the baggage of aesthetic effeteness that the novel assigns him, in time-honored coding for closeted gayness; Daniel Day-Lewis makes him a triumph of insufferability, until his dignity in relinquishing Lucy, as in the book, renders him moving.

Cecil's tendency to contain and devitalize life is rendered nicely onscreen in his National Gallery encounter with the Emersons: the camera films them statically against the backdrop of an Italian painting with figures moving across the foreground to emphasize the flatness of an Italy reduced to an indoor, aesthetic setting, so different from the depth of field and movement in the numinous Sacred Lake scene. Moreover, the one exception to Cecil's indoorness, his constrained kiss of Lucy at the lake, registers as the antithesis of George's passion not just in the Fiesole kiss (which a screen flashback recapitulates) but also in the male baptism in the same location.

Like Philip making Caroline into a Madonna, Cecil seems unfamiliar and uncomfortable with woman as a flesh-and-blood creature, as George eventually warns Lucy—in words suggesting yet another repression. In Forster's version, George says, "'He is for society and cultivated talk. He should know no one intimately, least of all a woman'" (193), which the film amends more explicitly to, "He's the sort who can't know anyone intimately, least of all a woman. He doesn't know what a woman is." Here again feminism and homoeroticism seem more aligned than opposed: Cecil cannot feel passion for, or connect with, anyone of either gender. It is no coincidence, then, that Forster has Lucy cite Cecil's refusal to play tennis with Freddy as her immediate cause for rupturing the engagement: in being "'no athlete'" (197)—or "no good for anything but books" in the film—Cecil compounds his priggishness by rejecting society's most approved venue for meaningful physical connection between men.

If Cecil is "an unreconstructed Philip, simplified and cast as a villain" and even "the author's rejected self" (Rosecrance 101), Freddy Honeychurch is a Philip-like Gino, with the "Italian" traits of spontaneity, energy, honesty, singing, and gregariousness packaged into English boyishness. In other words, he is Gino's British counterpart as a child of nature even as he structurally resembles Philip in being a "boy" who discovers a male rapport that can be couched in terms of brotherhood(-in-law). Like Caroline and Philip vis-à-vis Gino, Lucy and Freddy take gendered routes to intimacy with George, but because Freddy already resembles his comrade, he far outstrips his sister in the process. Granted, in this second Italian narrative it is almost exclusively in the Sacred Lake scene that "growing friendship between . . . two males is allowed to elbow conventional marriage into the background" (Land 65); but after assigning magic to "identity of positions" between Lucy and George (52), Forster offers as much mirroring between Freddy and George as between the fated lovers. In addition to opposing Cecil's courtship and endorsing George as "'topping'" (158), Freddy takes physical liberties with Lucy (in sibling horseplay), sprawls indecorously on the grass, studies anatomy in acceptance of the human body, cuts through social decorum to essentials (the bathe), and recognizes the kindness in Miss Bartlett (in his account of her cooking him an egg). Eventually the narrator points out rather gratuitously, "Neither George nor Freddy was truly refined" (152).

Besides relaying his energetic physicality, childlike frankness, and attachment to Lucy, Merchant-Ivory give Freddy overlong, straight hair like George's and make him, rather than Lucy, the one to scoff at Mrs. Honeychurch's snobbery about "the right sort of people" (131). On the one hand, Lucy's obvious affection for Freddy and affinity with his values stress her need for a temperamentally similar lover and husband; on the other, as Lucy's male counterpart in youthful rebellion and desires, Freddy subliminally helps to establish George's role as "an idealized love object for both male and female characters" (Rosecrance 102). After all, Lucy's comment to Cecil about bathing in the Sacred Lake until discovered by Charlotte (123) is an indirect parallel between kissing George and bathing; as such, it not only links her own two sensual experiences but also hints at possible displacement of desire in the men's swim. In the same vein, the screen Freddy's frequent presence at Lucy's side at the piano implies not only their closeness but also his parallel capacities to be "stirred up" (Mr. Beebe's screenplay term) by both music and men. Hence Freddy's pronounced role in Lucy's two courtships seems a British version of tabooed ambiguities already hinted at in the Italian driver's lie that Persephone is his sister.

The third member of the bathing party, Mr. Beebe, is the one to lose the most homoerotic resonance in transposition to the screen. But then the novel itself dampens the early drafts' original homoeroticism, only mildly noting Mr. Beebe's distance from women, his Paulinian "belief in celibacy" (219), and his withdrawal from George and Lucy once they become engaged. As Summers notes, latent homosexuality seems a likely deduction following the narrator's early remark about Beebe's view of females: "Girls like Lucy were charming to look at, but Mr. Beebe was, *from rather profound reasons,* somewhat chilly in his attitude towards the other sex, and preferred to be interested rather than enthralled" (38; emphasis added). Back in England, Freddy relays Beebe's telling comparison of himself to the repressed Cecil, "'My Vyse is an ideal bachelor . . . he's like me, better detached'" (98). And toward the close of the novel, Mr. Beebe confesses that Greece is beyond his capacities in Michelangelesque terms already associated with George's male beauty: "Italy is heroic, but Greece is god-like or devilish—I am not sure which. . . . The ceiling of the Sistine Chapel for me" (208).

Essentially, the film adaptation dispenses with the homoerotic implications in Beebe's portrait beyond the Sacred Lake scene. But the space
remains for pairing off the male characters into earthily homoerotic and
effetely repressed. Thus, for example, although Mr. Beebe's comparison of
Cecil to himself disappears, the two characters often share a pinched intonation, a constrained pitch, resembling the "ups and downs" that Lucy deplores in Cecil's voice (184)—a tightness contrary to opera's full-throated
connotations. Also, amazingly enough, Merchant-Ivory have Beebe hesitate before undressing at the lake with the same surreptitious glance that
Cecil executes there before awkwardly kissing Lucy. Alongside Beebe's
manifest if unverbalized similarity to Cecil in aestheticism and bachelor-
hood, such almost subliminal links evidently leave the pair's repression open
to both a heterosexual and a queer interpretation. Finally, to those aware of
actor Simon Callow's uncloseted persona in England, the screen Mr. Beebe
cannot help taking on a uniquely cinematic homosexual identity.

In comparing the Italies of *Where Angels Fear to Tread* and *A Room
with a View,* Rosecrance finds the former endowed with social realia, the
latter one-dimensionally rendered from Forster's surface impressions on
his first visit (103). But actually both Italies, not only on page but also on
screen, belong to an identical tradition of a homoeroticized Mediterranean,
a "green world" whose alien horizons serve so well for representing the
Otherness of male love. Granted, Forster uses characters' responses to Italy
as a gauge of their moral worth; he also hints at the insular, imperialist
attitudes of the British abroad, which eventually become his far more pal-
pable target in *A Passage to India.* For that matter, even in *A Passage to
India* Forster still uses Italy for a spiritual-sensual measure, making it Cyril
Fielding's "training-ground" and his brief stay in Venice "an aesthetic and
thus a moral norm for gauging India" (Fussell 136). But Forster's psychosexual development, or in Edwardian parlance, his "inversion," dovetailed
with mythic constructs of Northern and Southern cultures to code his Italy's
exotic Otherness for homoerotic self-discovery above all else—in these two
novels and ultimately in the screen adaptations. By honoring equally his
emphasis on the foreign place for, and on foreign *dis*placement of, desire,
Sturridge and Merchant-Ivory have translated one of Forster's enduring preoccupations and most characteristic indirections to the screen. Like the novels
before them, these films steeped in the myth of the homoerotic Mediterranean cannot be reductively labeled gay propaganda; rather, they are richly
queer texts, or as Aldrich puts it, "artistic creations with gay themes, accessible to all publics but holding special meaning for those who empathise
most directly with their characters or situations" (8).[7]

NOTES

1. The Labouchère Amendment, passed into law in 1885 and repealed only in 1967, criminalized sexual activity between men in all circumstances and set a maximum of two years' imprisonment with hard labor—the penalty that Oscar Wilde incurred in 1886 (Koestenbaum, *Double* 3). Joseph Bristow notes that although the amendment started out as an attempt to safeguard youth of both sexes from corruption, it crystallized the concept of, and attitude toward, male homosexuality for late-nineteenth- and twentieth-century England. The term "gross indecency"—especially after Wilde's trial—became most closely associated with the "love that dare[d] not speak its name"(48-49); yet Henry Labouchère's original intention had been to punish *non*consensual acts with minors under thirteen (234).

2. Of course, Mrs. Herriton is a matriarch in service to a misogynist patriarchy whose standards she supports, as witness her comment to Philip, "'[Italy] may be full of beautiful pictures and churches, but we cannot judge a country by anything but its men'" (72). In this respect, she resembles *A Room with a View*'s Mrs. Honeychurch, who depreciates women more than once, telling Sir Harry, "'Beware of women altogether. Only let to a man. . . . Men don't gossip over tea-cups. . . . If they're vulgar, they somehow keep it to themselves. It doesn't spread so'" (120). The flight of both male and female youth from the mother's masculinist domination tends to align homoeroticism and feminism.

3. The mythological analog in the bathing scene is Forster's description of the men "rotat[ing] in the pool breast high, after the fashion of the nymphs in Gotterdämmerung" (150). Meyers's observation on this passage extends to the previous one too: "Forster hellenizes nature to blend with the classical ideal of manly love" (93). Obviously, the feminizing of the men into nymphs veils even as it exposes the homoeroticism.

4. Even more obviously linked to the Sacred Lake scene, and to the Neptune fountain, is the narrator's ultimately phallic description of violets running down the terrace "in rivulets and streams and cataracts, irrigating the hillside with blue . . . this terrace was the well-head, the primal source whence beauty gushed out to water the earth" (80). In the film, it is perhaps a variation on this parallel between sexuality and setting that the lush flaxen (or barley-colored) tresses of "Persephone" match the hue of the fertile field in which George kisses Lucy.

5. And later, when George kisses Lucy after tennis, the camera frames them tightly against the greenery of trees in a close-up that erases their English surroundings and, along with them, English constraints on passion.

6. Presumably the greater "natural man" context makes it acceptable for George to resemble a statue by Michelangelo, but *not* acceptable for Cecil to see Lucy as a Leonardo.

7. My thanks to Helena Goscilo and Laura Fasick for their helpful readings of early drafts.

WORKS CITED

Aldrich, Robert. *The Seduction of the Mediterranean: Writing Art and Homosexual Fantasy.* New York: Routledge, 1993.

Beauman, Nicola. *E. M. Forster: A Biography.* New York: Knopf, 1994.

Bristow, Joseph. "Wilde, Dorian Gray, and Gross Indecency." *Sexual Sameness: Textual Differences in Lesbian and Gay Writing.* Ed. Joseph Bristow. New York: Routledge, 1992, 44-63.

Colmer, John. *E. M. Forster: The Personal Voice.* London: Routledge and Kegan Paul, 1975.

Doty, Alexander. *Making Things Perfectly Queer: Interpreting Mass Culture.* Minneapolis: U of Minnesota P, 1993.

Fletcher, John. "Forster's Self-Erasure: *Maurice* and the Scene of Masculine Love." *Sexual Sameness: Textual Differences in Lesbian and Gay Writing.* Ed. Joseph Bristow. New York: Routledge, 1992, 64-90.

Forster, E. M. *A Room with a View.* 1908. New York: Vintage, n.d.

———. *Where Angels Fear to Tread.* 1905. New York: Vintage, 1959.

Furbank, P. N. *E. M. Forster: A Life.* 2 vols. New York: Harcourt Brace Jovanovich, 1977-78.

Fussell, Paul. *Abroad: British Literary Traveling Between the Wars.* New York: Oxford UP, 1980.

Koestenbaum, Wayne. *Double Talk: The Erotics of Male Literary Collaboration.* New York: Routledge, Chapman and Hall, 1989.

———. *The Queen's Throat: Opera, Homosexuality and the Mystery of Desire.* New York: Vintage, 1993.

Land, Stephen K. *Challenge and Conventionality in the Fiction of E. M. Forster.* New York: AMS, 1990.

LaValley, Albert. "The Great Escape." *American Film* 10 (April 1985): 29-34, 70-71.

Levine, June Perry. "Two Rooms with a View: An Inquiry into Film Adaptation." *Mosaic* 22.3 (1989): 67-84.

Martin, John Sayre. *E. M. Forster: The Endless Journey.* Cambridge, Eng.: Cambridge UP, 1976.

Meyers, Jeffrey. *Homosexuality and Literature 1890-1930.* Montreal: McGill-Queen's UP, 1977.

Nelson, Scott R. "Narrative Inversion: The Textual Construction of Homosexuality in E. M. Forster's Novels." *Style* 26 (Summer 1992): 310-26.

Orrey, Leslie, ed. *The Encyclopedia of Opera.* New York: Charles Scribner's Sons, 1976.

Rosecrance, Barbara. *Forster's Narrative Vision.* Ithaca: Cornell UP, 1982.

Sedgwick, Eve Kosofsky. *Between Men: English Literature and Male Homosocial Desire.* New York: Columbia UP, 1985.

Summers, Claude J. *E. M. Forster.* New York: Ungar, 1987.

Nostromo: Economism and Its Discontents

Paul Delany

MATERIAL INTERESTS

Nostromo begins by establishing two moral registers and continues to alternate between them. Chapter 1 tells of the treasure seekers of Azuera, figures of romance whose ghosts remain to haunt the Golfo Placido. In chapter 2, the narrative focus changes to the arrival of the "commercial activity" (43) of the Oceanic Steam Navigation Company in the gulf. This comes as a falling-off from the novel's melodramatic beginning; and a tone of disappointment and denigration will carry on through Conrad's exposition of Costaguana's predominant commercial enterprise, the San Tomé mine. The counterpoint between these two registers reflects the duality of imperialism, which mingles imaginative and material projects, adventure and consolidation, power and profit; it also points us towards the shift, in *Nostromo*, from Conrad's earlier treatment of imperialism to a neo-colonialism more characteristic of the twentieth century than of the nineteenth.

We are all familiar enough with the critique of imperialism as a morally flawed project of domination over cultures expediently defined as inferior; and familiar, too, with Conrad's tentative exculpation of imperialism by virtue of the "redeeming idea"—some higher purpose that makes imperialism more than just the pursuit of power or money and honors the ethical imperative of Britain's civilizing mission (Parry, *Conrad*). But in reading *Nostromo,* attention should also be paid to a critique from a different quarter: not from leftist moral condemnation, but from the long tradition of economic liberalism that opposed the rise of the British Empire. This tradition decries the direct exercise of power by a stronger against a weaker state; instead, it understands progress as the peaceful extension of modernizing economic rationality. In the eighteenth century, Adam Smith argued that it was counterproductive for Britain to enforce a monopoly on trade with its North American colonies, because capital would always be employed more efficiently in open markets than in closed ones, and because keeping rivals out of American markets required huge military expenses (2:105-29, 130-31). Cobdenite liberalism, a century later, sustained the claim that Britain would be more prosperous as a free trade power than as an imperial one. "Cheapness," Cobden said, "and not the cannon or the sword, is the weapon through which alone we possess and can hope to defend or extend our commerce. . . . armies and ships cannot protect or extend commerce; whilst, as is too well known, the expenses of maintaining them oppress and impede our manufacturing industry" (*Writings* 299, 307).[1] Cobden believed that U.S. reliance on economic incentives to promote trade was wiser than Britain's policy of "trade follows the flag." He praised Washington's call, in his farewell address: "The great rule of conduct for us in regard to foreign nations is, in extending our commercial relations, to have with them as little *political* connection as possible." America was a *democratic* nation, Cobden argued, whose motives were commercial; England was *aristocratic,* which meant motives like pride, power, and imperialism.

Schumpeter, finally, writing during the First World War, defined imperialism as an aristocratic reaction against the secular trends of rationalization and modernization:

> Imperialism thus is atavistic in character. It falls into that large group of surviving features from earlier ages that play such an important part in every concrete social situation. In other words, it is an element that stems from the living conditions, not of the present, but of the past—or, put in terms of the economic interpretation of history, from past rather than present relations of production. . . . If our theory is correct, causes of imperialism should decline in intensity the later they occur in the history of a people and of a culture. (*Imperialism* 65)

In Schumpeter's theory, the industrial revolution creates an "economically oriented leadership" that becomes "democratized, individualized, and rationalized" (66, 68), as economic competition gradually supersedes "the primitive contingencies of physical combat":

> In a purely capitalist world, what was once energy for war becomes simply energy for labor of every kind. Wars of conquest and adventurism in foreign policy in general are bound to be regarded as troublesome distractions, destructive of life's meaning, a diversion from the accustomed and therefore "true" task.
>
> A purely capitalist world therefore can offer no fertile soil to imperialist impulses. (69)

Marxists argued that imperialism was on the rise, as the last resort of a "late" capitalism that needed to conquer new markets to prop up a declining rate of profit (Lenin, Hobson). Schumpeter argued the precise opposite: imperialism was a precapitalist survival tactic that would wither away as capitalism became a purely rational economic system. Aristocratic values were by definition archaic, and sure to be undermined by the advance of commercial modernity. This meant, in the long run, free trade, the dissolution of special interests in a global economic system, and commercially motivated pacifism instead of atavistic wars.

The ideology of Smith, Cobden, and Schumpeter is *economism:* that economic values are, in the long run, most peaceful, most productive, and most worthy to prevail over all other social goals. British foreign policy after 1815 was heavily influenced by economist principles. The Reciprocity of Duties Act of 1823 encouraged commercial treaties between England and other countries willing to open their markets, and was followed by Cobden's crowning achievement, the repeal of the Corn Laws in 1846.[2] Throughout the nineteenth century, Britain moved steadily toward free trade and, as the world's greatest economic power, presided over huge increases in international trade, global capital movements, and cultural exchange between nations.[3] Even the empire was run with a frugal administration and without tariff preference.

No critic of Conrad could overlook his disdain for "material interests," and much of this disdain may well stem from his aristocratic disposition to judge the pursuit of profit irredeemably base.[4] What I want to argue here is that the phrase "material interests" in *Nostromo* is not just a vague label for "business," "greed," or even "capitalism." Rather, the phrase identifies a specific ideological and institutional formation: the Cobdenite *system* of free-trade economism that was espoused by the Liberal party and that determined British trade policy from 1846 to 1914. Anyone with the slightest interest in politics would be aware of Cobdenite principles; on the personal level, Conrad's first publisher, T. Fisher Unwin, was married to Cobden's

youngest daughter and drew Conrad's attention to his father-in-law's intellectual legacy.[5] Most important for our present purpose is that Conrad was
for twenty years an agent of the free-trade system, in his capacity as an officer of
the merchant navy. Yet there is a remarkably sustained exercise of false consciousness in the way he seized on the chivalric code of the sea while denigrating the economic function to which that code was, after all, ancillary. In his
essay on the loss of the *Titanic,* Conrad wrote: "I have seen commerce pretty
close. I know what it is worth, and I have no particular regard for commercial
magnates" (*Life and Letters* 289). In such remarks, he assumed that an officer
on a merchant ship is—by virtue of his code of duty—superior to and morally
separate from the trade that he is in fact engaged in.

THE MODERNIZATION OF COSTAGUANA

Nostromo's Costaguana is not an imperial possession. Free of Spanish rule
for nearly a century, it has fallen into a destructive polarization between
liberal aristocracy and populist dictatorship. The breaking of this opposition can only come from an external intervention, whose instrument will be
the San Tomé mine.

The history of the mine recapitulates centuries of Latin American development: from an imperialism of mere plunder to a failed policy of national autarchy to incorporation by globalizing capitalism.[6] When first
worked, it might as well have been in the Congo as in Latin America:
"Worked in the early days mostly by means of lashes on the backs of slaves,
its yield had been paid for in its own weight of human bones. Whole tribes
of Indians had perished in the exploitation; and then the mine was abandoned, since with this primitive method it had ceased to make a profitable
return" (75). The mine was later expropriated by the government and shut
down; and the site reverted to jungle. When Charles Gould decides to re-
open the mine, it is in the service of a comprehensive project of modernization of Costaguana:

> "What is wanted here is law, good faith, order, security. Anyone can
> declaim about these things, but I pin my faith to material interests.
> Only let the material interests once get a firm footing, and they are
> bound to impose the conditions on which alone they can continue to
> exist. That's how your money-making is justified here in the face of
> lawlessness and disorder. It is justified because the security which it
> demands must be shared with an oppressed people. A better justice
> will come afterwards. That's your ray of hope." (100)

Before *Nostromo,* Conrad had contrasted the mindless greed of "material
interests" to the redeeming *idea* of paternalist colonialism. But now the

material interests have an idea too: a Cobdenite vision of economic liberalism, internationalism, and democracy. Mrs. Gould doesn't see how "awful materialism" (99) can have any ideals, but in this earlier part of the novel her husband seems to have the best of their argument:

> For the San Tomé mine was to become an institution, a rallying-point for everything in the province that needed order and stability to live. Security seemed to flow upon this land from the mountain-gorge. The authorities of Sulaco had learned that the San Tomé mine could make it worth their while to leave things and people alone. This was the nearest approach to the rule of common sense and justice Charles Gould felt it possible to secure at first. In fact, the mine, with its organization, its population growing fiercely attached to their position of privileged safety, with its armoury, with its Don Pepe, with its armed body of *serenos* . . . was a power in the land. (119-20)

Before Gould's initiative, power in Sulaco—as exercised by successive caudillos—was absolute, ruthless, and entirely self-interested. This new power claims only a negative agency, to protect an economic space of liberalism where wealth, civic order, and productivity will be able to flourish together.

Yet *Nostromo* ends with a chorus of condemnation against Charles Gould and his American financier Holroyd, the agents of this modernizing capitalism. Mrs. Gould, Dr. Monygham, and Nostromo, who make up the party of conscience, are of diverse temperament. For one, dislike of instrumental economic reason is associated with her femininity and her genteel origins (93); one is an intellectual skeptic; one an existential outsider. The new state of Sulaco divides into an economist party of function and an idealist party whose various critiques are enunciated from positions of ineffectual detachment from the institutions that exercise power.

Mrs. Gould's judgment on her husband's work is expressed in a characteristically Conradian idiom:

> There was something inherent in the necessities of successful action which carried with it the moral degradation of the idea. She saw the San Tomé mountain hanging over the Campo, over the whole land, feared, hated, wealthy; more soulless than any tyrant, more pitiless and autocratic than the worst Government; ready to crush innumerable lives in the expansion of its greatness. He did not see it. He could not see it. (431)

Yet if Mrs. Gould sees her husband as sealed up within a perspective that is impermeable to other views, her own critique is equally self-enclosed. Earlier, the narrator had observed that "even the most legitimate touch of materialism was wanting in [her] character" (93). If Gould's disposition did not allow him to see any evil in the mine, his wife's did not allow her to see any good. Further, their disagreement is implicated in a familiar marital dynamic of jealousy and dissociation: the mine has become, for Mrs. Gould, an erotic rival. She and Gould shared the "brief intoxication" of romantic love, a union of soul and sense, but in the long run the mine displaced her as the object of Gould's passion—"she would never have him to herself." His love of the mine appears to her as "soulless," no more than "hard, determined service of the material interests" (431). Yet Mrs. Gould also wanted exclusive possession of her husband, so as to subdue him to her own absolutist moral idealism. Her resentment of the mine includes a desire to reclaim her husband from the "man's world" of economic power and bring him into her own domestic sphere. Nor does she offer any alternative vision of statecraft. Like the Belgian fiancée in *Heart of Darkness,* Mrs. Gould's spiritual authority is inseparable from her ignorance and her literal distance from the arenas—the jungle, the mine—of violent conflict or crisis.

No feminine (or feminized) idealist could provide a full articulation of Conrad's worldview, and Mrs. Gould's scorn for her husband's enterprise is itself vulnerable to more pragmatic judgments. Her refined and luxurious way of life aligns her with the rentier, one who shuns the contamination of the marketplace even as she allows agents of coarser moral fiber to work her capital. And her idealism carries weight in society because of her proximity to the throne from which economic power is exercised; if she were married to someone ordinary, who would attend to her?

Dr. Monygham's anticapitalism is similarly conditioned by his quietist temperament and privileged social position. He complains, "There is no peace and no rest in the development of material interests"—interests that, for him, lack "the continuity and the force that can be found only in a moral principle" (423). Yet the previous rulers of Costaguana have been far more malignant than Gould, so where is Monygham to find an anti-economic regime of continuous virtue, free from the self-corrupting dynamic of idealism?

Nostromo, faithful to his populist idealism, comes to see the mine as "hateful and immense, lording it by its vast wealth over the valour, the toil, the fidelity of the poor" (417). But the immensity is precisely what he must acknowledge, relative to his own present resources. Modernizing global capitalism may be without an intrinsic principle of rectitude, but its dynamic is so comprehensive as to render futile any individualist attempt to mount an opposition to it. It is precisely that futility that gives Nostromo the rationalization for keeping his boatload of silver. His vacillation between Giselle and Linda Viola, and his consequent casual death, confirm his post-revolutionary loss of authority. Whether he has the silver or not, he remains a superfluous man in an era of consolidation; his censoriousness is a product of his superfluity, just as much as his dishonesty is.

THE KNITTING MACHINE

There is a,—let us say,—a machine. It evolved itself (I am severely scientific) out of a chaos of scraps of iron and behold!—it knits. I am horrified at the horrible work and stand appalled. I feel it ought to embroider,—but it goes on knitting. You come and say; "This is all right: it's only a question of the right kind of oil. Let us use this,— for instance,—celestial oil and the machine will embroider a most beautiful design in purple and gold." Will it? Alas, no? You cannot by any special lubrication make embroidery with a knitting machine. And the most withering thought is that the infamous thing has made itself: made itself without thought, without conscience, without foresight, without eyes, without heart. It is a tragic accident—and it has happened. (Conrad, *Letters* 1:425)

Edward Said has understood this machine to be Conrad's emblem of the mindlessness of human destiny (*Beginnings* 133). But the mindlessness may be of a more literal kind, if we place the knitting machine in its historical role as one of the first makers of the Industrial Revolution. The mechanical loom epitomizes the *impersonality* of the new economic system, overriding any individual projects and preferences that try to confront it. The machine serves a "material interest" without any dimension of conscience (the "embroidery" that it will never produce). It is supremely effective in its destruction of traditional economic relations, yet entirely without higher purpose.

That effectiveness includes a highly strategic sense of its own local deployment. Mrs. Gould and Nostromo, like other organicists who oppose the machine, typically view it as constant in its operation, a monotonous and cumulative engine of tyranny. But the industrial system of Sulaco displays a kind of intelligence in choosing to develop one space and ignore another. Antonia Avellanos wants the Sulacans to do something about the "cruel wrongs" suffered by those who remain in Costaguana:

'Annex the rest of Costaguana to the order and prosperity of Sulaco,' snapped the doctor. 'There is no other remedy.'

'I am convinced, Senor Doctor,' Antonia said, with the earnest calm of invincible resolution, 'that this was from the first poor Martin's intention.'

'Yes, but the material interests will not let you jeopardize their development for a mere idea of pity and justice,' the doctor muttered, grumpily. 'And it is just as well perhaps.' (422)

The rulers of Sulaco wish to consolidate their domain as an enclave of economic order, putting off the modernization of Costaguana to a later date. Sulaco will be a proving ground for the emergent neo-colonialism of the United States, which operates through finance capital and Protestant missionaries rather than direct political domination. In Costaguana and most other parts of South America, caudillo regimes will remain the political norm. Their resistance to the forces of Cobdenite globalization will be given voice by such figures as Gamacho, of the Costaguanan "Nacionalistas," for whom the Great Powers, "by introducing railways, mining enterprises, colonization, and such other shallow pretences, aimed at robbing poor people of their lands" (332).[7]

The expansion of modernizing capitalism may appear to the peasants as robbery, but the underlying process is a prolonged and patient work of incorporation. Any continent-wide triumph of Cobdenite liberalism remains far beyond the horizon at the end of *Nostromo* (as it still does today, though surely it has come nearer). Yet its critics within the novel view it as an achieved ideal, and one that is already beginning to fester, since it rests on nothing more than "covetousness which, in its universal extent, measures the moral misery and the intellectual destitution of mankind" (377). Mrs. Gould and Dr. Monygham acknowledge that peace, order, and good government have been achieved in Sulaco; what they resent is that these are *by-products* of industrialization, rather than benefits conferred by a paternalist aristocracy, or a disinterested "service class" like that which ran the British Empire. When Nostromo denounces the regime as merely the latest form of dictatorship, he overlooks the diminution of personal authority in its rule and the corresponding predominance of an international system of production and exchange. Sulaco is being rapidly and successfully "Europeanized," but as a commercial rather than an aristocratic society, through "[m]aterial changes swept along in the train of material interests" (417). What is generated by the requirements of industry can scarcely act as an internal restraint on it. Nonetheless, that system is generating its own countervailing forces, as "other changes more subtle, outwardly unmarked, affected the minds and hearts of the workers" (417) . These are the stirrings of class-consciousness: instead of fighting for the Goulds, as they did during the war of secession, the workers are girding themselves to fight for their collective economic interest.[8]

The evolution of the miners—from personal loyalty to their master to self-interested market agents—corresponds to the economizing of the society as a whole. Paternalism yields to laissez-faire individualism, and foreign relations shift from postimperial nationalism to neo-colonialism. Conrad was all too familiar with the mechanisms of international capital (he lost the major part of his inherited capital by speculating in South African gold mines), and he made financiers into centers of interest in *The Inheritors* (1901) and *Chance* (1913).⁹ As a novelist, he could be expected to personalize the emergent global economic system by showing its moral effects on individuals like Gould or Nostromo. Yet even if one reads Conrad as aligning himself with the indictments of modernizing capitalism made variously by Mrs. Gould, Dr. Monygham, and Nostromo, nothing in the conclusion of the novel suggests that revolutionary socialism can offer a better future, any more than the restoration of the agrarian aristocracy. The chief engineer of the Sulaco railway argues that transcendence lies as a potential in any material task: "things seem to be worth nothing by what they are in themselves. I begin to believe that the only solid thing about them is the spiritual value which everyone discovers in his own form of activity" (275). But it is an engineer who speaks, not a captain; and if he were believed, all vocations could lead equally to salvation, and no one need be troubled by the baser interests that their activities served. Populism is certain, on its past record, to spiral downward into corruption and terror. We are left, it would seem, with a Conrad whose dislike of the Gould/Holroyd regime incorporates a broad cynicism about any alternatives, and a conviction that the forces now prevailing in Sulaco are impregnable.

Indeed, when in debate with a pure idealist like Cunninghame-Graham, Conrad liked to argue that material interests were universal and irresistible:

> You with your ideals of sincerity, courage and truth are strangely out of place in this epoch of material preoccupations. What does it bring? What's the profit? What do we get by it? These questions are at the root of every moral, intellectual or political movement. Into the noblest cause men manage to put something of their baseness; and sometimes when I think of You here, quietly You seem to me tragic with your courage, with your beliefs and your hopes. Every cause is tainted: and you reject this one, espouse that other one as if one were evil and the other good while the same evil you hate is in both, but disguised in different words. (*Letters* 2:25)

Conrad here reduces the deeper motives of both Right and Left to the pursuit of similarly base ends: money or power desired for their own sakes, once the screen of idealism has been removed. Hence the great Conradian theme of *corruption,* whether of grandiose national ideals or individual dreams. Yet if this is true, any moral critique of Cobdenism is either quixotic (because human nature cannot be changed) or hypocritical (because if the critics got into power, they would soon discard their "disinterested" principles).¹⁰

NOSTROMO AND GLOBALIZATION

Literary accounts of the relation between the West and its "periphery" have been dominated by the high imperialism of the later nineteenth century and by the dissolution of the European empires after 1945. The West and its Others have been framed in the perspective of nationalism, with the rich cultural possibilities it has made available (whether hegemonic or oppositional): from the literature of "prestige" or "service" imperialism, whose great names are Kipling, Forster, Orwell, and the Conrad of *Heart of Darkness* or *Lord Jim,* to the contemporary post-colonial literature that has arisen from the continuing links between periphery and metropolis.

Nostromo stands apart from these traditions as the single major novel in English that engages not imperialism, but the rival formation of Cobdenite liberalism and internationalism. Cobden's vision of a peaceful, commercial, and multilateral world system anticipates the current arguments of the "End of History" school.[11] "Free trade! What is it?" Cobden asked, "Why, breaking down the barriers that separate nations; those barriers behind which nestle the feelings of pride, revenge, hatred, and jealousy, which every now and then burst their bounds and deluge whole countries with blood" (quoted in Hutchinson 29). Whatever Conrad's reservations about Cobdenism, he does not oppose it in the name of protecting any indigenous cultural identity for Costaguana. That country is modernized by metropolitan intervention, just as the later critique of that modernization comes from the same source, as enlightenment humanism or radicalism (Colás 390). Conrad's representation of Costaguana remains rigorously Eurocentric, and he presents the action of *Nostromo* as a heroic narrative of the replacement of indigenous backwardness by a European modernizing order. The criticisms of that order are no less European than their object: they arise from traditional oppositions between aristocratic and commercial values, between master and slave, and between moral ideals and material interests.

Conrad represents fully and faithfully the logic of transition from the regime of the caudillos to that of Cobdenite economic rationality. But Cobden, in his time, was driven by resentment of the prestige culture of the British aristocracy, with its unearned privileges and its anti-economic values. Conrad is not a radical in that sense and still esteems such romantic projects as Gould's desire to restore his family's honor (a quintessentially aristocratic motive). The industrial modernization of Sulaco provides the occasion for those with "higher" agendas to make displays of existential heroism that are, it must eventually be recognized, peripheral to the relatively mundane transition that is going to be repeated in many other "backward" regions as they are incorporated into global neo-liberalism. It is of the essence of such transitions—seen in retrospect, at least—that they are not revolutions, and that they are incompatible with grand narratives of personal leadership, agency, or teleology.

After Sulaco's war of secession, Charles Gould is represented as a new kind of caudillo, all the more oppressive for the efficient economic rationality on which his power depends. Yet this gives Gould and Holroyd a degree of agency that is at odds with their actual economic function. The personality cult of an old-fashioned caudillo could not extend beyond his frontiers, and political or economic concerns would always be subordinated to his need for absolute personal power. The caudillo, by definition, claims an organic relation with his nation; but that which legitimates his rule internally deprives him of any plausible claim to authority in neighboring countries, who will be fearful of any pretensions he may have to regional hegemony. It is inappropriate, then, to equate the rule of the caudillos with that of internationally oriented capitalists like Gould and Holroyd. The economic modernization of Sulaco is the product of its integration with an emergent global system of trade and capital mobility—a system of which Gould and Holroyd are the managers rather than the masters. By opening Sulaco to the international market, they reduce proportionately the sovereignty of whoever rules it.

It is of course true that Holroyd has religious and nationalist ambitions that are close to megalomania. The issue (as in *Heart of Darkness*) is whether these aims are continuous with his economic aims or represent a turning away from them. With his "temperament of a Puritan and an insatiable imagination of conquest," Holroyd carries the torch of a global "Manifest Destiny" for "the greatest country in the whole of God's Universe. . . . We shall be giving the word for everything: industry, trade, law, journalism, art, politics, and religion, from Cape Horn clear over to Smith's Sound, and beyond, too, if anything worth taking hold of turns up at the North Pole" (94).[12] The list ascends from the material interests of industry and trade to the ideal interests of religion at the top; but how are these elements interconnected? Holroyd claims "the introduction of a pure form of Christianity" into South America as his transcendent goal, but Conrad seems to consider him a religious hypocrite, whose true motives are crudely commercial.

Parry makes Holroyd exemplary of a specific historical moment, of messianic high imperialism:

> Not until the late nineteenth century . . . did imperialist rhetoric invent an exorbitant and anomalous idiom of messianic utilitarianism and bellicose mysticism, where the positivist and aggressive phraseology of compulsory universal modernization is joined with the

anachronistic and chimerical lexicon of chivalry, 'a mandate of destiny', and 'a high and holy mission' serving as ideological pillars of the west's planetary ambitions. ("Dystopia")

Holroyd's particular strain in this rhetoric is that of American exceptionalism, whereby the United States has a sacred destiny in the world, distinct from the base aims of European imperialism. Conrad thought exceptionalism was humbug—except when it came to Britain where, in some moods, he would argue strenuously for the possibility of imperial disinterestedness (*Letters* 2:230). The issue I hope to resolve in my conclusion is whether high imperialism should be seen as a single movement, integrating a mixture of economic and ideological aims, or whether (following Cobden and Schumpeter) we should try to distinguish between economic and anti-economic motives within it.

Nostromo Today

The Cobdenite era began to dissolve with the protectionist policies of Britain's trade rivals in the years leading to World War I and culminated in Britain's abandonment of free trade in 1931. By 1934, total international trade had shrunk to one third of its level in 1929 (Hutchinson 258). The two world wars were indeed the "deluges of blood" that Cobden predicted if countries chose military rivalry over peaceful commerce. The Bretton Woods agreement of 1945 can now be seen as the inauguration of a second Cobdenite era in world history, whose salient features include multilateral tariff reduction and growth of trade, the end of empire, the economic integration of Europe since 1963 and of North America since 1992, and the fall of the autarchic Communist bloc in 1989. All of these developments now culminate in a triumphant economism, what Frederick Buell calls "the new global system."

This system was first theorized by Immanuel Wallerstein, Raul Prebisch, and André Gunder Frank as oppressively neo-colonial, the Western world perpetuating dominance over its periphery by economic fraud rather than imperial force. The critique of globalization in *Nostromo* thus anticipates later denunciations of transnational capitalism as the enemy of local cultures or exploited classes. Recently, however, mainstream economic opinion has become more respectful of the efficacy of the "new international division of labour." To Buell, the rise of countries like Taiwan, South Korea, Hong Kong, and Singapore represents "the death knell of the previous era of nationalism: national development under the protective stewardship of the state has come to seem inhibited, rather than advanced, and integration with the global system—in some ways nationalism's precise opposite—has become the hope" (116). Peter Worsley sees in such developments what "earlier generations of theorists on the Left had deemed to be impossible—the industrialization of Third World economies under capitalism" (quoted in Buell 115-16).

Conrad's friend Cunninghame-Graham saw the economic incorporation of the periphery as a recurrent and deplorable effect of imperialism. In his essay "Bloody Niggers," he denounced "material and bourgeois Rome . . . conquering the world . . . and by its sheer dead weight of commonplace, filling the office in the old world that now is occupied so worthily by God's own Englishmen" (quoted in Watts 144). Conrad shared Cunninghame-Graham's fear that European investment in Latin America would create in the New World the same sordid industrial society that had already taken over the Old, and that "Yankee Conquistadores" would repeat the crimes of their Spanish predecessors (144).[13] But the idea of the modernizing capitalist as a new conquistador blurs the distinction between Cobdenite globalizing liberalism and the kind of imperialism by force and pillage practiced in the Congo.[14] The original conquistador was scarcely an "economic man" in the sense of the Protestant thrift and rationality of Weberian capitalism: one should distinguish between plunder and productivity, and between domination and free exchange. Yet Conrad typically sees these as two sides of an integral process, each motive being naturally absorbed into the other. In both *Heart of Darkness* and *Nostromo,* material interests begin to work for constructive ends, but soon accommodate themselves to baser instincts. The economic sector cannot maintain its autonomy; it is the instrument of a will to power that precedes the appearance of "economic man," and whose dynamic is always a striving for "positional superiority" (in Edward Said's terms) of one individual, class, race, or nation over another.

The Cobdenite ideal makes politics superfluous; its opposite is the view that politics determines everything, including the operations of so-called free markets. Evidently, great nations have often proved unwilling to follow a pure Cobdenite policy of free trade with peripheral regions. Having political, cultural, and military—as well as economic—power, they have always been tempted to deploy it to "capture" or "defend" markets to which they assert a claim. Nonetheless, it is a long step from saying that imperial nations manipulate markets to saying that markets don't matter and imperialism is only about power. In *Burmese Days,* for example, the timber merchant Flory argues that the whole political and ideological face of imperialism is no more than a screen for economic interests:

> "I don't want the Burmans to drive us out of this country. God for-
> bid! I'm here to make money, like everyone else. All I object to is
> the slimy white man's burden humbug . . . the lie that we're here to
> uplift our poor black brothers instead of to rob them. . . .
>   The official holds the Burman down while the businessman goes
> through his pockets. . . . The British Empire is simply a device for
> giving trade monopolies to the English—or rather to gangs of Jews
> and Scotchmen." (37-38)

Neither Orwell nor his creation, Flory, consider that business might be a
legitimate activity in itself, still less that it could carry out the civilizing
mission it professes in *Nostromo*. Nonetheless, *Burmese Days* takes it for
granted that business motives are central to imperialism. The striking achievement of Said's *Orientalism* (and of its sequel, *Culture and Imperialism*)
does not obviate its equally striking occlusion of the economic motives for
European expansion into the East. If it is a truism that there were a mixture
of material and spiritual motives for the Crusades, it is hardly likely that this
duality of aim ceased to operate after 1291. Yet *Orientalism* assumes a
Western power that reproduces itself regardless of Western economic interest, or that is in excess of any adequate economic justification. Behind
Orientalism stands Foucault's obsession with vertical relations of domi-
nance/submission as virtually the only kind of social bond, combined with
the post-structuralist privileging of *difference* as the ground of meaning. In
examining the massive Western project of ideological dominance over the
East, one should not ignore the economic "will to profit" that accompanies
the political "will to power." Thus Benita Parry criticizes in the post-
colonial "discourse analysis" of Spivak and Bhabha

> a shared programme marked by the exorbitation of discourse and a
> related incuriosity about the enabling socioeconomic and political
> institutions and other forms of social praxis. Furthermore, because
> their theses admit of no point outside discourse from which opposi-
> tion can be engendered, their project is concerned to place incendi-
> ary devices within the dominant structures of representation and not
> to confront these with another knowledge. ("Problems" 43)

Implicitly, Parry places "discourse analysis" in the mode of utopian socialism derided by Lenin—where ideas systematize themselves spontaneously,
free of any material determination. If economics is recognized at all, it is as
"just another discourse"; so that neo-liberalism, for example, is no more
than a rhetoric to be exploited by ruling elites.
    Orientalism thus takes its place at the opposite pole from the liberal
economic model that posits a formal equality and community of interest
between buyers and sellers. Post-colonial focus on difference would seem

to make Orientalism incurable, since difference determines, without residue, the relations between persons, races, and nations—and also, monoto-
nously, serves the ends of domination. Against this, the Cobdenite perspective
argues that patterns of dominance in the global system are much less simple
or stable than, say, British imperial control over its Eastern possessions in
the nineteenth century. A rapidly shifting international division of labor ac-
commodates the rise of newly industrializing countries, and inflicts a relative decline on the established centers of Europe and North America. The
nation itself loses much of its coherence under the pressures of globalization—a dissolution anticipated in the fate of Costaguana in *Nostromo.*

What verdict, then, may be pronounced on the modernizing capitalism
of *Nostromo?* Many recent critics have emphasized the narrative, symbolic,
or moral incoherence of the novel——projecting the nihilism of *Heart of
Darkness* forward into the darkness that so often lies over the Golfo Placido.
I would argue that a more coherent reading emerges when we look forward
to the later twentieth-century world system, rather than backward to Leopold's
Congo. Conrad's essay "Autocracy and War" (1905), an important coda to
Nostromo, both defines his quarrel with Cobdenism and differentiates his
position from contemporary *Orientalism.*[15] Conrad identifies a moment of
optimism in Victorian thought around the time of the Great Exhibition (1851)
and the repeal of the Corn Laws (1846):

> A swift disenchantment overtook the incredible infatuation which
> could put its trust in the peaceful nature of industrial and commer-
> cial competition.
>   Industrialism and commercialism . . . stand ready, almost eager,
> to appeal to the sword as soon as the globe of the earth has shrunk
> beneath our growing numbers by another ell or so. (142)

Looking at the past decade of imperial and commercial rivalry, Conrad observes: "Germany's attitude proves that no peace for the earth can be found
in the expansion of material interests which she seems to have adopted exclusively as her only aim, ideal, and watchword" (151). His frighteningly
accurate prediction of the intentions of the great powers seems to confirm
Dr. Monygham's diagnosis, that economic motives are intrinsically restless
and aggressive.

Yet Conrad fails to inspect the links in his causal chain from 1846 to
1914. Cobden and Schumpeter posited a rational global trading system that
would eventually overcome the bias of prestige societies toward belligerent
expansionism. In a world of free trade, nations would only handicap themselves by spending on armaments in the hope of "conquering" or "protecting" overseas markets. That a world war followed the Cobdenite era does

not prove that Cobdenism was the "cause" of it: Cobden's ideals may have
been abandoned or betrayed, like those of any other revolution.

The opposition between Cobdenism and imperialist war is well illustrated in Werner Sombart's 1915 polemic *Merchants and Heroes:*

> [Sombart] welcomed the "German War" as the inevitable conflict
> between the commercial civilization of England and the heroic cul-
> ture of Germany. His contempt for the "commercial" views of the
> English people, who had lost all warlike instincts, is unlimited. Noth-
> ing is more contemptible in his eyes than the universal striving after
> the happiness of the individual; and what he describes as the leading
> maxim of English morals: be just "that it may be well with thee and
> that thou mayest prolong thy days upon the land" is to him "the most
> infamous maxim which has ever been pronounced by a commercial
> mind." . . . Claims of the individual are always an outcome of the
> commercial spirit. (Hayek 170)

Sombart, who began as a socialist and became a Nazi supporter in the
1930s, assumed that capitalism, and especially the English variety, was synony-
mous with the rise of Cobdenite pacifist internationalism since the Napoleonic
wars.[16] If the individual pursuit of wealth was the final purpose of social
organization, the state would tend to shrink, and the nation would have no
powerful embodiment of its collective will. Yet late-nineteenth-century capitalists proved susceptible to messianic appeals to national destiny that made
economics the instrument of other national ambitions.

H. G. Wells registered this shift of opinion in his dining club "The
Coefficients," which met from 1902 to 1908:

> I was still clinging to the dear belief that the English-speaking com-
> munity might play the part of leader and mediator towards a world
> commonweal. It was to be free-trading, free-speaking, liberating flux
> for mankind. . . . But the shadow of Joseph Chamberlain lay dark
> across our dinner-table, the Chamberlain who, upon the "illimitable
> velt" of South Africa had had either a sunstroke or a Pauline conver-
> sion to Protection and had returned to clamour influentially for what
> he called Tariff Reform, but what was in effect national commercial
> egotism. (762-63)

Observing the European arms race and the turn toward protectionism
that led up to the First World War, Conrad blamed it on the inner dynamic of
the material interests.[17] Into economic projects—like any others—men will
always "manage to put something of their baseness," and turn them to ill
ends. To Johnson's quip that "[t]here are few ways in which a man can be
more innocently employed than in getting money," Conrad implicitly responded that men are without innocence in anything they do—or, at least,

are never innocent over the full course of an undertaking. Economism could not be the exception to history's tragic cycle of idealism and corruption, nor could there be an "end" to this history in any utopian era of global enrichment without limit or relapse. The condemnation of Gould's handiwork in Costaguana thus includes the expectation that it will culminate in another and larger war.[18] But the question remains whether Cobdenism ends in war, or whether war is inevitable when man tires of being *homo economicus.*

NOTES

1. Cobden goes on to show that the costs of the navy far outweigh any possible profit from the trade it protects, and that "no class or calling of society can derive permanent benefit from war" (328). Marx and Engels were perhaps echoing Cobden's formula when they spoke of cheapness as the "heavy artillery" used by the great trading nations to penetrate less developed societies (*Manifesto* 7).

2. See Platt 86ff. The Navigation Acts, which protected British merchant shipping, were repealed in 1849.

3. In addition to the ideological shift toward economic liberalism, technical revolutions in transport and communications such as steamships, the telegraph, and the telephone contributed to the growth of international exchanges.

4. On aristocratic disdain for trade, see, for example, Weber.

5. While Conrad was on his honeymoon in 1896, Unwin sent him the special issue of the *Daily News* celebrating the fiftieth anniversary of the repeal of the Corn Laws, to which Unwin was a contributor. Conrad, however, disliked both Unwin's business practices and his Liberal politics.

6. The mine's product, silver, follows a similar evolution: first as booty for the Spanish, then as a national treasure that cannot be exploited, finally as the abstract medium of circulation for a global monetary system. *Heart of Darkness* presents a more immediate object of desire in ivory, an organic substance used for adornment.

7. The same opposition, though on different grounds, comes from the reactionary landed interest, "all these Don Ambrosios this and Don Fernandos that, who seemed actually to dislike and distrust the coming of the railway over their lands" (64).

8. The miners are Indians, who in the war of secession embraced European universalism: "In a very few years the sense of belonging to a powerful organization had been developed in these harassed, half-wild Indians. They were proud of, and attached to, the mine. It had secured their confidence and belief" (336). Conrad notes their movement into an oppositional *economic* consciousness, but does not imagine them reverting to a particularist cultural identity.

9. The financiers in these novels are the Duc de Mersch, whose project is a railway across Greenland, and de Barral, whose Sceptre Trust goes bankrupt. For Conrad's involvement with mining as promoter and speculator, see Karl 355-56, 376.

10. For Gareth Jenkins, this puts Conrad effectively on the Right: "[he] endorses, quietly but irrefutably, a particular type of class undertaking and a bourgeois-democratic revolution, no matter how fragile and brief the achievements of the society born therefrom" (174). My own conclusion, it will appear, is somewhat different.

11. See Fukuyama—who, however, never mentions Cobden or identifies economism as an ideology.

12. The original claim of Manifest Destiny, in the 1840s, was that the United States would expand until it reached the Pacific. Smith's Sound is the strait that divides Ellesmere Island, in the Canadian Arctic, from Greenland; so that Holroyd's United States would rule from north to south, as well as east to west.

13. The context of Conrad's exchange with Cunninghame-Graham was the American campaign to detach Panama from Colombia; this succeeded in November 1903, when Conrad was still writing *Nostromo*.

14. Arif Dirlik posits a similar shift from force to incentive in the rise of "trilateralism" after the U.S. defeat in Vietnam: "A policy of attracting revolutionary or socialist states within the orbit of capitalism rather than containing them militarily" (48).

15. *Nostromo* appeared in October 1904; "Autocracy and War," a reflection on Japan's victory over Russia, was published in the *Fortnightly Review* of July 1, 1905.

16. Britain had, of course, used force in defense of its interests from time to time; but Cobden argued that the existence of mutual commercial advantage would make it less likely that nations would resort to force.

17. He saw the only practical solution in the division of the world into "spheres of trade" ("Autocracy" 142), so that each of the Great Powers could develop its sphere without coming into conflict with the others.

18. Akin to the Chilean civil war over nitrate, mentioned in *Nostromo* 93-94. See Montéon.

WORKS CITED

Buell, Frederick. *National Culture and the New Global System.* Baltimore: Johns Hopkins UP, 1994.

Cobden, Richard. *The Political Writings.* Vol. 1. London: William Ridgeway, 1868.

Colás, Santiago. "Of Creole Symptoms, Cuban Fantasies, and Other Latin American Postcolonial Ideologies." *PMLA* 110 (May 1995): 382-96.

Conrad, Joseph. "Autocracy and War." *Notes on Life and Letters.* London: J. M. Dent, 1921.

———. *The Collected Letters of Joseph Conrad.* Ed. Frederick Karl and Laurence Davies. 4 vols. to date. Cambridge, Eng.: Cambridge UP, 1983- .

———. *Nostromo: A Tale of the Seaboard.* 1904. London: Penguin, 1990.

Dirlik, Arif. *After the Revolution: Waking to Global Capitalism.* Middletown, Conn.: Wesleyan UP, 1994.

Frank, André Gunder. *Capitalism and Underdevelopment in Latin America: Historical Studies of Chile and Brazil.* New York: Monthly Review Press, 1960.

Fukuyama, Francis. *The End of History and the Last Man.* New York: Free Press, 1992.

Hayek, Friedrich. *The Road to Serfdom.* London: Routledge and Kegan Paul, 1976.

Hobson, J. A. *Imperialism.* London: Allen and Unwin, 1938.

Hutchinson, Keith. *The Decline and Fall of British Capitalism.* Hamden, Conn.: Archon, 1966.

Jenkins, Gareth. "Conrad's *Nostromo* and History." *Literature and History* 6 (Autumn 1977): 138-78.

Karl, Frederick. *Joseph Conrad: The Three Lives.* London: Faber and Faber, 1979.

Lenin, V. I. *Imperialism, the Highest Stage of Capitalism.* Peking: Foreign Languages, 1973.

Marx, Karl, and Friedrich Engels. *The Communist Manifesto.* Ed. David McLellan. Oxford: Oxford UP, 1992.

Montéon, Michael. *Chile in the Nitrate Era: The Evolution of Economic Dependence,* 1880-1930. Madison: U of Wisconsin P, 1982.

Orwell, George. *Burmese Days.* Harmondsworth: Penguin, 1967.

Parry, Benita. *Conrad and Imperialism: Ideological Boundaries and Visionary Frontiers.* London: Macmillan, 1983.

———. "Narrating Imperialism: *Nostromo*'s Dystopia." *The Gravity of History: Reflections on the Work of Edward Said.* Ed. Keith Ansell-Pearson, Benita Parry, and Judith Squires. London: Lawrence and Wishart, forthcoming 1996.

———. "Problems in Current Theories of Colonial Discourse." *Oxford Literary Review* 9.1-2 (1987): 27-58.

Platt, D. C. M. *Finance, Trade, and Politics in British Foreign Policy 1815-1914.* Oxford: Clarendon, 1968.

Prebisch, Raúl. *Capitalismo Periférico: Crisis y Transformación*. Mexico City: Fondo de Cultura Económica, 1984.

Said, Edward. *Beginnings: Intention and Method.* New York: Basic Books, 1975.

———. *Culture and Imperialism.* New York: Viking, 1994.

———. *Orientalism.* New York: Vintage, 1979.

Schumpeter, Joseph. *Imperialism: Social Classes.* 1919. Cleveland: World Publishing, 1955.

Smith, Adam. *An Enquiry into the Nature and Causes of the Wealth of Nations.* Chicago: U of Chicago P, 1976.

Wallerstein, Immanuel. *The Modern World-System.* New York: Academy, 1974.

Watts, Cedric, and Laurence Davies. *Cunninghame-Graham: A Critical Biography.* Cambridge, Eng.: Cambridge UP, 1979.

Weber, Max. *Economy and Society: An Outline of Interpretive Sociology.* Ed. G. Roth and C. Wittich. New York: Bedminster Press, 1968.

Wells, H. G. *Experiment in Autobiography: Discoveries and Conclusions of a Very Ordinary Brain (Since 1866).* 1934. London: Faber, 1984.

The Secret Agent's (T)extimacies: A Traumatic Reading Beyond Rhetoric

Michael Mageean

"'He's all there. Every bit of him. It was a job'" (Conrad 70).

These three phrases, spoken "with stolid simplicity" by a police constable over mangled human remains spread out on a table in the morgue of a Greenwich hospital, bear witness to one of the most violent events in modern literature: the physical obliteration of Winnie Verloc's brother, Stevie, blown to bits when the bomb he had been carrying to the Greenwich observatory prematurely detonated. Another police official, Chief Inspector Heat, stares dumbfounded, paralyzed before the "heap of nameless fragments . . . heap of mixed things, which seemed to have been collected in shambles and rag shops. . . . A sort of a heap of rags, scorched and blood stained, half concealing what might have been an accumulation of raw material for a cannibal feast" (70). The constable's and inspector's radically different readings of Stevie's remains (as a "he" versus a "heap") enact the perennial uncertainty as to how violence can be read. Deictically, violence can never be "present" in itself; we can only indicate that something has been violated in reference to a previous state or identity. The constable is obliged to qualify his original deictic statement ("'He's all there'") by describing the drastic "present" dispersion of a once integral body ("'every bit of him'"). Reference to any violent event is always inherently dispersed between the deictic and mimetic registers, as we are forced to posit the violated object retroactively in an originary unviolated state ("'him'"). Any perception we have of violence is unavoidably mimetic: there can be no "violence" without the retroactive reference to that which has been violated, precisely that which is now irrevocably absent.

Conventionally, mimesis attempts to stabilize an absent referent as "re-present"; but the purpose of referring to a violated object is to expose it as irrecoverably absent precisely because of the violation. The violent event enacts a temporal rupture within mimetic representation itself, a split between a "before" (unviolated) state and an "after" (violated) state. This unavoidable intervention of a temporal dimension necessitates an automatic shift to the diegetic (narrative) register. In *The Secret Agent,* the constable is constrained from simply mimetically describing the human being's fragmented status ("'Every bit of him'"); he must account for how the "bits" were assembled into their present configuration ("'It was a job'"). Every mimetic representation of violence inevitably is extended over time as a diegetic narrative.

The overdetermined nature of the constable's revisionary statements betrays how systematically violence destabilizes referentiality, as they exhaust the three primary registers customarily used regarding objects: deixis (when the object is present and only needs to be indicated), mimesis (when the object is not present and needs to be described), and diegesis (when the object is not present and the story of its absence needs to be recounted). Each register is successively split and destabilized by the dynamics that violence introduces even on the linguistic level. When one tries to describe violence, the attempt to treat the violated object as a normal object only reveals the successive limitations of each register, each step generating an excess, a residue that the next level tries (unsuccessfully) to recoup. The stolid constable's three statements constitute a distancing from the bomb's detonation, becoming, in a sense, a synecdoche for the aporetic structure of the entire novel. As J. Hillis Miller remarks, "the disappearance of [Stevie] is the central event of the novel, but it is never directly described. Stevie's end is hinted at, imagined, and approached from various perspectives. It is recounted by various people, but remains hidden, a blank place in the center of the narrative" (51).

Given the fundamental structure of violence, such an aporia is inevitable. If conventional mimesis and diegesis set up an exchange between a "present" description and an absent referent, representation of violence is organized around an impossible circulation between two mutually constitutive yet mutually exclusive *absences:*

1. the absent/past unviolated state of that-which-has-been-violated; and
2. the "present" state, which is defined entirely in terms of its absence from the former, unviolated state.

By definition, these two absences cannot coexist and are irreducible to each other (being dispersed on either side of the decisive aporia opened by the violent event), and yet they define each other, can exist only in relation to each other in terms of the insuperable impasse inaugurated between them by the violent breach. Linguistically, violence is not a stable relation between two signifiers; rather, violence creates dizzying *valences* between two empty placeholders designating the radical absence of any stable entity. The "heap of nameless things" on the Greenwich hospital table can be referred to only as a violated "he" precisely because the heap is demonstrably no longer in human form. There would have been no sense of violation had the constable referred to the remains on the table as an inert "it"; referentiality would have functioned as it does with any conventional object ("It's all there. Every bit of it. It was a job"). It is precisely the abyssal incommensurability between the "heap" on the table and the pronoun "he" which allows us to gauge how thorough a violation has occurred.

The term Sigmund Freud applied to the inherent incommensurability within representation of violence was "trauma": "an experience which within a short period of time presents the mind with an increase in stimulus too powerful to be dealt with or worked off in a normal way" (*Introductory Lectures* 340-41). Trauma inaugurates what Georges Bataille would characterize as a general economy of exorbitance and excess that cannot be contained within the three conventional referential registers. As Cathy Caruth, elaborating upon Freud's insights, remarks, "It is the fundamental [symbolic] dislocation implied by all traumatic experiences that is both a testimony to the event and to the impossibility of its direct access" through representation (8). Ultimately, it would seem that the representation of violence is less that of an object than of this obdurate impasse in representation.

This impasse causes Chief Inspector Heat to bypass the constable's referential statements by resorting to rhetorical figures. His reading of Stevie's remains in terms of such metaphors as "an accumulation of material for a cannibal feast" is symptomatic of the impulse to figure the violently disfigured by torquing language itself. Once violence has exhausted the three basic referential registers, there seems to be no alternative but for language to turn back upon itself and to enact within itself the splits and ruptures encountered in the other registers.

As Gerard Genette points out in *Figures of Literary Discourse,* rhetorical figures have always been characterized as being a "hiatus" (47):

A figure is a gap in relation to usage, but a gap that is nevertheless part of usage (48). . . . The definition of the figure [is] a gap between sign and meaning (49). . . . Where there is choice, combination of words, turn of thought, there must be at least two terms to compare, two words to combine together, a space in which thought can operate. So the reader is able to translate implicitly one expression by another, and to assess their gap, their angle, their distance (51). . . . The value of a figure is not given in the words that make it up, since it depends on the gap between those words and those which the reader perceives, mentally, beyond them. . . . This space constitutes the figure. (54)

The hope the rhetorical register offers is that the ruptured structure of tropes and figures may be analogical to the impasse encountered by the referential registers when attempting to represent violence. After all, a trope is an indeterminate oscillation between two ordinarily incommensurable terms that nevertheless stabilizes a certain meaning across the gap constituted by their mutual conjunction. And, indeed, many have commented on the "violent" effects innate to rhetorical figuration: "In metaphor there is always some shock or surprise resulting from the realization of non-equivalency" between the two terms (D. MacCannell 133).

In fact, I would suggest that violence, and the inability of the referential registers to contain its effects, may be the primary reason why we need to resort to rhetoric at all. If objects could be stabilized, and merely "be," today *or* yesterday, present *or* absent, the three basic referential registers would be sufficient. But because objects can be violated, can be sundered by the dizzying ambi-valences of violence's absences, we have to resort to the arsenal of rhetorical devices that displace one thing onto another across the gaps within language. Thus, after the constable's employment of the three basic referential registers has failed to stabilize the violent effects of Stevie's traumatic obliteration, Chief Inspector Heat has recourse to a series of metaphors and metonymies by means of which he characterizes Stevie's remains as, variously, "a sort of mound," "an accumulation of raw material for a cannibal feast" (Conrad 70), "a heap of mixed things, which seem to have been collected in shambles and rag shops," "a heap of nameless fragments," and "the byproducts of a butcher's shop [for] an inexpensive Sunday dinner" (71).

In "Inhibitions, Symptoms and Anxiety," Sigmund Freud, recalling his case study of Little Hans's phobia toward horses, explains the formation of the neurotic symptom as a "displacement . . . [that] constitutes an alternative mechanism which enables a conflict due to ambivalence to be resolved" (25). Through the phobic symptom, the subject attempts to gain control over an impression that originally had been too overwhelming: "The ego, which [originally] experienced the trauma passively, now repeats it actively in a weakened version, in the hope of being able to direct its course" (102). In Hans's case, his ambivalence toward his father, arising from castration fear, caused his metaphoric displacement of this anxiety onto horses: the phobic horror of being bitten by a horse constituted "a single instinctual repression" from a "convergence of . . . two instinctual impulses that have been overtaken by repression—sadistic aggressiveness towards the father and a passive attitude toward him—[which] form a pair of opposites" (29).

While an entire essay could be written analyzing why Heat applies alimentary/cannibal metaphors to Stevie's remains, for the purposes of our inquiry, what is more significant is the *structure* of his substitutive metaphors. Much like Hans, Heat is caught within an irreducible ambi-valence, the double absence inherent in violence, vacillating between "he" (the absent former state of that-which-has-been-violated) and "heap" (the "present" state which is defined entirely in terms of its absence from the former state). Conrad describes Heat's traumatic inability to reconcile himself to the valences set off between those two syllables:

> It seemed impossible to believe that a human body could have reached that state of disintegration without passing through the pangs of inconceivable agony. No physiologist, and still less of a metaphysician, Chief Inspector Heat rose by the force of sympathy, which is a form of fear, above the vulgar conception of time. . . . The inexplicable mysteries of conscious existence beset Chief Inspector Heat. (71)

It is precisely Heat's own inability to correlate "he" with "heap" within a stable referential economy that compels him to torque language itself by resorting to metaphors of ability (indeed, there's almost a bulimic symbolic exchange here, as Heat tries simultaneously to ingest and abject his own revulsion). Analogous to Little Hans's displacement of his ambivalent feelings toward his father onto the substitutive metaphor of the devouring horse, Heat's displacement of the anxiety arising from the ambi-valences of violence onto alimentary images enacts his attempt to master the traumatic impressions that so overpower him. So universal is this torquing of language to cope with the traumatic linguistic effects of violence that even the stolid constable himself has recourse to a simile when he describes the explosion itself as *"something like* a heavy flash of lightning in the fog" (70). And countless examples of automatically resorting to rhetoric in describing violence can be gleaned from everyday discourse: "It hit me like a ton of bricks . . . like a truck . . . like an express train," et cetera.

But of course, just as neurotic symptoms ultimately fail to control the traumatic emotional ambivalences (as the subject instead becomes controlled by the obsessive-compulsive imperatives of the symptom), so too there are ultimately limitations to rhetoric's ability to re-present violence—as Heat himself acknowledges when he remarks acutely, "The first term of the problem was unreadable—lacked all suggestion but that of atrocious cruelty" (Conrad 72). Heat has run up against the structural impasse inherent in violence: if a conventional trope traverses the "gap between sign and meaning" (Genette 49) by positing an analogous differential relationship between signifiers, this rhetorical relation becomes radically evacuated when applied to the (dis)figuration of violence. Rather than witnessing to an oscillation of two signifiers across the gap that separates them, the figuration of violence is asked to span a gap between two *absences* absolutely incommensurable with each other. As a result of violence's double structure, its ambi-valence, in which what "is" is represented only in terms of that which it no longer is, each term functions only as the radical evacuation of the other. Terming Stevie's remains "material for a cannibal feast" only draws attention to the insuperable gap between the "heap" and the "he," only exacerbates the irreversible aporia that separates the two absences within violence's structure.

Rhetoric seems to mark the ultimate traumatic limit of language—a point Conrad marks explicitly when he writes of "death, whose catastrophic character cannot be argued away by sophisticated reasoning or persuasive eloquence" (174). The differential, out-of-phase valences of violence undermine not merely the referential capacities of language but ultimately the figural as well. In "figuring" violence, we are not able to stand even on the precarious bridge of an "indeterminable oscillation of meaning" between two signifiers by which conventional rhetorical figures straddle the gaps within language. All violent (dis)figuration can establish is that there is no "first term," no stable object—as Freud remarks about traumatic anxiety, it has a quality of "indefiniteness and lack of object" (*Inhibitions* 100). Instead, there is only an irreducible aporia, a fathomless ambi-valence, between two mutually exclusive absences (what is no longer versus what is experienced now purely in terms of what it no longer is). Indeed, perhaps trauma should not be seen as a phenomenological experience in and of itself so much as a linguistic dilemma arising from the referential and symbolic limitations of language. Perhaps the signifier "violence" itself is a rhetorical figure—specifically, a catachresis—for a linguistic predicament so thoroughly overwhelming to the referential capacities of language that it cannot even be imagined, much less named. A radically negative anti-mimesis? A mimesis of negation? Negimesis?

And yet, even in acknowledging the symbolic impasse constituted by
the radical absence of a "first term" in violence, Chief Inspector Heat per-
sists in trying to "read" the effects of violence—assisted, of course, by the
sedulous, stolid constable. In a scene that recalls the chorus in Seneca's
Phaedra advising King Theseus to reassemble his son's shattered body parts
("You, sir, shall set in order these remains / Of your son's broken body, and
restore / the mingled fragments to their place. Put here / his strong right
hand. . . ." [V:1285-88]), the constable suggests that Heat reassemble the
body to reconstitute the unviolated "first term": "'here he is—all of him I
could see. Fair. Slight—slight enough. Look at that foot there. I picked up
the legs first, one after another. He was that scattered you didn't know where
to begin'" (Conrad 72). The earnest constable seems to believe that if Humpty
Dumpty's pieces can be put back together, the "first term" will become
legible. After all, the components are all present: "'And here he is all complete, velvet collar and all. I don't think I missed a single piece as big as a
postage stamp'" (73).

But Heat declines the constable's suggestion. Rather than trying to re-
late the pieces, such as the velvet collar, to each other in a futile attempt to
reconstitute an irrecoverable whole, he instead focuses on the collar as a
fragment "complete in itself like a porcupine" (to quote Schlegel's profound
non sequitur in *Athenaeum Fragment* 206). Whereas the constable's "Classical" reading of Stevie's remains is guided by an earnest belief in an integral whole, Heat's reading is informed more by Romantic irony, which takes
into account the system shattering irreversibility of violence. As Maurice
Blanchot writes: "Only a discontinuous form suits romantic irony, since it
alone can arrange the . . . imperative and indecision of unstable and divided
thought, and, finally, for the mind, the obligation to be systematic and the
horror of system" (171).

On one level, Heat's mind is arrested, paralyzed before the meaningless "horror of system" manifested by the violence of Stevie's disintegration; but on another level, "his trained faculty of an excellent investigator,
who scorns no chance of information" (Conrad 71-72) remains faithful to
the "obligation to be systematic" by resisting the temptation of the constable's
complacent assurance in totality and instead attending to what does not fit
into a system: the anomalous, the residual, the exorbitant fragment. Freud
too based psychoanalysis on the presumption that trauma, the very excess
of any system, may nevertheless proceed by a systematic process of distor-
tion in the form of anomalous fragments of speech and behavior called neurotic symptoms. Whereas the constable, guided by an integral logic of
synecdoche (relating part to whole), would have the Chief Inspector plumb

the depths of that "heap of nameless things," Heat, as if intuiting Winnie Verloc's article of faith that depths "do not bear much looking into," instead plucks from the surface of the heap an exorbitant fragment that will eventually render the details of the ghastly violence if not representable, at least readable:

> Overcoming his physical repugnance, Chief Inspector Heat stretched out his hand without conviction for the salving of his conscience, and took up the least soiled of the rags. It was a narrow strip of velvet with a larger triangular piece of dark blue cloth hanging from it. He held it up to his eyes. . . . He moved to one of the windows for a better light. His face, averted from the room, expressed a startled intense interest while he examined closely the triangular piece of broad cloth. By a sudden jerk he detached it, and only after stuffing it into his pocket turned round to the room, and flung the velvet collar back onto the table. "Cover up," he directed the attendants curtly. (73)

In textual terms, what *has* Heat recovered? As any reader familiar with the novel knows, the triangular piece of broadcloth is a lapel upon the underside of which has been "stitched carefully . . . a square piece of calico with an address written on it in marking ink. . . . Only the number 32 and the name of Brett Street were written in marking ink" (98). On the diegetic plot level, the address label functions as a metonymy that will lead Heat to the identity of the man blown up in the explosion in Greenwich Park that morning. On a thematic level, the triangular shape of the cloth has a certain ironic resonance with Verloc's code name, secret agent Δ—"as if Fate," indeed, "had thrust that clue into [Heat's] hands" (73). On a rhetorico-figural level, the sewn address label may be read as a metaphor for Winnie's Eurydicean attempt to secure Stevie from danger by means of an umbilical thread. Various symbolic ganglia link the address label to major characters in the text. But how is the label linked to the actual victim, Stevie, himself?

Significantly enough, the label contains only Verloc's address, unaccompanied by, as would be expected, a name. Too easily overlooked is that nowhere in the entire text is Stevie provided with a last name (-of-the-father). Despite Winnie's fervently held fantasy that Verloc and Stevie "might be father and son" (142), Stevie cannot legally assume the Verloc name as his sister had. On the other hand, Conrad quite deliberately avoids revealing Winnie's "maiden" name which the mother (who likewise remains nameless) carries. Systematically, throughout the text, Stevie's patronymic seems to be as absent from the symbolic order as it is from the address label; as if the address-label-without-a-name materializes Stevie's incapacity to constitute a positive term within symbolic exchange.

Stevie is only referred to by the diminutive assigned him by his mother and sister. For both of them, Stevie seems to register symbolically only insofar as he is threatened with the Oedipal wrath of the name-of-the-father (regardless whether Stevie's father or Verloc wields it): "The endeavour to keep him [Stevie] from making himself objectionable to the master of the house put no inconsiderable anxiety into these two women's lives. 'That boy,' as they alluded to him softly between themselves, had been a source of that sort of anxiety almost from the very day of his birth" (35). The address-label-without-a-name is but the final tactic in Winnie's strategy to shield Stevie from the name-of-the-father. Throughout the text, Stevie always already inhabits his prospective absence, as Winnie and her mother apprehensively perceive him purely in terms of his possible negation. While he has reached the legal age of majority, Stevie is habitually referred to as "'the boy,'" "'the peculiar boy,'" or (most frequently) "'the poor boy.'" Ironically, the only time Stevie is referred to as a man is when his mangled remains are lying in that heap on the Greenwich hospital table: "the man, whoever he was, had died instantly" (71).

And yet, Stevie does seem to be safe only so long as his sister and mother are able to keep him inconspicuous, unincorporated as a human subject within Verloc's symbolic frame of reference. For, prior to the few weeks preceding the bombing, "Verloc extended as much recognition to Stevie as a man who is not particularly fond of animals may give to his wife's beloved cat" (35). The catastrophe of the bombing is precipitated when Winnie tries to force her hapless brother into an Oedipal "father and son" relation with Verloc. For only at that point does Verloc begin to suspect that Stevie may occupy the position of "being loved for himself" (215) that Verloc had believed himself to hold in Winnie's eyes.

So, in the address-label-without-a-name, Conrad has provided quite an odd troping of Stevie's symbolic situation. Through it, Stevie's pervasive identity, as a potential absence, crystallizes into his actual physical annihilation. By means of the address-label-without-a-name, we may discern the abyssal structure of the "blank place in the center of the narrative" (*Poets* 51) around which Hillis Miller maintains the entire narrative accretes. Stevie is granted a place in the narrative's symbolic economy only insofar as he is subject to obliteration. By the absence of any name on the address label, even Stevie's provisional status in the symbolic order (as "'the poor boy'") is retroactively exposed as having been absence all along. In this abyssal trope, which does not so much "turn" as implode, may be detected the dizzying play of the ambi-valence characteristic of the representational struc-

ture of violence. Has Conrad formulated a type of rhetorical trope that can
finally contain violence's valences?

Hardly. Try as we might, the address-label-without-a-name refuses to
operate as a conventional metaphor, metonymy, or rhetorical trope. As tropes,
metaphors and metonymies function by establishing a certain reciprocal
relation between two signifiers. But the address-label-without-a-name establishes no such reciprocal identification: quite the contrary, it pointedly
manifests an obdurate asymbolic blockage. Picking up on Freud's definition of trauma as a stimulus too overwhelming for the mind to cope with,
the French psychoanalyst Jacques Lacan has discussed such points of symbolic impasse as the intrusion of the Real that resists all symbolization; as a
residue that witnesses to the subject's evacuation from the symbolic order.
As we have seen, the state prior to the violation is irrecoverable. Traumatic
anxiety is the compulsive repetition of this unrepeatability, resulting from
the irreversibility of violence. As Gilles Deleuze points out in *Difference
and Repetition,* Freud's key insight into repression is that one repeats the
past precisely because one does not remember it, is unable to re-present it:
"The less one remembers, the less conscious one is of remembering one's
past, the more one repeats it" (14-15). Lacan too remarks that Freud maintained that "what cannot be remembered is repeated in behavior" (*Fundamental Concepts* 129). If metaphors establish a stable symbolic transfer
between two terms, trauma only repeats the insistent running into a symbolic impasse between two absences.

In *Tarrying with the Negative,* Slavoj Zizek distinguishes the decisive
difference between rhetorical tropes and the traumatic Real: "Inversion . . .
is the fate of every successful metaphor. . . . The Real designates the very
remainder which resists reversal" (42-43). Stevie's address-label-without-
a-name, far from stabilizing meaning in the manner of a conventional trope,
seems rather to witness to the "radical annihilation of the entire symbolic
texture through which 'reality' is constituted" (Zizek, *Sublime Object* 132),
since it witnesses not merely to Stevie's physical obliteration in the explosion, but also to Stevie's never having had a stable place in the symbolic
order in the first place. The nameless address tag organizes the entire text
around an abyssal play of absences: not only the physical evacuation of
Stevie from "ground zero," but the establishment of Stevie as always already an absolute cipher himself: a site of the radical evacuation of the
symbolic order. His obsessive drawing of zeroes within zeroes is all too
reflective of his symbolic status. If the address-label-without-a-name functions as a metaphor for anything, it is for the radical failure of metaphor to
contain the double absence of violence.

According to Zizek, to designate such a "traumatic element which cannot be symbolized, integrated into the symbolic order . . . Lacan coined a neologism: *L'extimité*—external intimacy, which served as a title for one of Jacques-Alain Miller's Seminars" (*Sublime Object* 132). Lacan's earliest use of the term seems to be in *Seminar VII: The Ethics of Psychoanalysis, 1959-60,* when he refers to "the central place [in the symbolic order] as the intimate exteriority or 'extimacy,' that is, the Thing [*das Ding*]" (139). In a 1986 seminar dedicated to elucidating the enigmatic term, the example that Jacques-Alain Miller provides of an "extimacy" (as Lacan's neologism has been translated) is, ironically enough, that of a bomb. A previous seminar session having been canceled because of a bomb threat, Miller points out that, regardless of whether the bomb did or did not actually exist, the mere signifier "bomb" still "could produce its effect" of trauma within the symbolic order (126). As such, Miller defines an extimacy as a signifier for

an object absolutely incompatible with the presence of the subject; it implies a physical disappearance of bodies that . . . represent the subject. If you can sit down opposite a painting and chat with people next to you, it is not so with the bomb [extimacy]; when you speak about this type of object, the subject disappears . . . at the very moment when this object crops up via the signifier "Bomb!," the Other is emptied, disappears. Only the object remains, the object in the desert. ("Extimité" 127)

With that concluding "Ozymandias"-esque image, Miller may or may not be alluding to the advice given Freud by a patient on how to catch lions in the desert: "Take a desert and put it through a sieve and the lions will be left over" (*Interpretation* 499). However, that is as good a conception of the logic of the extimacy as any other. For the irony is that, whether there are actually lions in the desert or not, the entire desert becomes filtered through their very absence. Such is the situation of the symbolic order in relation to this most exorbitant residue at the core of its operation: the extimacy is "the point of the Real at the very heart of the subject which cannot be symbolized, which is produced as a residue, a remnant, a leftover . . . that is more than the subject, yet simultaneously constitutive of the subject" (Zizek, *Sublime Object* 180). As such, like the lions in the desert, an extimacy "is an entity which, although it does not exist (in the sense of "really" existing, taking place in reality), has a series of properties—it exercises a certain structural causality, it can produce a series of effects in the symbolic reality of subjects" (163).

I suggest that the address-label-without-a-name functions in the text of *The Secret Agent* as an extimacy—or, since we are discussing a literary text, a (t)extimacy. As a residue of the traumatic encounter with the Real exemplified by the bomb's detonation, the address tag stands for the radical evacuation of Stevie from the symbolic order; but the lack of a name on the tag stands as a materialization of the absolute symbolic blockage that had always already characterized Stevie's identity within the symbolic order all along. There seems to be no other way of accounting for the paradox that Stevie is situated as a "man" within the symbolic order only upon his having been violently evacuated from it and physically reduced to a heap of mutilated fragments. Following Miller's observation that the extimacy is absolutely inimical to the subject's existence, I would argue that a (t)extimacy can attain symbolic status only by symbolizing the absolute evacuation of the subject.

For instance, in Stendhal's *Red and Black,* Julien, awaiting execution in his cell, contemplates a (t)extimacy posed by Danton on the eve of his execution: "It's a funny thing, the verb guillotine can't be conjugated in all its tenses. One can very well say, I will be guillotined, you will be guillotined, but it's impossible to say: I have been guillotined" (389). The first person present perfect tense of the verb "to guillotine" is a (t)extimacy because it and the subject cannot coexist in the symbolic order—as an impossible performative, it remains ever a traumatic excess designating the evacuation of the subject from the symbolic order. However, that very asymbolic impasse nevertheless produces certain traumatic effects in the symbolic order, as manifested by its paradoxical unrepresentability. Epitaphs, according to Paul de Man, pose a similar paradoxical asymbolic double bind: "It is always possible to anticipate one's own epitaph, even give it the size of an entire *Prelude,* but never possible to be both the one who wrote it [the epitaph] and the one who reads it in the proper setting, that is, confronting one's own grave as an event of the past" (201, n8).

Like neurotic symptoms, (t)extimacies *are* readable by their traumatic effects; they just are not representable in the conventional linguistic registers (deixis, mimesis, diegesis, rhetoric). They remain forever exorbitant, in excess of the subject; and yet they witness to the subject's fundamental constitution in the symbolic order, by marking precisely the absolute negation of the subject. Lacanian theory defines the Real as "that which resists symbolization absolutely" (Zizek, *Sublime Object* 69), and (t)extimacies mark the precise points of symbolic impasse: the points where the (t)extimacy's attainment of symbolic efficacy constitutes absolute evacuation of the subject—as in "I have been guillotined," or an epitaph, or, indeed, an address-label-without-a-name that only becomes readable after its "first term" has been blown to bits. Thus, a (t)extimacy is the most excessive yet most essential aspect of the subject.

But *how* can (t)extimacies be read within the symbolic order if they are unrepresentable within it? As Joan Copjec observes, in order to protect the subject from the traumatic Real, the symbolic order must abject the Real: "The symbolic, in other words, must include the negation of what it is not" (121). However, how can the Real be negated "since the Real is, by definition, that which has no adequate signifier"?

> The answer is, through repetition, through the signifier's repeated attempt—and failure—to designate itself. The signifier's difference from itself, its radical inability to signify itself, causes it to turn in circles around the Real that is lacking in it. It is in this way—in the circumscription of the real—that its non-existence or its negation is signified *within* the symbolic. (121)

One could hardly ask for a better enactment of this repetition compulsion than Stevie obsessively "drawing circles, circles, circles; innumerable circles, concentric, eccentric; a coruscating whirl of circles that by their tangled multitude of repeated curves, uniformity of form, and confusion of intersecting lines suggested a rendering of cosmic chaos, *the symbolism of a mad art attempting the inconceivable"* (Conrad 40; emphasis added). However, in light of Copjec's insight, we may recognize that what is significant about the circles is not so much, as we suggested earlier, their signification of "zero," but rather their insistent, automatic repetition. Like a neurotic symptom, a (t)extimacy is not readable in its referential or symbolic meaning, but rather in its anomalous textual effects of repetition, *insistance de la lettre,* overdetermination, fetishistic disavowal. And yet, unlike a neurotic symptom, which witnesses, in a distorted manner, to a repressed personal trauma, a (t)extimacy manifests the dreadful, dreadful object, the primordial *das Ding,* upon which is premised simultaneously the very constitution and the absolute dissolution of the subject (and, ultimately, of the symbolic order itself). The instant the (t)extimacy attains symbolic access, the subject is no longer around to witness its success. Thus, in his cyclical obsessive-compulsion, Stevie, unwitting draftsman and draftee, cartographer of catastrophe, seems to be insistently plotting targets, targets, targets within targets, drawing a bead on the extimate negation at the center of his very being. One morning in Greenwich Park, stumbling about in the fog, he will inadvertently hit the bull's-eye.

I have been making rather sweeping claims for (t)extimacies as being integral components of the symbolic order, but so far I have focused only on one character. Perhaps Stevie, as a "blank space at the center of the narrative," is arguably an anomalous case. As a figure radically evacuated *avant la lettre* from the symbolic order, Stevie's symbolic status may well be thematized by a nameless address tag; but do any of the novel's other characters accrete/dissolve around similarly insistent (t)extimacies?

What of the putative title character of the novel, Adolf Verloc, alias secret agent Δ? Throughout the novel, the object with which Verloc seems most associated is his omnipresent round hat. Most conspicuously, Conrad emphasizes Verloc's penchant for dining at home while wearing his hat: "He got up heavily, and came to his dinner in his overcoat and with his hat on, without uttering a word (34). . . . [Verloc] sat down to consume [his dinner] without conviction, wearing his hat pushed back on his head (134). . . . He ate as if in a public place, his hat pushed up off his forehead" (139).

At home, Verloc is a tourist: "It was not devotion to an outdoor life, but the frequentation of foreign cafes which was responsible for that habit, investing with a character of unceremonious impermanency Mr Verloc's steady fidelity to his own fireside" (134). Far from signifying mere impoliteness, Verloc's metonymic association with his hat becomes a systematic metaphor for his innate rootlessness, his "unceremonious impermanency" being his residual holdout against being "thoroughly domesticated" (11, 191). So significant is Verloc's inseparability from his hat that the first time Verloc removes it at home—when "Stevie pounced upon [the hat], and bore it off reverently into the kitchen" (140)—seems to constitute the point when Verloc initially realizes that Stevie could be of some use to him. As if reading his mind, Winnie adds, "*'You* could do anything with that boy, Adolf. . . . He would go through fire for you. He—'" (140). The entire bomb plot seems to hatch from Stevie's sedulous care for Verloc's hat—after all, if "'that boy'" can be relied upon to handle Verloc's precious hat, perhaps he may be entrusted with an even more delicate package.

However, just before Verloc's death, his hat is detached from him for the final time, as Conrad's description grants it an oddly personified autonomy: "Mr Verloc flung himself heavily upon the sofa, disregarding the fate of his hat, which, as if accustomed to take care of itself, made for safe shelter under the table" (194-95). In "A Connection Between a Symbol and a Symptom," Freud established that a hat, by virtue of its being both "a symbol of the genital organ, most frequently the male" and "a continuation of the head, though detachable," could become a locus of castration anxiety symptom formation (162-63). As such, Verloc's severance from his hat would, at first glance, seem to be a prolepsis of castration. However, once the hat's "master" is killed, Conrad's text seems to transform the hat into a placeholder for the absolute evacuation of the subject, Verloc, from the symbolic order. As Winnie gazes, paralyzed like Heat before Stevie's remains, upon her husband's corpse, she reflects on the manifest "unreadability" of the "first term":

> He had been the master of a house, the husband of a woman, and the murderer of her Stevie. And now he was of no account in every respect. He was of less practical account than the clothing on his body, than his overcoat, than his boots—*than that hat lying on the floor.* He was nothing. . . . He was less than nothing now. (200; emphasis added)

"That" hat-without-its-wearer is really no different than the address-label-without-a-name: each image functions as a blunt materialization of the radical evacuation of the subject from the symbolic order—indeed, we may well correlate the *"round* hat . . . rock[ing] slightly on its crown in the wind of [Winnie's] flight" (199; emphasis added) with Stevie's "coruscating whirl of circles" (76). No differently than Stevie's nameless address tag had been a desperate attempt on Winnie's part to "suture" Stevie's empty identity within the symbolic order, so too Verloc's omnipresent hat had been an empty, stubborn gesture to deny the castration (of being "thoroughly domesticated") at the core of his inhabiting the symbolic order. However, no differently than Stevie's address-label-without-a-name incarnates the radical negativity at the center of his being, Verloc's hat-without-its-wearer materializes the castration that had conditioned his status in the symbolic order all along. No differently than the nameless address tag, the Verloc-less hat enacts the very symbolic impasse from which Verloc's entire symbolic economy had been organized to protect him: for embodied in that (t)extimate blockage of the hat-without-its-wearer is the radical evacuation of Verloc as a subject in the symbolic order—indeed, the radical evacuation of the symbolic order itself.

And yet it is crucial to mark the radical reversal enacted by the traumatic (t)extimacy, which distinguishes it from a conventional neurotic symptom. The point of the hat-without-its-wearer is not, ultimately, that Verloc is "castrated." Quite the contrary, as Winnie's rumination over his corpse makes clear, it is more accurate to say that the hat is "castrated" of Verloc. For the obdurate fact is that *there is no longer any Verloc to be castrated:* "He was nothing. . . . He was less than nothing" (200). "That hat," bereft of its habitual wearer, is an empty placeholder for a subject that no longer exists: "He was of less practical account than . . . that hat lying on the floor" (200). Like Danton's "I have been guillotined" or de Man's epitaph, it is impossible even to say "Verloc's hat" anymore. That the idea of a "castrated hat" strikes us as an absurdity is precisely an index of its functioning as a (t)extimacy. No differently than Stevie's nameless address label, the moment that Verloc's (t)extimacy attains symbolic status is precisely the moment the subject Verloc's removal from the circuit of symbolic exchange has been completed.

However, Verloc's (t)extimacy differs decisively from Stevie's (t)extimacy in that the ownerless hat starts out as a functional trope (metaphor) prior to its traumatic transmutation. In order to demonstrate how a trope can be transformed into a traumatic (t)extimacy, it will be necessary to explore the dynamics of the *en*trope.

To understand the semantic distinction between a trope and an entrope, let us take a standard example of a felicitous metaphor: "My love is a red rose." While "my love" and "a red rose" are demonstrably two separate terms, a certain frisson (or "shock," as Dean MacCannell would have it) of "indeterminate oscillation of meaning" is established by yoking the two generally unlike terms together: a reciprocal "bridge" is established between certain features shared by the two terms (such as "freshness," "youth," "loveliness," "vivid color," et cetera).

However, as Juliet Flower MacCannell points out in *Figuring Lacan,* the metaphor that equates "my love" with a "rose" only functions because of a prior exclusion (or repression) of all the features which "my love" and "rose" do *not* share:

> In the metaphoric mode it is only on the basis of a preceding negation, a linguistic "not," that "similarity" can be conceived. Whoever can associate love and roses . . . can do so only by dissociating hate and roses, and also, because they will have made a prior distinction between "rose" and "not rose." Only this law of non-coincidence between rose and all other entities, the principle of distinction and division, supports comparison—our familiar literary version of metaphor—of love as "like" a rose. (97)

Yet suppose we turn this "law of non-coincidence" inside out and activate one of the repressed, non-coinciding metaphors to which Flower MacCannell alludes? Suppose we make a symmetrical reversal of this metaphor into "My *lost* love is *a withered rose"?* While grammatically a metaphor, this trope strikes us as a particularly ungainly and inefficacious one, even a redundant absurdity (like a "castrated hat"). But why does this trope not "turn" with the reciprocal frisson productive of metaphoric meaning as "my love is a red rose" does? The reversal seems to be symmetrical (love/ lost love; red rose/withered rose). The connection between love and rose, while reversed, should still be intact on some level. It *should* work as a metaphor. Instead, we are left with a grotesque, infelicitous trope which, oddly, refuses to "turn."

What arrests the turning of "my lost love is a withered rose" is the double absence, the symbolic impasse, that we have identified as the ambi-valent linguistic structure of violent representation. Already, each separate image, "my lost love" and "a withered rose," is inhabited by the irreversible split within mimesis/diegesis discussed above. To refer to a "lost love," we must mimetically conjure up, across the unbridgeable rupture of loss, a re-presentation of an un-violated love which was, but is no longer. Similarly, a "withered rose" can only be gauged in relation to some re-presentation of a healthy, blooming "red rose" which once was, but is no longer. The law of non-coincidence, which underwrites successful tropes, when systematically reversed runs into the double absences, the ambi-valent structure, of violence.

The efficacy of a trope such as "my love is a red rose" is premised upon the suppression of "entropes"—as we will term (t)extimate "shadow" tropes within felicitous tropes—such as "my lost love is a withered rose." At the core of every successful trope lies an exorbitant residue of its semantic dissolution through the symbolic impasse created around the double absences of violent representation. Every felicitous trope can be negated, violated, to reveal at its very core a rigorously suppressed (t)extimate *en*trope.

For, as Copjec indicated, due to the traumatic Real's radical negativity, a (t)extimacy can never signify in itself. Grammatically, "my lost love is a withered rose" may well be a trope, but semantically the effect is more that of a radically negative tautology: non-x = non-y. Meaning cannot be stabilized as a productive, reciprocal "turning" trope; rather, semantically, an entropic equilibrium state has been established in which there is no directed symbolic energy available with which the trope could generate productive meaning. Within every successful metaphor inheres a metaleptic reversal that short-circuits the semantic reciprocity constitutive of the metaphor, and that threatens to empty out the entire symbolic order. Rhetoric can only function by repressing this (t)extimate "beyond rhetoric" that nevertheless inhabits its very foundation. In its symbolic impassability, an entrope is a metaphor that, even prior to its use, is always already a "dead" metaphor: a (t)extimacy that inhabits the core of every trope as violent, ambi-valent paralysis and the eventual dissolution of the entire symbolic order.

The entrope is a site of radical textual implosion: think of it as a semantic "dark star"—it attracts meaning only to crush it, to evacuate it. And, just like a dark star, we can never "see" what an entrope represents directly in the symbolic order; we can only "read" its effects through the disturbances of the symbolic order (repetition, overdetermination, *insistance de la lettre,* disavowal, et cetera) exerted by the entropic "gravitational" pull by which it empties any trope within its semantic orbit of all productive meaning.

Despite their radically disruptive effects in the symbolic order, entropes do not necessarily refer just to catastrophic objects such as bombs. The key to recognizing an entrope is to encounter an absolute symbolic blockage within a trope whose very resistance to "turning" in itself communicates certain definable textual effects—such as those we have discussed of an address tag that, pointedly, is lacking a name; or those of a hat that noticeably is missing its habitual wearer. Not that a (t)extimacy is always a text-ile either; a (t)extimacy can be a text, but pointedly emptied of its representational efficacy—for example, the journalistic phrase "The drop given was fourteen feet" (201, 203, 219) that insistently hounds Winnie Verloc to her watery death:

> That!—never! Never! And how was it done? The impossibility of imagining the details of such a quiet execution added something maddening to her abstract terror. The newspapers never gave any details except one, but that one with some affection was always there at the end of a meagre report. . . . It came with a burning pain into her head, as if the words "The drop given was fourteen feet" had been scratched on her brain with a hot needle. "The drop given was fourteen feet." (201)

It is not immediately clear why that particular phrase, as opposed to other aspects of the "meagre report," should so obsessively horrify Winnie: the reaction provoked in her by the journalistic phrase seems out of all proportion to its matter-of-fact nature. In trying to activate some referential meaning from the enigmatic phrase, the editors of the Cambridge edition of *The Secret Agent* contend that, according to their research in such sources as Charles Duff's *A New Handbook on Hanging,* "Winnie's gruesomely imagined drop would actually have produced decapitation" (Conrad 426, n. 201.30).

As informative as this fact may be, it still cannot account for Winnie's obsessive repetition of the phrase. Recall, as Deleuze and Lacan noted above, Freud established that we repeat traumatic experiences precisely because we cannot adequately re-present them. Conrad explicitly emphasizes that it is precisely *"the impossibility of imagining* the details of such a quiet execution" that "added something maddening to her abstract terror" (201; emphasis added). The very meagerness of the newspaper report causes her to fixate on the one concrete detail given; but it is crucial to recognize that this detail takes on a traumatic intensity that far exceeds its referential signification:

> These words ["The drop given . . ."] affected her physically. Her throat became convulsed in waves to resist strangulation; and the apprehension of the jerk was so vivid that she seized her head in both hands as if to save it from being torn off her shoulders. "The drop given was fourteen feet." No! that must never be! She could not stand *that*. The thought of it even was not bearable. She could not stand thinking of it. (201)

Decapitation is never explicitly mentioned in this passage—even attentive readers may miss its association with the fourteen-foot drop because Winnie cannot bring herself even to imagine its consequences in mimetic or symbolic terms. Precisely because she cannot attach words or images ("the thought of it even was not bearable") to the fourteen-foot drop, Winnie physically acts out a compulsive hysterical symptom—which, as Freud states, is "on the one hand an expectation of trauma, and, on the other, a repetition of it in mitigated form" (*Inhibitions* 102). Her seizing her head *"as if* [note the rhetorical distancing by means of a simile] to save it from being torn off her shoulders" (201), is an involuntary reflex, unmediated by any mimetic representation—only the empty deictic "that!" which apotropaically refers to something that simply can never be. Much like Danton's "I have been guillotined," Winnie's fourteen-foot drop is simply unthinkable within her symbolic economy.

In other words, Winnie's end-of-her-rope is an entrope. In her hysterical reaction to the phrase, Winnie has absolutely bypassed the imaginary and symbolic orders to confront the Real in all its traumatic obduracy. While she can envision Stevie's decapitated head (196), she cannot give word or image to her own decapitation. However, while "The drop given was fourteen feet" constitutes an absolute asymbolic blockage, it nevertheless produces powerful disruptions throughout Winnie's symbolic economy that can be read in her compulsive fixation on the phrase, the phobic repetition of that which must never be repeated because it simply never can be. The phrase only becomes a traumatic (t)extimacy the instant it acquires an automatic insistence of its own *purely as a phrase detached from any representational referentiality.* If Winnie could attach a stabilized signified ("decapitation") or mimetic representation (head dangling from swaying rope gripped tightly around severed spinal cord) to the phrase, the fourteen-foot drop would lose some of its phobic intensity. For, as Freud and Breuer discovered, hysterical symptoms are dispelled "when the patient had described the [traumatic] event in the greatest possible detail and had put the affect into words" (*Studies in Hysteria* 6). But so long as "The drop given was fourteen feet" remains unrepresentable within Winnie's symbolic economy, its very *in*significance will ensure it functions as a traumatic (t)extimacy insistently signifying only the prospect of her radical evacuation from the entire symbolic order. As in Ossipon's discovery of Verloc's corpse, something is missing from the entrope—and that Thing *(das Ding)* is precisely the subject, who is posited as the always already irrecoverable lost object beyond all object relations: beyond deixis, beyond mimesis, beyond diegesis . . . beyond even rhetoric.

We could explore more of *The Secret Agent's* (t)extimacies: such as Ossipon's *"an impenetrable mystery"* phrase—drawn, like Winnie's entrope, from a newspaper—which insistently haunts him into madness. Regarding the phrase, Conrad observes, in virtually a textbook definition of a (t)extimacy, that Ossipon "was menaced by *this thing* in the very sources of his existence" (228; emphasis added). However, it is time to return to the (primal) scene of Chief Inspector Heat paralyzed before the "heap of nameless fragments" which resemble "the raw material for a cannibal feast" (70) spread out on the Greenwich hospital table. Since Lacan's influential "Seminar on the 'Purloined Letter,'" it has become axiomatic that in reading detective fiction, we may view the detective as enacting an "allegory of reading"—that is, the detective models the methodology by which the text itself is to be read. Joseph Conrad's *The Secret Agent* is hardly a conventional detective novel (as it leaves the "mystery" hanging at the conclusion—from the "sandwich board" about Ossipon's neck!). Still, Chief Inspector Heat, by exhuming that anomalous piece of blue velvet cloth from the heap of human fragments, has modeled a unique methodology of reading for us: a *traumatic* reading. Following Heat's lead, by attending to textual fragments that do not fit into the novel's symbolic economy—an address tag without a name; a hat without an owner; non sequitur phrases from newspapers, divorced from their original context—we have been able to specify points of asymbolic blockage where "the first term . . . was unreadable" (72), but where we may discern, as Lacan remarks in "Metaphor of the Subject," a "new species of signification which disputation [rhetoric] cannot fathom, for it is unfathomable" (12). In this arena beyond rhetoric, beyond the signifier, we may sense the effects of the traumatic Realism that lies at the (t)extimate core of Winnie Verloc's governing idea that *das Ding* does not bear much looking into. Of course, (t)extimacies and their (dis)figural entropes have always been inherent in language—they are precisely what rhetorical tropes traditionally must repress to function felicitously. And, from Classical times, rhetoric has been dedicated to suppressing the entropes at its core with the compromise symbolic economies established by metaphors and metonymies. However, certain Modernist texts have been obsessively attracted to the (t)extimate entropes usually repressed by tropes. In a proto-Modernist text such as Herman Melville's "Bartleby the Scrivener," the phrase "I would prefer not to" takes on an insistence that seems to "mean" nothing other than marking the subject as a "dead letter," evacuated from the symbolic order.

Still, historically, "Bartleby" only became "readable" after Freud's psychoanalytic theories on traumatic insistence had become widely disseminated. In our "traumatic" reading of Conrad's *The Secret Agent,* we have not resorted to the theories of Freud and Lacan arbitrarily; rather, we have encountered certain points of asymbolic blockage in Conrad's text itself, and referred to psychoanalytic theories on trauma to account for the textual *effects* of these structural impasses. By no means do Freud and Lacan "explain" the impenetrable mysteries that Conrad's text poses, but they can alert us to the symptomatic effects of the violent ambi-valences that structure Conrad's text.

To speculate why Modernism should be attracted to the asymbolic blockages that Classical rhetoric had been dedicated to suppressing would require an essay on its own. We can but offer some preliminary suggestions. Nineteenth-century science was torn between two seemingly opposed theories of the universe, both proposed in the 1850s. As Gillian Beer writes in *Darwin's Plots,* Darwinian "evolutionary theory appeared to propose a more and more complex ordering [of the universe], while [Rudolf Clausius's] second law of thermodynamics emphasised the tendency of energy systems toward disorder," as every physical process consumed a quantity of energy that could never be reclaimed for productive work (16). In many ways, haunted by this vision of the irrecuperable and irrevocable at the core of every chemical reaction, much of modern science has attempted to reconcile Darwin's progressivism with Clausius's pessimism. And the evolution/entropy enigma became a powerful metaphor in many other disciplines, as the paradoxical sense that society was growing more intricate and ordered, yet simultaneously more chaotic and inexplicable emerged as the Modernist sensibility par excellence. Sigmund Freud's theory of the Unconscious was one modern solution posed to the dilemma: while conceding that there is a mental sphere that is inaccessible to direct conscious apprehension, Freud posited that this irrecuperable realm nevertheless exercised determinable conscious *effects* that could be "read," if never exhaustively explained.

Joseph Conrad's *The Secret Agent* explores the evolution/entropy dilemma on a thematic level—most overtly in the two chapters devoted to confrontations between the progressivist Ossipon, disciple of Lambrosian eugenics, and the Professor, dedicated to accelerating the slide into entropy by developing the "perfect detonator." However, Conrad's most innovative staging of the entropy paradox is on the tropological level (the Chief Inspector's very name is a sly thermodynamic pun). For, by centering so much of the novel's text precisely on tropes that fail to "turn" as tropes should, Conrad has opened his text to the traumatic effects of the evacuation of the subject from the entire symbolic order. In their inexplicable compulsive repetition, such entropes may well be seen as constituting a type of linguistic "death drive."

Certain texts by Conrad, Kafka, and other Modernists have always obdurately resisted traditional "rhetorical" readings. There always seems to be some peripheral residue in their texts beyond the imaginary and symbolic registers; a residue that, nevertheless, seems to insist at the inexplicable core of the texts. Or, as Kafka wrote about Prometheus's rock: "There remained that inexplicable mass of rock. The [Prometheus] legend tried to explain the inexplicable. As it came out of the substratum of truth it had in turn to end in the inexplicable" (152).

It is time we attend to such symbolic impasses and blockages, learn to read these unrepresentable (t)extimacies and entropes, and subject these Modernist texts to the "traumatic" readings—beyond mimesis, beyond diegesis, beyond even rhetoric—that they have so insistently, obsessively demanded.

WORKS CITED

Beer, Gillian. *Darwin's Plots: Evolutionary Narrative in Darwin, George Eliot and Nineteenth-Century Fiction.* London: Routledge, 1983.

Blanchot, Maurice. "The Athanaeum." Trans. Deborah Esch and Ian Balfour. *Studies in Romanticism* 22.2 (1992): 163-72.

Breuer, Joseph, and Sigmund Freud. *Studies on Hysteria: The Standard Edition of the Complete Psychological Works of Sigmund Freud.* Ed. James Strachey. Vol. 2. London: Hogarth, 1981.

Caruth, Cathy, ed. "Introduction: Psychoanalysis, Culture and Trauma 1." *American Imago: Studies in Psychoanalysis and Culture* 48.1 (1991): 1-13.

———. "Introduction: Psychoanalysis, Culture and Trauma 2." *American Imago: Studies in Psychoanalysis and Culture* 48.1 (1991): 417-23.

Conrad, Joseph. *The Secret Agent: A Simple Tale (The Cambridge Edition of the Works of Joseph Conrad).* 1907. Ed. Bruce Harkness and S. W. Reid. Cambridge, Eng.: Cambridge UP, 1990.

Copjec, Joan. *Read My Desire: Lacan Against the Historicists.* Cambridge, Mass. : MIT Press, 1994.

Deleuze, Gilles. *Difference and Repetition.* Trans. Paul Patton. New York: Columbia UP, 1994.

de Man, Paul. *Romanticism and Contemporary Criticism: The Gauss Seminar and Other Papers.* Ed. E. S. Burt, Kevin Newmark, and Andrzej Warminski. Baltimore: Johns Hopkins UP, 1993.

Freud, Sigmund. "A Connection Between a Symbol and a Symptom (1916)." *The Collected Papers of Sigmund Freud.* Trans. and ed. Joan Riviere. New York: Basic Books, 1959, 162-63.

————. *Inhibitions, Symptoms and Anxiety.* Trans. Alix Strachey. Ed. James Strachey. New York: W. W. Norton, 1989.

————. *The Interpretation of Dreams.* Trans. James Strachey. New York: Avon, 1965.

————. *Introductory Lectures on Psycho-Analysis.* Trans. and ed. James Strachey. New York: W. W. Norton, 1989.

Genette, Gerard. *Figures of Literary Discourse.* Trans. Alan Sheridan. New York: Columbia UP, 1982.

Kafka, Franz. *The Basic Kafka.* Ed. Erich Heller. New York: Washington Square, 1979.

Lacan, Jacques. *The Four Fundamental Concepts of Psycho-Analysis.* Trans. Alan Sheridan. Ed. Jacques-Alain Miller. New York: W. W. Norton, 1981.

————. "Metaphor of the Subject." Trans. Bruce Fink. *Newsletter of the Freudian Field* 5.1-2 (1991): 10-15.

————. *The Seminar of Jacques Lacan: Book VII, The Ethics of Psychoanalysis, 1959-60.* Trans. Dennis Porter. Ed. Jacques-Alain Miller. New York: W. W. Norton, 1992.

MacCannell, Dean. *Empty Meeting Grounds: The Tourist Papers.* New York: Routledge, 1992.

MacCannell, Juliet Flower. *Figuring Lacan: Criticism and the Cultural Unconscious.* Lincoln: U of Nebraska P, 1986.

Miller, J. Hillis. *Poets of Reality: Six Twentieth-Century Writers.* Cambridge, Mass.: Belknap/Harvard UP, 1965.

Miller, Jacques-Alain. "Extimité." Trans. Françoise Massardier-Kenney. *Prose Studies* 11.3 (1988): 121-31.

Schlegel, Friedrich. *Philosophical Fragments.* Trans. Peter Firchow. Minneapolis: U of Minnesota P, 1991.

Seneca (Lucius Annaeus). "Phaedra (or Hippolytus)." *Four Tragedies and Octavia.* Trans. E. F. Watling. Middlesex: Penguin, 1984, 97-150.

Stendhal. *Red and Black: The Norton Critical Edition.* Trans. and ed. Robert M. Adams. New York: W. W. Norton, 1969.

Zizek, Slavoj. *For They Know Not What They Do.* New York: Verso, 1991.

———. *The Sublime Object of Ideology.* New York: Verso, 1991.

———. *Tarrying with the Negative.* Durham, N.C.: Duke UP, 1993.

Notes on the Contributors

Patrick Brantlinger, editor of *Victorian Studies* from 1980 to 1990, is Professor of English at Indiana University. He is author of several books, including *Rule of Darkness: British Literature and Imperialism, 1830-1914* (1988), *Crusoe's Footprints: Cultural Studies in Britain and America* (1990), and *Fictions of State: Culture and Credit in Britain, 1694-1994* (1996).

Paul Delany is Professor of English at Simon Fraser University, Vancouver. His books include *D. H. Lawrence's Nightmare* (1978), *The Neo-Pagans* (1987), and, as editor or co-editor, *Hypermedia and Literary Studies* (1991), *The Digital Word* (1993), and *Vancouver: Representing the Postmodern City* (1994). His essay on Joseph Conrad in this volume emerges from his interest in the larger subject of English literature and money, which will be the focus of his next book.

Margaret Goscilo has taught literature and film as an assistant professor in Switzerland, France, Pennsylvania, Minnesota, and Vermont. Her publications include *The Bastard Hero in the Novel* (1990) and articles on gender studies and on the connections between the visual and narrative arts.

Jane Hotchkiss is a doctoral candidate in nineteenth-century British studies at the University of California, Davis. Her dissertation is on "wild children" and the literary child-of-nature in the Romantic and fin-de-siècle periods. She has published articles on Kate Chopin and Doris Lessing.

Carola M. Kaplan is Professor of English at California State University, Pomona. Among her publications are articles on E. M. Forster, Joseph Conrad, Henry James, and T. E. Lawrence in essay collections and in such journals as *Twentieth-Century Literature, Conradiana,* and *Texas Studies in Literature and Language.* She is currently writing a book, *Cultural*

Crossdressing: Englishness and Otherness in Joseph Conrad, E. M. Forster, T. E. Lawrence, and Christopher Isherwood.

Shoshana Milgram Knapp, Associate Professor of English at Virginia Polytechnic Institute, has published articles on such figures as Anton Chekhov, Fyodor Dostoevsky, George Eliot, W. S. Gilbert, Ursula K. Le Guin, Vladimir Nabokov, Ayn Rand, George Sand, Herbert Spencer, and Leo Tolstoi. Her articles on "Victoria Cross" appear in the *Dictionary of Literary Biography, News-Stead,* and *Rediscovering Forgotten Radicals.*

John Lucas is Professor of English at Loughborough University. His books include studies of Charles Dickens, Elizabeth Gaskell, and Arnold Bennett; as well as *The Literature of Change, English Poetry: From Hardy to Hughes, Romantic to Modern,* and *England and Englishness: Poetry and National Identity 1688-1900.* Publisher of Shoestring Press, he is also a recognized poet, winner of the Aldeburgh Poetry Festival Award in 1990 for his collection *Studying Grosz on the Bus.*

Michael Mageean teaches at Loyola Marymount University, Los Angeles. He recently received his Ph.D. from the University of California, Irvine. His dissertation, *Traumatic Readings: Violence and Rhetoric,* investigates how rhetoric—from Classical texts through Elizabethan revenge tragedy to the novel—attempts to compensate for the failure of mimesis to represent violence in literature.

Jean-Michel Rabaté, Professor of English and Comparative Literature at the University of Pennsylvania, has published books about James Joyce: in English, *James Joyce: Authorized Reader* (1991) and *Joyce upon the Void: The Genesis of Doubt* (1991). In addition, his books include studies of Samuel Beckett, Thomas Bernhard, and Ezra Pound. His recent treatments of literary theory and Modernism include *The Ghosts of Modernity* (1996) and, as editor, *Roland Barthes and the Arts of Seeing* (forthcoming).

Anne B. Simpson is Associate Professor of English at California State University, Pomona. Her work centers on late Victorian and Edwardian literature as reconceived from the perspective of current feminist and poststructuralist theories. She has published articles on H. G. Wells, Arnold Bennett, Matthew Arnold, and Thomas Hardy in such journals as *Essays in Literature, Reader, Works and Days, American Imago,* and *Victorian Literature and Culture.*

Robert Squillace is currently Associate Director of Composition at Columbia University. He has also taught at Lafayette College and Wittenberg University. In addition to editing the Penguin edition of Arnold Bennett's *Riceyman Steps* (with Edward Mendelson) and contributing the essay "Bennett, Wells, and the Persistence of Realism" to *The Columbia History of the British Novel,* he has published essays on Thomas Hardy and V. S. Pritchett. His book *Modernism, Modernity and Arnold Bennett* is forthcoming.

Wilfred H. Stone, Professor of English Emeritus, has been at Stanford University since 1950 and is the author of *The Cave and the Mountain* (1966), which won the Christian Gauss Award; as well as other books and articles on Victorian and near-Victorian subjects. One of his central concerns is with the future of the planet. His scholarly interests include Bloomsbury and the literature of World War I. He is currently writing chapters on George Eliot and Henry James for a book to be called *Fiction and the Market Society.*

Marianna Torgovnick is Professor of English at Duke University, where she teaches twentieth-century British literature, the novel, and cultural criticism. She is known for her interdisciplinary work in art and anthropology, and also for writing memoir and scholarly work that can be read by general audiences. Her most recent books include *Gone Primitive: Savage Intellects, Modern Lives* (1990), *Crossing Ocean Parkway* (1994), and *Primitive Passions: Men, Women, and the Quest for Ecstasy* (forthcoming 1997). The essay printed here developed from her work on ecstatic traditions in the West and their relationship to Western primitivism.

Index